SPIRIT-FILLED LIFE®
NEW TESTAMENT
COMMENTARY SERIES

ROMANS

David P. Seemuth

Jack W. Hayford and David P. Seemuth
General Editors

NELSON REFERENCE & ELECTRONIC
A Division of Thomas Nelson Publishers
Since 1798
www.thomasnelson.com

Spirit-Filled Life New Testament Commentary Series: Romans

Copyright © 2005 by David P. Seemuth

Published in Nashville, Tennessee, by Thomas Nelson, Inc.

Book design and composition by *A&W Publishing Electronic Services, Inc.*, Chicago, Illinois

Spirit-Filled Life New Testament commentary series: Romans/David P. Seemuth
   Jack W. Hayford and David P. Seemuth, general editors
   ISBN 0-7852-4942-7
Printed in the United States of America
1 2 3 4 5 6 7—09 08 07 06 05

CONTENTS

FOREWORD

Welcome to the Spirit-Filled Life® New Testament Commentaries. It has been my desire to combine solid biblical scholarship with a passionate embrace of kingdom living principles in a format accessible to pastors, students, and other readers of God's Word. If you have picked up this commentary you probably wish to become a more equipped servant of God through the thorough understanding of the Spirit's revealed Word to us.

God has led me at this stage of life to pour myself into the training of people fit for the task of kingdom ministry. Of course, this does not mean ministry in the "professional" sense. Ministry (service for the Master) occurs when people are moved by the Holy Spirit to advance as equipped warriors in a spiritual battle with evil forces to help deliver people from the realm of darkness and bring them into the kingdom of the Beloved Son of God. We know that this refers to outreach and evangelism. But such ministry extends far beyond that.

People must embrace the fullness of the kingdom of God for every aspect of life. Only by Spirit-filled living and moving will people be able to comprehend and connect with such a life. And only by Spirit-filled ministry will such work occur in the lives of others.

Key to the advancing of such kingdom ministry is the ministry of God's Word. To this end I have brought together individuals of significant biblical scholarship who also have an understanding of what it means to live the Spirit-filled life in order to form the Spirit-Filled Life® New Testament Commentary series. It should come as no surprise that biblical scholarship and an understanding of the Spirit-filled life are put together. Solid intellectual discovery of the Word of God leads to conclusions about the Spirit-filled life consistent with experience of God's empowering Spirit. The two are not to be in conflict. And they are not, in fact, in conflict. God's truth in the revealed Word (given by the Holy Spirit) is the same truth given in Spirit-empowered living. The Holy Spirit is the common denominator!

Some of the distinctives you will see in this series are:

- A commitment to renew our confidence in God's Word through solid scholarship in tune with current issues in New Testament studies
- A commitment to realized kingdom living through practical insights and application of God's Word.
- A commitment to reflect the inspiration of the text through seeing the Holy Spirit as Author even though God used human writers

- A commitment to reveal kingdom principles God has built into the Scriptures

Of course we know that the real purpose for knowing God's Word is to be transformed and equipped by it. We are not simply to accumulate intellectual facts about the Word. The end of study is not *knowledge* but *knowing God* by His Holy Spirit. This series will help you do just that.

So, it is with my joy to present these commentaries to you for your edification. May God use these to build you up for His service.

—*Jack W. Hayford*

PREFACE

No new work on the Epistle of Paul to the Romans stands alone. Many have mined the depths of this part of God's Word with wonderful results for the church of Jesus Christ as a whole as well as for individuals. Any author is indebted to previous writers who have helped form basic understandings and profound thoughts. But as I have worked through this epistle afresh the beauty of God's mercy burned with new intensity and clarity in ways that need present attention in this age. As people with a firm commitment to the authority of God's Word and the importance of dedicated attention to scholarship, we must always be seeking greater insights into the majesty of God's revelation. I hope that this volume in the Spirit-Filled Life® New Testament Commentaries will lead students of the Word to greater depths of understanding of Romans, application of God's principles to our lives, and richer worship of the One who justly judges, redeems by grace, and gives us power to live for Him.

My thanks go out to those who have had profound impact upon my own life in preparation for writing this commentary. Specifically, I am grateful to William Larkin, Jr., who showed me the joy of intense study of God's Word, to D. Stuart Briscoe, who showed me the delight of spreading God's Word, and to Jack W. Hayford, who showed me the depths of loving the Spirit who gave us God's Word. Certainly each will find some of their own marks upon my own thinking that come through in this commentary and I am sure each will see places where I fall short. But such is the nature of writing. I am grateful to God for each of these dear men who are dedicated servants of our Lord Jesus Christ.

Special thanks is due to my copy-editor, Daniel Partner, and to Managing Editor Lee Hollaway at Thomas Nelson Publishers, who were very patient with me in this endeavor and persevered in this work.

Finally, this work would not have been completed without the support of my wife, Karen, and the wonderful prodding of my children, Daniel and Kristin.

In His Service,
David P. Seemuth

INTRODUCTION

Few people would deny the impact of Paul's formative letter to the Romans in the life of the Christian church throughout history. This has often been felt in times of the church's greatest need. At the same time, it has satisfied the yearnings of individual believers seeking greater understanding of the faith. The Holy Spirit has used this mighty writing to convict people of sin, bring them new awareness of the grace of God, and provide wonderful glimpses of a way of life that worships and pleases God. For example, Augustine, the great fourth-century defender of the faith, was still a young man when unusual circumstances prompted him to read Romans chapter 13. This was a turning point for Augustine; he came to grips with his sin, surrendered to the Lord Jesus Christ, and began a life of faith that greatly influenced the church throughout the ensuing centuries.

Martin Luther was in agony as he confronted his sin and realized his total inability to dispel the terror of living under the watchful eye of God. Yet when Luther understood the grace of God through reading Romans 1:17, his life was transformed. As a result, most of Europe entered into the Protestant Reformation. John Wesley, the founder of Methodism, found in Romans the catalyst for his conversion and went on to profoundly change English society. Countless similar stories can be recounted to underscore the importance of this letter in church history.

The Book of Romans in Christian Theology

As we study this amazing epistle, we must understand the apostle Paul, since his writings dominate the New Testament. Indeed, Paul's understanding of the words and works of God have been central for the

THE CONVERSION OF AUGUSTINE OF HIPPO

From *The Confessions of Saint Augustine*, A.D. 401

I cast myself down I know not how, under a certain fig-tree, giving full vent to my tears; and the floods of mine eyes gushed out an acceptable sacrifice to Thee. And, not indeed in these words, yet to this purpose, spake I much unto Thee: and Thou, O Lord, how long? how long, Lord, wilt Thou be angry for ever? Remember not our former iniquities, for I felt that I was held by them. I sent up these sorrowful words: How long, how long, "to-morrow, and tomorrow?" Why not now? why not is there this hour an end to my uncleanness?

So was I speaking and weeping in the most bitter contrition of my heart, when, lo! I heard from a neighbouring house a voice, as of boy or girl, I know not, chanting, and oft repeating, "Take up and read; Take up and read. " Instantly, my countenance altered, I began to think most intently whether children were wont in any kind of play to sing such words: nor could I remember ever to have heard the like. So checking the torrent of my tears, I arose; interpreting it to be no other than a command from God to open the book, and read the first chapter I should find. For I had heard of Antony, that coming in during the reading of the Gospel, he received the admonition, as if what was being read was spoken to him: Go, sell all that thou hast, and give to the poor, and thou shalt have treasure in heaven, and come and follow me: and by such oracle he was forthwith converted unto Thee. Eagerly then I returned to the place where Alypius was sitting; for there had I laid the volume of the Apostle when I arose thence. I seized, opened, and in silence read that section on which my eyes first fell: Not in rioting and drunkenness, not in chambering and wantonness, not in strife and envying; but put ye on the Lord Jesus Christ, and make not provision for the flesh, in concupiscence. No further would I read; nor needed I: for instantly at the end of this sentence, by a light as it were of serenity infused into my heart, all the darkness of doubt vanished away.

formation of the church. Terms such as *justification, sanctification, redemption*, and *glorification* are illuminated in the letters of Paul. The understanding of the nuances of these terms brings a believer to a profound place of praise for the awesome works of God.

It is crucial to understand the Epistle to the Romans as a whole before examining its parts. A proper understanding of the flow of the entire book provides safeguards for scriptural interpretation yet does not limit God's Word. Throughout Romans, Paul uses key building blocks to build his case. A view of these helps the reader to see the smaller parts of the epistle and understand how they fit into the larger scheme of Paul's gospel. Thus, a preliminary look at the concepts of sin, faith, the Mosaic Law, the work of the Holy Spirit, the role of Israel in God's plan, practical insights into the Christian's walk of faith and other critical points will help guide the study of this book.

Paul—The Human Author of Divine Scripture

The Book of Acts chronicles the rise of a man who would change the world through his obedience to the Lord Jesus Christ. But Paul didn't start out this way. At first, he thought that God wanted him to eliminate those who participated in a sect called "the Way" (Acts 9:2). This group identified with Jesus, a man who had been crucified and, they claimed, had risen from the dead. But many within the established religious leadership harshly rejected these people because of the scandal of the Cross. To them, a crucified person could not please God. Paul, who was then named Saul, joined those who vigorously rejected the disciples of Jesus. He gave hearty consent to the stoning of Stephen and "made havoc of the church, entering every house, and dragging off men and women, committing them to prison" (Acts 8:3).

Paul was trained as a rabbi, a teacher and biblical interpreter in first-century

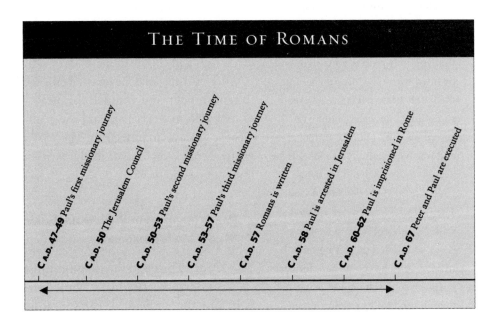

THE TIME OF ROMANS

C.A.D. 47-49 Paul's first missionary journey

C.A.D. 50 The Jerusalem Council

C.A.D. 50-53 Paul's second missionary journey

C.A.D. 53-57 Paul's third missionary journey

C.A.D. 57 Romans is written

C.A.D. 58 Paul is arrested in Jerusalem

C.A.D. 60-62 Paul is imprisoned in Rome

C.A.D. 67 Peter and Paul are executed

Judaism. He excelled in this role but totally missed the point of the Old Testament, even though it was the focus of his life. A radical event dramatically changed Paul's life.

The Book of Acts records this remarkable event. Paul was on his way to Damascus to persecute the disciples of Jesus when Jesus Himself appeared to him. Through this miracle, Paul realized his persecution of Jesus' disciples was actually the persecution of the Lord Jesus Christ Himself. Paul was blinded during his encounter with Christ, was led into Damascus, and was ushered into the kingdom of God by a faithful servant of Jesus named Ananias. Acts 9:17–22 states:

And Ananias went his way and entered the house; and laying his hands on him, he said, "Brother Saul, the Lord Jesus, who appeared to you on the road as you came, has sent me that you may receive your sight and be filled with the Holy Spirit." Immediately there fell from his eyes something like scales, and he received his sight at once; and he arose and was baptized…. Immediately he preached the Christ in the synagogues, that He is the Son of God. Then all who heard were amazed and said, "Is this not he who destroyed those who called on this name in Jerusalem, and has come here for that purpose, so that he might bring them bound to the chief priests?"

But Saul increased all the more in strength, and confounded the Jews who dwelt in Damascus, proving that this Jesus is the Christ.

From that time, Paul was an apostle to the Gentiles; fearless in his proclamation that Jesus truly is Messiah, the Promised One, in whom Israel should place its hope and through whom the Gentiles have access to the Father.

The Timing of Paul's Letter to the Romans

While there is no specific date in this letter, Paul evidently wrote to the Romans from Corinth while on his third missionary journey. At that time, Paul was on a mission to deliver money, which had been gathered in the Gentile churches, to the poor believers in Jerusalem (Rom. 15:22–29). Paul mentioned this in 1 Corinthians 16:1–3 and 2 Corinthians 8:1—9:1. After visiting the believers in Rome for refreshment and mutual encouragement (Rom. 1:11, 12), Paul was planning to travel to Jerusalem. Therefore, the letter was most likely written about A.D. 56 or 57.

Paul's Intention in Writing the Letter to the Romans

Paul's Epistle to the Romans must be understood first as a whole unit before the individual parts can be examined. When Paul wrote this letter, he was mindful that he had never visited the church at Rome (1:9–13), though he longed to be among them. Because of his lack of intimate contact with the believers in Rome, the letter exhibits a different tone from some of his other epistles. For instance, because Paul had spent significant time in Corinth, he was well aware of some of the concerns that existed in the Corinthian church. Paul pointedly addressed some of the issues confronting the church there and demonstrated extensive knowledge of their situation. The first letter to the Corinthian church is a classic example of an "occasional" letter, written to address issues raised by a specific historical circumstance. Most of Paul's letters exhibit such occasional nature whether written to an individual or a church. But the Epistle to the Romans shows little specific information about either the Roman context or even of Paul's immediate life situation. This has led scholars to debate the intention of the letter.

Some read into the situation of the letter and posit the idea that there were extensive Jew vs. Gentile problems in the Roman church. There is certainly a focus on Jews and Gentiles in the Epistle to the Romans, yet there are few links with the specifics of the believers in Rome. Virtually nothing is said regarding such a conflict in Rome. Others view the letter as primarily a treatment of justification by faith. While this was a key theme of the Protestant Reformation, and the Epistle to the Romans loomed large in the writings and teachings of the Protestant Reformers, such a reduction of the whole letter to one theological theme is inadequate. Still others think that the letter was written to give a summary of theology for the Roman believers. Yet certain key theological themes present in other letters such as the Resurrection of Christ (1 Cor. 15), the Second Coming of Christ (1 Thess. 4—5; 2 Thess. 2—3) and the supremacy of Christ (Col. 1) receive scant mention in Romans.

The Theme of the Letter to the Romans

The purpose of the letter to the Romans can be deduced from the flow of thought in the letter. There is widespread agreement that the theme of the letter is found in 1:16, 17. Paul, in typical form, first follows the conventions of first-century letter writing by identifying himself and his recipients in 1:1–7. While Paul explains more about his calling to the Romans than in other letters (see commentary on 1:1–6) due primarily to their lack of knowledge of Paul, the opening of the letter is in standard form. Next, the "thanksgiving" part of the letter, which is common in Paul's writing, is contained in 1:8–13. Thus, we find the epistle's theme after the important, though customary, opening remarks of the letter.

THE CAREER OF THE APOSTLE PAUL (1:5)

Origin:	Tarsus in Cilicia (Acts 22:3)
	Tribe of Benjamin (Phil. 3:5)
Training:	Learned tentmaking (Acts 18:3)
	Studied under Gamaliel (Acts 22:3)
Early Religion:	Hebrew and Pharisee (Phil. 3:5)
	Persecuted Christians (Acts 8:1–3; Phil. 3:6)
Salvation:	Met the risen Christ on the road to Damascus (Acts 9:1–8)
	Received the infilling of the Holy Spirit on the street called Straight (Acts 9:17)
Called to Missions:	Church at Antioch was instructed by the Holy Spirit to send out Paul to the work (Acts 13:1–3)
	Carried the gospel to the Gentiles (Gal. 2:7–10)
Roles:	Spoke up for the church at Antioch at the council of Jerusalem (Acts 15:1–35)
	Opposed Peter (Gal. 2:11–21)
	Disputed with Barnabas about John Mark (Acts 15:36–41)
Achievements:	Three extended missionary journeys (Acts 13—20)
	Founded numerous churches in Asia Minor, Greece, and possibly Spain (Rom. 15:24, 28)
	Wrote letters to numerous churches and various individuals that now make up one-fourth of our New Testament
End of life:	Following arrest in Jerusalem, was sent to Rome (Acts 21:27; 28:16–31) According to Christian tradition, released from prison allowing further missionary work; rearrested, imprisoned again in Rome, and beheaded outside of the city.

THE LIFE OF PAUL

Paul was born at Tarsus, the chief city of Cilicia (southeast Asia Minor). He was a citizen of Tarsus, "no mean city," as he called it (Acts 21:39). He was also born a Roman citizen (Acts 22:28), a privilege that worked to his advantage on several occasions during his apostolic ministry. Since Paul was born a Roman citizen, his father must have been a Roman citizen before him. "Paul" was part of his Roman name. In addition to his Roman name, he was given a Jewish name, "Saul," perhaps in memory of Israel's first king, a member of the tribe of Benjamin, to which Paul's family belonged.

His Jewish heritage meant much more to Paul than Roman citizenship. Unlike many Jews who had been scattered throughout the world, he and his family did not become assimilated to the Gentile way of life that surrounded them. This is suggested when Paul describes himself as "a Hebrew of the Hebrews" (Phil. 3:5), and confirmed by Paul's statement in Acts 22:3 that, while he was born in Tarsus, he was brought up in Jerusalem "at the feet of Gamaliel," the most illustrious rabbi of his day (Acts 5:34). Paul's parents wanted their son to be well-grounded in the best traditions of Jewish orthodoxy.

Paul proved an apt pupil. He outstripped many of his fellow students in his enthusiasm for ancestral traditions and in his zeal for the Jewish law. This zeal found a ready outlet in his assault on the infant church of Jerusalem. The church presented a threat to all that Paul held most dear. Its worst offense was its proclamation of one who had suffered a death cursed by the Jewish law as Lord and Messiah (Deut. 21:22–23). The survival of Israel demanded that the followers of Jesus be wiped out.

The first martyr of the Christian church was Stephen, one of the most outspoken leaders of the new movement. Luke told how Paul publicly associated himself with Stephen's executioners and then embarked on a campaign designed to suppress the church. Paul himself related how he "persecuted the church of God beyond measure and tried to destroy it" (Gal. 1:13).[1]

---

[1] Ronald F. Youngblood, general editor; F. F. Bruce and R. K. Harrison, consulting editors, *Nelson's New Illustrated Bible Dictionary:* An authoritative one-volume reference work on the Bible with full color illustrations [computer file], electronic edition of the revised edition of *Nelson's Illustrated Bible Dictionary*, Logos Library System, (Nashville: Thomas Nelson) 1997, © 1995.

Obviously, this letter is about the gospel of Jesus Christ. But we must understand what Paul means by this term and how the idea of *gospel* encompasses the power of God to salvation, the righteousness of God, and the existence of a people who live by faith. While these may seem like very familiar concepts, the letter qualifies them. It is the task of the reader of Romans to understand the meaning of these themes in the context of the epistle. The flow of the epistle is very deliberate in explaining these key concepts.

While Paul delineates the theme of the letter in 1:16, 17, the body of the letter begins at 1:18 and concludes at 15:13. Closing remarks begin at 15:14 and extend to the end of the epistle. The body of the letter contains the crucial concepts introduced by the theme. Paul addresses these concepts in deliberate style through meticulous argumentation. Oftentimes readers of this letter miss the movement of thought. So, it is important that we can see this movement and trace its paths before getting into the particulars of the text.

Guiding the Theme with Questions

The style of argumentation in the Epistle to the Romans is called *diatribe*. This technical form of debate was often used in the first century. Such a form is not hard to see in Romans. The essence of diatribe is to make a point and then propose questions that either challenge that point, like a verbal combatant, or lead into the next step of argument. A brief look at some of these questions will show how important this is for the apostle Paul. The imaginary verbal combatant is introduced in 2:1–5:

Therefore you are inexcusable, O man, whoever you are who judge, for in whatever you judge another you condemn yourself; for you who judge practice the same things. But we know that the judgment of God is according to truth against those who practice such things. And do you think this, O man, you who judge those practicing such things, and doing the same, that you will escape the judgment of God? Or do you despise the riches of His goodness, forbearance, and longsuffering, not knowing that the goodness of God leads you to repentance?

The context indicates that this imaginary questioner is probably of Jewish background, a receiver of the riches of God's goodness. His questions reveal a person who has a stake in the status and grace possessed by the Jewish people.

Here then are some of the questions that are contained in Romans:

- What advantage then has the Jew, or what is the profit of circumcision? (3:1)

- For what if some did not believe? Will their unbelief make the faithfulness of God without effect? (3:3)
- But if our unrighteousness demonstrates the righteousness of God, what shall we say? Is God unjust who inflicts wrath? (3:5)
- What then? Are we better than they? (3:9)
- Where is boasting then? It is excluded. By what law? Of works? (3:27)
- What then shall we say that Abraham our father has found according to the flesh? (4:1)
- Does this blessedness then come upon the circumcised only, or upon the uncircumcised also? For we say that faith was accounted to Abraham for righteousness. How then was it accounted? While he was circumcised, or uncircumcised? (4:9, 10)
- What shall we say then? Shall we continue in sin that grace may abound? Certainly not! How shall we who died to sin live any longer in it? Or do you not know that as many of us as were baptized into Christ Jesus were baptized into His death? (6:1–3)
- What then? Shall we sin because we are not under law but under grace? (6:15)
- Or do you not know, brethren (for I speak to those who know the law), that the law has dominion over a man as long as he lives? (7:1)
- Who will deliver me from this body of death? (7:24)

- What shall we say then? Is there unrighteousness with God? (9:14)
- What shall we say then? That Gentiles, who did not pursue righteousness, have attained to righteousness, even the righteousness of faith; but Israel, pursuing the law of righteousness, has not attained to the law of righteousness. Why? (9:30–32a)
- How then shall they call on Him in whom they have not believed? And how shall they believe in Him of whom they have not heard? And how shall they hear without a preacher? (10:14)
- Has God cast away His people? (11:1)
- Have they stumbled that they should fall? (11:11)

Proving the Righteousness of God

It is fascinating that Paul moves his argument along by questions asked by an imaginary questioner. The nature of these questions, as seen above, indicates a concern over whether or not God's ways are righteous. Many of the questions deal with the righteousness of God's actions in judging the sinner (particularly the Jew) and in providing a way of righteousness for the Gentile. Paul argues vigorously that justice is maintained throughout God's plan of redemption through Christ.

We must keep in mind Paul's concern for upholding God's justice throughout all His actions in judging, justifying, and dealing with the believer.

But the concern for justice doesn't end here. Paul must relate how God continues to be just and merciful to Israel. Thus, chapters 9—11 are not a parenthetical aside but crucial to the argument in the epistle. This is often missed in the study of this letter.

Since we see the emphasis on the justice and righteousness of God in Romans particularly in the first eleven chapters, it is important that the theme of the letter is consistent with this. In fact, in the good news of the kingdom of God the righteousness of God prevails. This righteousness is from faith to faith—that is, totally on the basis of faith. God's justice is manifested in this gospel message.

God's Righteousness Is Revealed in Judgment

The letter to the Romans develops the concept of God's righteousness. The first portion of the letter (1:18—3:20) meticulously argues that God is absolutely righteous and just. The standard for the Gentiles is implicit knowledge of God as revealed through creation (1:18–32). The behavior of the Gentiles is vile and despicable. Such sinfulness stems from a rejection of the knowledge of God. The Jews stand in hypocritical judgment of the Gentiles for such behavior, but because they break the law, they also are wicked (2:1—3:8). God metes out punishment based on law. It matters little whether a person is Jew or Gentile,

everyone is a law-breaker; all receive due punishment for their sins (3:9–20). God does not show favoritism.

God's Righteousness Is Revealed in Salvation

If Romans ended at chapter 3, verse 20, there would only be despair. But Paul answers the need of humanity through the wonderful turning point of 3:21. In 3:21—5:21, Paul points out the amazing provision that God has made for sinful people. There is a new way to be right with God that is not law-dependent. It is the way of righteousness through the obedience of Christ. This addresses the penalty of sin for those who embrace the Savior by faith. Thus, God's righteousness is fully met in Christ.

Romans chapter 4 uses the examples of Abraham and David to illustrate that this righteousness is consistent with God's way of working and meets the need for God's justice. In chapter 5, the era of righteousness by faith is shown to be totally superior to the era of the law. The law cannot bring righteousness to a sinner but grace can.

God's Provision for Practical Righteousness by the Spirit

How does this relate practically to the believer's need for righteous behavior? Chapters 6 through 8 deal with this issue. They show that, since a sinner cannot obtain righteousness through the law, so also practical righteousness cannot be obtained through keeping the law. Paul wishes the believers to see the absolute freedom from sin that is based purely on the work of Christ (6:1–23). This freedom is gained not through law but by grace. But Paul recognizes the believer's tendency to continue in a law orientation even though he or she is actually righteous in Christ. So, in chapter 7, Paul makes the case that law-oriented living only brings frustration, not practical freedom from sin. The only answer for the daily living of those who have embraced Jesus Christ by faith is to live in accordance with the Holy Spirit's movement in their lives. Chapter 8 is the believers' freedom manifesto. There is freedom from the law, freedom from sin, freedom from condemnation, freedom to live as God intended. It is a glorious freedom, full of hope for the future and strength for today.

God Is Righteous in Dealing with Israel

But the question of Israel's place in all of this argumentation is still at hand. Is God just in His dealings with Israel since He has provided a way of righteousness apart from the Old Covenant? Paul answers with a resounding *yes*.

The righteousness of God is upheld because Israel's history is not yet finished. There is a future for Israel as God continues to work in her midst. That is the point of Romans 9—11. God's justice is upheld in His dealings all along the way with Israel. He dealt with Israel justly and graciously in the past, He continues to do so in the present, and He guarantees a wonderful future for Israel. The only thing Paul can do at the end of all of this is break out in praise of God for His wonderful plan (11:33–36).

God's Justice and Mercy Lead to a Life in the Spirit

Having proved the wonderful mercy and justice of God in providing salvation for all people, Paul moves on to provide the practical ramifications of his teachings. In Romans 12:1—15:13, Paul turns his attention to very important and straightforward instructions on how the believers are to live. This pattern is seen in other letters of Paul (see Ephesians, for example). Earlier in the letter, Paul establishes his theological foundation upon bedrock and allows the practical commands to follow. It is amazing to see in Romans 12:9–21 a plethora of commands for the church to follow. It is as if they were held back until the theological foundations were established. Now Paul is free to let them burst forth. These last chapters are abundantly practical and provide essential marching orders for the church at Rome.

The progression of the letter to the Romans is logical and consistent with Paul's main concerns. When seen as a whole, it is evident that every aspect of the letter is crucial to proving Paul's point. Yet, the apostle also does not neglect practical instructions for living according to the Holy Spirit.

Chapter 1

Romans 1:1–32

PAUL AND THE BELIEVERS IN ROME

The Theme of the Epistle

Paul begins his letter in the customary fashion. He includes the description of the author, the recipient, and a blessing as well as a thanksgiving. While customary in form, the contents describe the apostle in ways that compel us to look at his Lord rather than his work. Paul describes himself and the church at Rome only in relation to the living God. He gives a standard blessing that is not a collection of empty, religious words spoken at religious functions, but words full of richness and meaning to those who have experienced the grace and peace of God for themselves.

Paul, a bondservant of Jesus Christ, called to be an apostle, separated to the gospel of God which He promised before through His prophets in the Holy Scriptures, concerning His Son Jesus Christ our Lord, who was born of the seed of David according to the flesh, and declared to be the Son of God with power according to the Spirit of holiness, by the resurrection from the dead. (1:1–4)

Paul, perhaps the best-known apostle, identifies himself here as a

WORD STUDY
APOSTLE

Apostle—*a special messenger of Jesus Christ; a person to whom Jesus dele-gated authority for certain tasks.* The word "apostle" is used of those twelve disciples whom Jesus sent out, two by two, during His ministry in Galilee to ex-pand His own ministry of preaching and healing. It was on that occasion, evi-dently, that they were first called "apostles" (Mark 3:14; 6:30).

The word "apostle" is sometimes used in the New Testament in a general sense of "messenger." For instance, when delegates of Christian communities were charged with conveying those churches' contributions to a charitable fund, they were described by Paul as "messengers [apostles] of the churches" (2 Cor. 8:23). Jesus also used the word this way when He quoted the proverb, "A servant is not greater than his master, nor he who is sent [literally, "an apostle"] greater than he who sent him" (John 13:16). Jesus Himself is called "the Apostle ... of our confession" (Heb. 3:1), a reference to His function as God's special Messenger to the world.

The word "apostle" has a wider meaning in the letters of the apostle Paul. It includes people who, like himself, were not included in the Twelve, but who saw the risen Christ and were specially commissioned by Him. Paul's claim to be an apostle was questioned by others. He based his apostleship, however, on the direct call of the exalted Lord who appeared to him on the Damascus Road and on the Lord's blessing of his ministry in winning converts and establishing churches (1 Cor. 15:10).

Apparently, Paul also counted James, the Lord's brother, as an apostle (Gal. 1:19). This James was not one of the Twelve; in fact, he was not a believer in Je-sus before the Crucifixion (John 7:5). It was the resurrected Lord who "appeared to James" (1 Cor. 15:7) and presumably commissioned him for his ministry. When Paul says Jesus was seen not only by James but also by "all the apostles" (1 Cor. 15:7), he seems to be describing a wider group than "the Twelve" to whom Jesus appeared earlier (1 Cor. 15:5).

As pioneers in the work of making converts and planting churches, apostles were exposed to special dangers. When persecution erupted, they were the pri-mary targets for attack (1 Cor. 4:9–13). Paul, in particular, welcomed the suffer-ing he endured as an apostle because it was his way of participating in the suffering of Christ (Rom. 8:17; 2 Cor. 1:5–7).

The authority committed to the apostles by Christ was unique. It could not be transmitted to others. The apostles could install elders or other leaders and teachers in the churches, and they could authorize them to assume special responsibilities; but apostolic authority could not be transferred. Their authority has not come to us through their successors; it has come through their writings, which are contained in the New Testament.[2]

bondservant of Jesus Christ. A relationship with the King of kings can only be characterized as the utmost of subordinate relationships. Of this, the apostle is sure. Indeed, Paul punctuates this slave-King relationship using three aspects of the Lord's name. Royalty fills this designation, for the essence of the idea of the Christ, i.e. Messiah, is found in the promises that a new King shall come and rule the kingdom. This King emerges from the seed of David and inherits David's throne forever. This kingdom never ends, nor does the reign of its King. With this in mind, it is no wonder that the essential posture of the believer, even one as great as Paul, is to be one of humble service.

It is, therefore, important that we never regard the name Jesus Christ simply as a first name-last name convention. Certainly many assume that

this is the case. But the title *Christ* is too important. It is not simply a name. Christ came in the flesh, died, and was raised from the dead, and rules over us as the Promised One. Submission to Him as the King highlights the Spirit-filled life. Paul learned this well in his encounter with Jesus on the road to Damascus (Acts 9). Then he asked the right question: "Who are you, Lord?" (Acts 9:5). No advance can be made in the Christian life without an understanding of this fundamental principle: The Lord is my Master and I am His bondservant.

With this established, Paul moves on to describe himself. This section is larger than in his other letters since Paul did not have a direct relationship with the believers in Rome. He found it necessary to connect with his readers in other ways. One example of this is found in Romans 16 where it is obvious that he knows many of the

2 Ronald F. Youngblood, general editor; F. F. Bruce and R. K. Harrison, consulting editors, *Nelson's New Illustrated Bible Dictionary: An authoritative one-volume reference work on the Bible with full color illustrations* [computer file], electronic edition of the revised edition of *Nelson's Illustrated Bible Dictionary*, Logos Library System, (Nashville: Thomas Nelson) 1997, © 1995.

Romans by name. This creates a link between himself and his readers.

But Paul's greatest link with the Roman believers is found in his distinct identification with God's Son. The bond between believers that exists through Christ far exceeds simple personal acquaintance. This is the fellowship of the Holy Spirit, which comes through mutual relationship with Jesus Christ. It overshadows natural connections or obstructions. Of this, we can be extremely grateful. The work of God the Spirit binds believers together despite geographical distance or even historical distance. The same Spirit is at work in this century just as He was at work in Paul's day.

Paul was called to be an apostle (1:7) and separated to the gospel of God (v. 8). His lowliest self-identification gives way to the highest calling of God: Paul is called and separated as an apostle with good news. This gospel is not just any good news. It is the history-altering message from God Himself. Paul dives into this deeply. His phrases bring out the grandeur of this gospel, which is precisely focused on the Son of God, the Lord Jesus Christ. Paul inextricably links his apostolic identity and ministry with the person of Christ. He likewise links the Roman believers' identity. Note how Paul structures his thoughts:

I. Paul ... separated to the gospel of God

A. Which He promised before through His prophets in the Holy Scriptures

B. Concerning His Son Jesus Christ our Lord

1. Who was born of the seed of David according to the flesh

2. And declared to be the Son of God with power

a. According to the Spirit of holiness

b. By the resurrection from the dead

3. Through Him, we have received grace and apostleship

a. For obedience to the faith among all nations for His name

b. Among whom you also are the called of Jesus Christ

This is all one sentence in the original Greek text, a style that Paul uses often. It is as if Paul wishes to move to the background in describing his authority as an apostle. So, he puts Christ forward. Paul diminishes in comparison. The minister leads with the message about the great King.

He points out that God has promised this through the prophets in the Holy Scriptures. The Holy Spirit ordained that we find the message of the gospel in the Old Testament. Isaiah 53 and Jeremiah 31 are primary "promise" texts; but Paul goes beyond these to include many Old Testament references about the new era of the kingdom of God, as we shall see. Romans is full of biblical texts showing how the mighty, saving work of God was foretold by the prophets.

God Himself designed this gospel. It concerns "His Son Jesus Christ our Lord" (1:3). Paul defines his understanding of Jesus like this: He is a human being named Jesus who is the Son of God, the Messiah-King, and the Master. It is highly probable that the term *Lord* further describes the nature of Jesus as being God Himself. The Greek word *kurios* is used to translate the Hebrew YHWH (Jehovah) in the Septuagint, the ancient Greek translation of the Old Testament. This strengthens the concept of deity to Paul's understanding of the man Jesus.

Yet, the humanity of Christ is also highlighted, though this is described after the divine attributes to securely fix the nature of Jesus prior to His Incarnation. Jesus does not become the Son of God through His birth; He already was God's Son.

Christ becomes flesh through an ordinary birth to an extraordinary lineage. Jesus is born into the line of the great king David because it is required of the Messiah-King to be of the seed of David. And so, He fulfills this prophecy. Jesus lived according to the flesh on earth. The phrase *according to the flesh* (Greek *kata sarka*) is often used in Paul's writing to describe a way of living that is not godly. Here it

CROSS REFERENCE
Acts 2:36–38

The speeches of Acts show us the importance of the proclamation of the Resurrection of Christ. In each of the major speeches of Acts, Luke, the author of Acts, highlights the Resurrection as the pivotal element that turned listeners toward repentance. In Acts 2, Peter preached Jesus as the resurrected One whom God has made both Lord and Christ. In other words, he told the crowd to come to grips with the fact that they put to death the One who is exalted by God the Father. The people were cut to the heart and wondered what to do in response. Peter urged them to repent, be baptized, and gave them the assurance that they would receive the Holy Spirit.

Luke presents the common elements of the account of Jesus' holy, sacrificial life, His unjust death at the hands of the religious authorities, the Resurrection of Christ as historical reality, the urgent plea to repent and believe in the Lord, and the response of the hearers. From this account of apostolic preaching we conclude that we must not shy away from the calling to believe in the Lord based upon the revelation of His Resurrection.

ACCENT ON APPLICATION
The Empowering Holy Spirit

We must always remember that the same Holy Spirit who empowered Jesus for holy living indwells us. This is an awesome thought! This very truth allows people who have Christ as Lord and Savior to live lives that please God. Kingdom living in practice requires that the King indwell a person. The Holy Spirit is the One who empowered Jesus for kingdom life on earth and who empowers us as well. It is improper to say that we cannot live a Christ-like life since we have the Spirit indwelling us. We will not attain total Christ-likeness this side of heaven, of course, but we will exhibit some of His life in the world by the presence of the Holy Spirit.

describes living as a human being. Examining this yields a view of Jesus in weakness. Jesus lived out a life on earth that was dramatic in word and deed but was characterized most by the humbling and suffering of the Son of God. Jesus was crucified as a common criminal. This is hardly the mark of royalty. His words did not exhibit philosophical wisdom in the eyes of the Greeks and this became a stumbling block to many. Of course, the story of Christ's earthly existence does not end at the Cross. The Resurrection is the pinnacle event that distinguishes Jesus from all others. Jesus the crucified one is also Christ the resurrected one. In this way God royally installs Jesus Christ as King for all to see. As Peter declared at Pentecost, "God made this Jesus, whom you crucified, both Lord and Christ" (Acts 2:36).

No longer does weakness characterize the existence of Jesus. We now see power. The work of the Cross obviously has God's approval; the Lord's words have obvious authority; and His works are signs of the kingdom, which arrived with power from on high.

We must not underestimate how powerful this concept of the vindication of Christ is for Paul. He was well aware of the criticisms pertaining to Jesus. He was a main persecutor of those who advocated following this Messiah, even agreeing with those who put Stephen to death. It made no sense to Paul that anyone would want to follow a cursed, crucified man. But he saw Jesus on the road to Damascus and heard about all of the post-resurrection sightings (1 Cor. 15:3–5) of Jesus which altered Paul's view forever. And our views are altered as well. It is not possible to conclude that Jesus was just a gifted teacher. Nor is it acceptable to assert that, as a miracle worker, God was with Him without also stating that He is the King and deserves total devotion. One cannot be halfway regarding Jesus. He either is the resurrected, God approved Savior-Messiah-Lord-King or He is none of those. This is the reason Paul goes to great lengths, both in terms of geographical travels, as well as in physical and emotional travail for the gospel. This is truly good news for all.

Another phrase in this verse is worth noting: Jesus was resurrected "according to the Spirit of holiness." This unusual phrase is only found in this verse. It would be easy to say that it refers to the Holy Spirit in another way. But that is probably not the whole story. Certainly, the Holy Spirit is active. Few doubt this. But the phrase *according to the Spirit of holiness* is intentionally in opposition to the phrase *according to the flesh*. Paul contrasts the simple humanity of Jesus with the unusual aspect of His life, that of His holiness. Jesus exhibited a way of life that distinguished Him from all others who have walked this earth. It is this quality of the life that is remarkable. He walks with absolute holiness by the power of the Holy Spirit. The Holy Spirit empowers Jesus to live in absolute purity before God.

God publicly rewarded Jesus for this absolute holiness and purity by raising Him from the dead. This is good news in two ways. First, we have access to eternal life through the

perfect life, death, and resurrection of Jesus. Second, we have access to Jesus' way of life, that is, to be totally controlled by the Holy Spirit and, thus, live in holiness before God. This is not hypothetical. The term *in Christ* is one of Paul's favorite phrases. It indicates that one is living with all of the benefits of Christ's life. Being empowered by the Holy Spirit for a way of life like Jesus' is to be normal, not peculiar. This is the message of Romans chapter 8.

Through Him we have received grace and apostleship for obedience to the faith among all nations for His name, among whom you also are the called of Jesus Christ; (1:5, 6)

In Romans 1:5, Paul continues to talk about what he received from God. These extend even to the Roman believers. For the Spirit of God through Paul highlights the grace and apostleship that are his in Christ but which have an impact upon others. There is no self-aggrandizement here in Paul. He does not lift himself high in order to gain accolades from the Romans. He points out that God's work is centered in him to accomplish his appointed task as apostle. The intended result of his apostleship is to gain "obedience to the faith among all nations." Paul refers not only to the obedience *to* the faith here, but also to the obedience that comes *from* faith. He knows there is no faith in Jesus that will not result in a changed lifestyle.

But this is not a law-oriented obedience. It is Spirit motivated and oriented; it is the way of the New Covenant; the way of the law written on the heart (Jer. 31:31–34). Within Paul's call to the Gentiles is his ministry to the Roman believers as well (vv. 6, 7) because they are among the nations who "are also the called of Jesus Christ." The same God calls Paul for apostleship and the Romans to the obedience of faith. The same Jesus is to be master of both Paul and the Romans.

The Roman believers are the beloved of God, living in the full blessing of the kingdom of God inaugurated by the installation of the King of kings through the Resurrection of Christ. Paul highlights this love later in this epistle (5:8; 8:39). The amazing realization that we live as the beloved of God brings out in us a sense of gratitude and peace towards God.

To all who are in Rome, beloved of God, called to be saints: (1:7a)

The Roman believers are called to be saints (v. 7). Ecclesiastical officials do not give this sainthood to some worthy Christian. No, every believer is called by God to be holy. In the Old Testament, certain utensils in the tabernacle and temple were set apart for special use and certain people were set apart for special service. The concept of a people who are set apart is at the heart of the calling of God for believers. This is not the odd way of people with a "holier than thou" attitude. It is the winsome way of the believer living the new kingdom lifestyle with all of its blessings, power, and responsibilities. People do not simply *will* this into

CROSS REFERENCE
James 2:23–26

"And the Scripture was fulfilled which says, 'Abraham believed God and it was accounted to him for righteousness.' ... For as the body without the spirit is dead, so faith without works is dead also." Both Paul and James point to Abraham as the pioneer who embraced righteousness by faith. James makes explicit what Paul implies in Romans 1:5—obedience is an outworking of faith. Of course, Paul further clarifies this in Romans chapters 6—8 by declaring that believers have freedom from the dominion of sin and have the power to live by the Holy Spirit.

ACCENT ON APPLICATION
Praying Beyond Ourselves

Few would deny the importance of prayer. But we should examine whether we are including brothers and sisters in Christ in other locations in our prayers. Obviously, Paul had a worldwide perspective on the Christian movement. Do we? Or are we simply thinking of our own personal problems and situations? Perhaps we are concerned only with our own congregation. Paul would have us be people on the lookout for what God is doing in the world-at-large.

existence. Later in the epistle, Paul is quite specific that God works by the Holy Spirit to bring this about. Simply giving moral imperatives for people to follow will not produce saints in the new era of the kingdom. Nothing short of a complete renewal of the person will bring this change about. God's way through Christ produces new life that brings forth the "obedience of faith" to which Paul calls the Gentiles.

Grace to you and peace from God our Father and the Lord Jesus Christ. (1:7b)

Here Paul combined common Greek and Hebrew greetings and brought them into the realm of the kingdom of God. The normal Greek greeting *charein* ("greetings") becomes *charis* ("grace"). The normal Hebrew greeting *shalom* becomes, in Greek, *eirene* ("peace"). God is the author of grace and peace through Christ Jesus.

Both grace and peace ought not to be expected by people. In a dramatic turn of events God has changed the destiny of the individual sinner. In Romans chapter two God says that all who break the law, whether the written law or the unwritten law of conscience, deserve His wrath. For there will be "indignation and wrath, tribulation and anguish, on every soul of man who does evil, of the Jew first and also of the Greek" (2:8, 9). But through the saving work of Christ and the response of faith on the part of the sinner this destiny is changed. Instead of wrath we receive peace "through our Lord Jesus Christ." Apart from Christ no peace is possible. The Roman believers share in grace and peace just as do all the churches.

Paul closes this introductory paragraph with a somewhat formal blessing. Yet for Paul there is nothing formal about "grace and peace from God our Father and the Lord Jesus Christ." Far from it, Paul relies upon this grace and peace every day in his own life. In this epistle, he calls the

Roman believers to understand this grace and peace and to live it out. We who have received grace in our salvation have experienced peace with God through our Lord Jesus Christ (5:1). And we are to live in the good of it at all times.

First, I thank my God through Jesus Christ for you all, that your faith is spoken of throughout the whole world. (1:8)

Paul's pastoral concern for a church he has not yet visited pours out in his first reflection on the believers in Rome. God has obviously done a great work among these followers of Christ. In the midst of the secular city of Rome, the center of the governmental structures of the Empire, the faith of these believers is

ACCENT ON APPLICATION
Romans 1:9

"Without ceasing I make mention of you always in my prayers."

With this verse, Paul provides a wonderful glimpse into his prayer life and, in so doing, presents prayer principles for believers. Christians gain three powerful examples from these simple words. We note the frequency, the focus, and the fashion of Paul's prayer life.

First, Paul prays without ceasing. This does not mean that he never did anything else! No, he prayed continually throughout the day. He developed a posture of continued prayer as part of his daily life. He practiced God's continual presence.

Second, he prayed with a focus on the needs of people elsewhere. He did not dwell on his own needs. He gave himself to the ministry of intercession for others. He knew of other people's needs and brought them before the Father.

Third, he had a regular time of specific prayer ("in my prayers"). His prayer was a planned activity, not a random activity. So we can ask: Do I have a regular sense of God's presence? Do I know the needs of others so that I may bring their needs before God? Do I have a regular time of daily prayer?

Examine whether you include brothers and sisters in Christ in other locations in your prayers. Obviously, Paul had a universal perspective on the Christian movement. Do you? Or are you only thinking of your personal problems and situations? Perhaps you are concerned only with your own congregation. Paul would have you on the lookout for what God is doing in the world-at-large, not your own small world.

being spoken of in all of the churches of Jesus Christ. We can't help but notice Paul's abundant joy as he thinks about what is happening among these believers. The encouraging words of verse 8 pave the way for further instructions for these now famous believers.

_____

For God is my witness, whom I serve with my spirit in the gospel of His Son, that without ceasing I make mention of you always in my prayers, making request if, by some means, now at last I may find a way in the will of God to come to you. (1:9, 10)

We move from a picture of Paul the apostle in 1:1–5 to a portrait of Paul the man of prayer. He prays without ceasing for these Roman believers. His prayer is for their benefit in two ways. First, he gives thanks for them to God. Second, he wishes for a mutually beneficial experience and an even fuller blessing from God, which they may receive from his presence among them. Yet it is always Paul's desire to be within God's will. We certainly may recall the scene in the Garden of Gethsemane when Jesus Himself prayed the Father that "this cup pass" from Him (Matt. 26:39). But even Jesus was careful to add "nevertheless, not as I will, but as You will."

Paul truly desired to be among the Roman believers. He would have enjoyed that though it may seem to be a bit selfish. But, like Jesus, he added the caveat that he wished only to be in God's will. The work of God must continue, but it does so by prayer. Paul was not lulled into thinking that by his own efforts the work of grace would continue. God intends that even the greatest of the apostles is great only if he prays before he works.

_____

For I long to see you, that I may impart to you some spiritual gift, so that you may be established—that is, that I may be encouraged together with you by the mutual faith both of you and me. (1:11, 12)

Here we see Paul's giving heart. His desire is to be a benefit to these believers. He sees the key to this in the ministry of the Holy Spirit among them. Primary in this regard is the Holy Spirit-directed ministry of Paul's own gift (Greek, *charisma*). But this is not simply any gift. It is a gift given by the Holy Spirit. Here Paul is probably referring to his gift of apostleship and ability to proclaim the Good News of the kingdom of God.

_____

Now I do not want you to be unaware, brethren, that I often planned to come to you (but was hindered until now), that I might have some fruit among you also, just as among the other Gentiles. (1:13)

While Paul elsewhere talks of spiritual gifts (I Cor. 12—14; Greek, *charismata*), here he speaks of a harvest of new believers among them. In so doing, there is mutual encouragement and a further establishing of the church in Rome. Whenever the gift of God is at work by the Holy Spirit, a mutual edification results and faith deepens. Paul's calling is to bring this message to the Gentiles. Of course Paul is not saying that the Roman church itself is deficient and needs correct preaching. Rather he simply wants the blessing of mutual ministry among the believers in Rome. Yet, God did not allow it. And this is God's prerogative! So, Paul's hope is to travel to be with them in Rome. This is a definite indication that Paul had never visited the church at Rome. He wishes that to change, if it is God's will.

I am a debtor both to Greeks and to barbarians, both to wise and to

WORD STUDY
WRATH

Wrath—*the personal manifestation of God's holy, moral character in exacting just judgment against sin.* Wrath is not impersonal nor is it irrational and fitful like anger. It is in no way vindictive or malicious. It is holy indignation—God's anger is directed against sin because of its destructive power and the havoc it wreaks in ruining His benevolent intent for man.

God's wrath is an expression of His holy love. If God were incapable of wrath, His love would be no more than a frail, maudlin sentimentality and the concept of mercy would be meaningless. Not only so, Christ's death on the Cross would have been a cruel and unnecessary expense.

The Bible reveals that human beings are "by nature children of wrath" (Eph. 2:3) and that "the wrath of God is revealed from heaven against all ungodliness and unrighteousness of men, who suppress the truth in unrighteousness" (Rom. 1:18). Thus, all people—either by nature or calculated enterprise—have earned judgment for sin. But there is promise, since Christ died. We can be "justified by His blood [and] be saved from wrath through Him" (Rom. 5:9). The magnitude of God's love is manifested in the Cross, where God's only Son experienced the wrath of God on sin by bearing it on our behalf.

Ultimately, "The day of the Lord's wrath" (Zeph. 1:18), identical with "the great day of the Lord" (Zeph. 1:14), will come upon this world. "The wrath of the Lamb" (Rev. 6:16) will be manifest through Jesus Christ, as it will fall on the ungodly at His Second Coming (1 Thess. 1:10; 5:9; 2 Thess. 1:7–10).

unwise. So, as much as is in me, I am ready to preach the gospel to you who are in Rome also. (1:14, 15)

The Holy Spirit has so worked in Paul that he senses a deep obligation, like an outstanding debt, to all Gentiles. The payment is made by his proclamation of the gospel. While Paul may have been quite comfortable with the Greeks (for he was raised in the Greek culture of Tarsus), he was also ready to speak to those who may be foreigners—the barbarians. He is ready to speak to anyone, regardless of his or her training or education. It was not Paul's business to decide who was ready to hear the message. He simply gave the message. Rome was the ideal place to reach many, many Gentiles from all walks of life. So, Paul's desire is clear; his mandate is clear; above this, he only hopes to soon visit his fellow-believers in Rome.

God's Righteousness Is Upheld in the Gospel

Romans 1:16, 17

For I am not ashamed of the gospel of Christ, for it is the power of God to salvation for everyone who believes, for the Jew first and also for the Greek. For in it the righteousness of God is revealed from faith to faith; as it is written, "The just shall live by faith." (1:16, 17)

Paul establishes the essence of his message in these introductory verses. The message for which Paul lives and by which he defines his existence is called the gospel, which means *the Good News*. Certain elements of this are clearly seen. First, this gospel is for both the Jew and the Greek. It is important for Paul to make the playing field level for each group because God sees them as equal in regards to sin (*guilty*; 1:18—3:20) and equal in regards to their ability to receive righteousness based on faith (*innocent*; 3:21—5:21). The very righteousness of God is contained in Paul's gospel and is received utterly by faith for those who believe. Paul has no reason to be ashamed of this gospel for in it God's righteousness is upheld. In no way is God seen to be either soft on sin or ungracious to the sinner. When dealing with humanity God upholds His own righteous standards and still provides salvation and abundant life to the repentant sinner who embraces His Son. It is this that Paul develops throughout the first eleven chapters of his letter to the Romans.

For I am not ashamed of the gospel of Christ, for it is the power of God to salvation for everyone who believes, for the Jew first and also for the Greek. (1:16)

The fact that Paul is not ashamed of the gospel relates to his absolute

ACCENT ON APPLICATION
Confidence in God's Ways

It is evident that Paul did not waver in proclaiming the gospel of the kingdom because he was convinced of God's perfect dealings with humanity. As we evaluate our own presentation of the message of the grace of God, are we as convinced as Paul was of the perfect blend of justice and grace in God? Or are we hesitant? Such certitude is of tremendous benefit when providing witness to those who have yet to embrace the kingdom message. Perhaps we must identify our own hesitance as a lack of belief in the absolute fairness of God in reference to His justice and mercy. Paul did not waver in his embrace of God's perfect treatment of humanity. If we have this settled in our minds, we can move ahead with bold presentation of the truth of the Christian gospel to others. There is no apology, no possibility of being ashamed of our message when this is understood and embraced.

confidence that God is always consistent with His righteousness and mercy. In no way does Paul hold back on this issue when he proclaims the gospel. The Good News of the kingdom of God is perfectly consistent with God's standard of righteousness. In no way is there injustice with God. This was Paul's message. Paul's boldness did not result from a mere bolstering of emotional fortitude. His firm declaration emanated from the theological certainty that God's way of providing salvation is just, merciful, and totally consistent with His nature and purposes.

For in it the righteousness of God is revealed from faith to faith; as it is written, "The just shall live by faith." (1:17)

In the gospel of Jesus Christ, God reveals a perfect way of redeeming individuals that is also perfectly consistent with God's own justice and righteousness. Sin cannot simply be ignored; justice demands that something be done about transgressions. The key to this is faith. The word *faith* (Greek, *pistis*) is used both for the ideas of *trust* and *belief* as well as *faithfulness*. As we will see in Romans 3:21—5:21, Paul speaks of the faith of the believer as well as the faithfulness of Christ. Both are, of course, crucial. But for now, it is important to set the stage for what is coming. For this we have Habakkuk 2:4, the very important biblical foundation for Paul's message: "The just shall live by faith." This has broad meaning.

QUESTIONS FOR PERSONAL REFLECTION AND GROUP DISCUSSION

Read Romans 1:1–17 and then answer the following questions.

1. According to Romans 1:1–6, how did Paul describe himself?

2. What do you learn about Jesus Christ from Romans 1:1–6? List four characteristics or truths.

3. What springs from your faith, according to Romans 1:5?

4. What are Paul's desires for the believers in the church at Rome?

5. Why is Paul not ashamed of the gospel?

6. What are the reasons that Paul thought the gospel reveals the righteousness of God?

7. Paul is an example of a person who understood what it is to have a life of ministry. What can you learn about his attitudes and actions from this section of Romans?

8. While you may not be ashamed of the gospel, you may not always exhibit boldness in your witness for Christ. Why is this the case? What hinders you?

9. How can you become more at ease and, in fact, eager to share the gospel with others?

10. Think of those with whom you would like to share the gospel but as yet have been unable to. Pray for these people this week.

    Evaluate your own attitude toward service for Christ in comparison to Paul's. What do you need to change or enhance?

God's Righteous Judgment of the Gentiles

Romans 1:18–32

It may seem odd that Paul begins his treatment of God's righteousness by speaking of the wrath of God. After all, where is the good news in this? Yet, if God can be counted on in judgment, then He can be relied upon in other ways. God is not arbitrary or capricious. This is proven in this section.

We start with those who were considered the worst offenders: the Gentiles. Though the list at the end of this chapter makes it clear that God must bring wrath upon those who practice heinous acts such as idolatry, sexual immorality, murder, hating God, etc. (vv. 28–31), the Spirit of God reveals that the first sin is not outward, but inward: The suppression of the truth about God. This posture of unrighteousness leads to the rejection of the knowledge of the revealed God. The refusal to acknowledge the truth ultimately leads to the behaviors listed below.

For the wrath of God is revealed from heaven against all ungodliness and unrighteousness of men, who suppress the truth in unrighteousness, because what may be known of God is manifest in them, for God has shown it to them.
(1:18, 19)

It is important to note that in this paragraph in the original Greek manuscript, *revealed* is the first word. This emphasis underlines the fact that the revelation of wrath is as much a part of the revelation of God as is righteousness

---

CROSS REFERENCE
1 Corinthians 1:20, 21

"Where is the wise? Where is the scribe? Where is the disputer of this age? Has not God made foolish the wisdom of this world? For since, in the wisdom of God the world through wisdom did not know God, it pleased God through the foolishness of the message preached to save those who believe."

Paul declares that the gospel of Christ is foolish from the world's point of view. Yet, worldly religious wisdom appeals to many who have not yet been redeemed. This should not be surprising. Even the Corinthian believers preferred the Greek philosophical ideas to a simple message of the Cross of Christ. They thought Paul should become more sophisticated in his thinking. Such preference for a worldly spirituality demonstrates the futility of the mind (Rom. 1:21).

CROSS REFERENCE
Galatians 5:19–21

"Now the works of the flesh are evident ..."
God gives us an organized and categorized list of vices in Galatians 5:19–21. While we might add more to the list, this section of Scripture includes sexual sins (adultery, fornication, uncleanness, lewdness), religious sins (idolatry and sorcery), relational sins (contentions, jealousies, outburst of wrath, selfish ambitions, dissensions, heresies, envy, murders), and indulgences of the body (drunkenness and revelries). Paul concludes by saying, "and the like," to include other sins not listed. We may add greed or covetousness to the list (Col. 3:5) and have a complete list. Often people have specific weaknesses in one or more of these *areas*. Specific focus of repentance, encouragement, prayer, and other means of support may be made by and on behalf of the person succumbing to such influences.

and grace. But God does not inflict wrath irrationally or without sufficient cause. The Spirit of God revealed to Paul that wrath and righteousness belong together because God's character in dealing with humanity is right. Any charge of injustice passes away in the light of the argument of these verses.

Paul states that there are two aspects of the revelation of God: The internal revelation (in them) and the external revelation (to them). Both are gracious works of God, which are later spurned. Here we see that God has given great revelation of Himself in the created realm. This manifestation from God presents itself as a movement of God without regard to whether humanity merits it or not. God simply gives this revelation of Himself. The particulars of the evidence are given in the next verse.

For since the creation of the world His invisible attributes are clearly seen, being understood by the things that are made, even His eternal power and Godhead, so that they are without excuse, because, although they knew God, they did not glorify Him as God, nor were thankful, but became futile in their thoughts, and their foolish hearts were darkened. (1:20, 21)

The phrase *since the creation of the world* is intended to signify not the one act of creation but the continuation of the revelation of God since that first day. He reveals Himself, and continues to reveal Himself through the created order. Paul then provides intentional irony by saying that God's invisible attributes are clearly seen. At the very least, God's dynamic power and order are seen in the things that are made. They exist out of nothing. He simply brings them into being. And so, through the created realm God impresses something wonderful on the minds of people: His eternal power and nature. God brings such things into the mind's eye. Thus, again, we see that the outward manifestation of God in creation is attested to, as it impresses itself upon the minds of people. This evidence of God and knowledge of God must be acted upon. Every person has a notion of God's greatness, power, and nature. The question is whether this is gratefully received and acted upon, or it is spurned.

The Gentiles spurned such knowledge of God so they are without excuse. Their actions betray their minds and their decisions. They refused to glorify God or even be thankful. Instead of the fullness of life that comes from the knowledge of God, they chose the emptiness and futility of mind that comes from rejecting God's revelation. The rejection leads to the darkening of the heart as well as the futility of the mind, which has no anchor in God's revelation. Justice is upheld in bringing wrath upon them.

Professing to be wise, they became fools, and changed the glory of the incorruptible God into an image made like corruptible man—and birds and four-footed animals and creeping things. (1:22, 23)

The irony continues: It is hard to grasp the incongruity of spurning the almighty God in all His glory and embracing inanimate idols! Yet that is exactly what was done. And it was called "wise" by the perpetrators! The foolishness shines like the noonday sun yet it is not seen by those who attempt to embrace life without the anchor of the knowledge of God. They create their own gods and call it wise in the face of the only wise God of creation who reveals Himself to humanity. God Himself created the "birds and four-footed animals and creeping things" and yet images of such things are assigned glory by humans. It is bad enough to worship such things as animals themselves; but it is totally absurd to erect "dumb idols" as Paul calls them in 1 Corinthians 8 and call them gods. Such is the wisdom that is without God's revelation.

Therefore God also gave them up to uncleanness, in the lusts of their hearts, to dishonor their bodies among themselves, who exchanged the truth of God for the lie, and worshiped and served the creature rather than the Creator, who is blessed forever. Amen. (1:24, 25)

Verse 24 begins a three-fold action of the Almighty God. God has decided to allow humanity to reap the consequences of the choices made. Certainly, the glorification of the Almighty would have brought blessing. Embrace of the revelation of God would have brought true wisdom. Recognition of the divine attributes of God would have brought perspective on life. But where there is refusal to acknowledge God's rightful place, then God allows people to get what they want. Unfortunately, this spells disaster for humanity.

Rejection of God's revelation, whether by an unbeliever or a believer, can only be done at peril.

Embrace of the full knowledge of God secures a place of protection and joy. But God gave those who refused to acknowledge Him what they wanted—"uncleanness, in the lusts of their hearts." Again, the internal precedes the external. Certainly the dishonoring of their bodies is heinous, but internal uncleanness and foul-heartedness comes first.

Paul, by the Spirit, reminds his readers that this points to false worship. Anytime we "exchange the truth of God for a lie," as he says, we are in extreme peril. The worship and service of the creature makes the physical

WORD STUDY
FOOL, FOOLISHNESS

Fool, Foolishness—*a stupid person or a senseless act.* In the Bible, the most foolish person of all is one who denies the reality of God the Father: "The fool has said in his heart, 'There is no God'" (Ps. 14:1; 53:1). Like the Book of Proverbs, where "fool" denotes a person who is morally and spiritually deficient, Jesus contrasted wise and foolish persons. Persons who keep His sayings are wise; those who do not are foolish (Matt. 7:24–27). The use of the word "fool" in Matthew 5:22 is a special case. Jesus warned against using the word fool as a form of abuse. This word expressed hatred in one's heart toward others; therefore, Jesus condemned the use of the word in this way.

Paul called the preaching of the crucified Christ "foolishness" in the eyes of unbelievers. For believers, however, the message of the cross is the power and wisdom of God (1 Cor. 1:23–24).[3]

---

[3] Ronald F. Youngblood, general editor; F. F. Bruce and R. K. Harrison, consulting editors, *Nelson's New Illustrated Bible Dictionary: An authoritative one-volume reference work on the Bible with full color illustrations* [computer file], electronic edition of the revised edition of *Nelson's Illustrated Bible Dictionary*, Logos Library System, (Nashville: Thomas Nelson) 1997, © 1995.

WORD STUDY
HOMOSEXUAL

Homosexual—*a person who is attracted sexually to members of his or her own sex.* Homosexual behavior is prohibited in Scripture (Lev. 20:13) and was a major cause of the divine judgment against Sodom and Gomorrah (Gen. 19:4–5, 12–13). The apostle Paul listed homosexuals among "the unrighteous" who would not inherit the kingdom of God (1 Cor. 6:9), and declared that God's wrath stands against such behavior, whether practiced by men or women (Rom. 1:26–27).[4]

realm the center of life rather than a testimony that points to the greatness of God. This causes unclean thoughts to arise in the hearts of people. Uncleanness of heart then leads to horrible behavior. But Paul brings people back to the center. It is God almighty who is the Creator of the physical realm, and therefore its Master and the focus of worship. He is the blessed one who brings blessing. But to reject the blessed one is to reject His blessings as well.

_____

For this reason God gave them up to vile passions. For even their women exchanged the natural use for what is against nature. Likewise also the men, leaving the natural use of the woman, burned in their lust for one another, men with men committing

what is shameful, and receiving in themselves the penalty of their error which was due. (1:26, 27)

Here again, God allows people to reap the natural consequences of their choices. Rejection of God and His way leads to a path of pain as the blessing of God is withheld and people are left to their vile passions. The word that is here translated "vile passions" is also used in Revelation 16:15 to describe the shame of those who are not looking for the Lord's Coming in the last days. They will be found naked and ashamed. Thus, the people here in Romans 1:24 are described as shameless. They do not flinch to live out such attitudes in the midst of daily society.

These passions include the lustful burning of women after women and men for men. The Greek world was

4   Ronald F. Youngblood, general editor; F. F. Bruce and R. K. Harrison, consulting editors, *Nelson's New Illustrated Bible Dictionary:* An authoritative one-volume reference work on the Bible with full color illustrations [computer file], electronic edition of the revised edition of *Nelson's Illustrated Bible Dictionary*, Logos Library System, (Nashville: Thomas Nelson) 1997, © 1995.

known for its acceptance of homosexuality. It even at times praised this
over heterosexual relations. It was, in
some quarters, presumed to be a
higher form of love. Of course, the
Spirit of God puts such vile notions to
rest. But we must be careful here. It is
not that homosexuality is regarded as
the worst of sins; in fact, it is simply a
natural result of the rejection of the
knowledge of God. Paul also shows
other actions to be the result of the rejection of God's revelation. Homosexual actions are only a symptom of the
path of darkness. The choice of that
path is the real act of defiance.

That these people are "receiving in
themselves the penalty of their error
which was due" is not an indication of
any special punishment that would
come upon a homosexual. No, it is
simply stating that God is just in
bringing wrath upon anyone who rejects the revelation of God. The behavioral practice simply highlights
that judgment will properly come
upon such people.

While it would be easy for people
to read Paul's argument and say, "Yes,
idolatry and sexual perversion brings
God's wrath," this would be an improper reading of the Holy Spirit's intention. The rejection of the knowledge of God is the first sin. This brings
forth outward behavior that is rightly
judged. Nonetheless, lest anyone thinks
that he or she is free from the judgment of God because of a lack of such
idolatry or immorality, Paul moves on

to a third manifestation of darkness
seen in the behavior of the Gentiles.

And even as they did not like to retain God in their knowledge, God
gave them over to a debased mind,
to do those things which are not
fitting; being filled with all unrighteousness, sexual immorality, wickedness, covetousness,
maliciousness; full of envy, murder, strife, deceit, evil-mindedness;
they are whisperers, backbiters,
haters of God, violent, proud,
boasters, inventors of evil things,
disobedient to parents, undiscern-
ing, untrustworthy, unloving, un-
forgiving, unmerciful; who,
knowing the righteous judgment of
God, that those who practice such
things are deserving of death, not
only do the same but also approve
of those who practice them.
(1:28-32)

We must be clear that these verses
do not describe a progression of depravity, but the continuing manifestation of the fruit of rejecting the
knowledge of God; the natural consequences of such refusal to acknowledge God continue. In this section,
the more run-of-the-mill sins come
to light. These vices are clearly against
God's law and deserve punishment.

God gave people over to a debased
mind because they did not want to
reckon with God. They found that the

knowledge of God did not fit their own minds. Therefore, God allowed their minds to yield what debased minds yield: actions that are not fitting. It is important here to maintain the divine perspective: Wrong behavior results from wrong thinking; wrong thinking results from hearts hardened toward God; hard heartedness towards God results from the rejection of the revelation of God that should lead to the worship of God. Too often people point at the behavior of others and simply ask people to stop what they are doing. But here

Paul does not ask people to stop behaving in a certain way. He simply points out the proper verdict: guilt requiring God's just wrath.

The specific vices listed are arranged in four groups. The first two groupings are qualified with the words "full of" indicating the depth of the problems in these areas. The third group aggressively states what people do to propagate wickedness and the final group denotes what people don't do. This last group contains the negating "un-" before the attribute.

WORD STUDY
KNOWLEDGE

Knowledge—*the truth or facts of life that a person acquires either through experience or thought.* The greatest truth that a person can possess with the mind or learn through experience is truth about God (Ps. 46:10; John 8:31–32). This cannot be gained by unaided human reason (Job 11:7; Rom. 11:33). It is acquired only as God shows Himself to man—in nature and conscience (Psalm 19; Rom. 1:19–20); in history or providence (Deut. 6:20–25; Dan. 2:21); and especially in the Bible (Psalm 119; Rev. 1:1–3).

Mental knowledge by itself, as good as it may be, is inadequate; it is too capable of only producing pride (1 Cor. 8:1, 13:2). Moral knowledge affects a person's will (Prov. 1:7; Phil. 3:11–12; 1 John 4:6). It is knowledge of the heart, not the mind alone. The Book of Proverbs deals primarily with this kind of knowledge. Experiential knowledge is that gained through one's experience (Gen. 4:1; 2 Cor. 5:21; 1 John 4:7–8).

The apostle Paul's wish for the church at Colosse was that they might increase in the "knowledge of God" (Col. 1:10).[5]

---

5   Jack W. Hayford, *Hayford's Bible Handbook* [computer file], electronic ed., Logos Library System, (Nashville: Thomas Nelson) 1997, © 1995.

QUESTIONS FOR PERSONAL REFLECTION
AND GROUP DISCUSSION

Read Romans 1:18–32 and answer the following questions.

1. Why is the wrath of God directed to the godlessness and wickedness of men?

2. How has God revealed Himself to us according to Romans 1:20?

3. What should have been our response to this knowledge of God?

4. What was the actual response to this knowledge (1:21–23)?

5. With what did the people exchange the glory of God?

6. Contained in 1:24–28 is a list of God's responses to those who have rejected His gracious revelation. In each case is the phrase *God gave them up*. To what did God give them up?

7. God is certainly just in His actions. Yet some may object that a person may be ignorant of God and thus cannot worship Him. Can God expect a person to worship Him? Why? In what way is a person without excuse?

8. How would you respond to people who may say that if they knew what was right, they would do it?

9. Judging from Paul's list in verses 26–32, would you say that twenty-first century humanity is worse, better, or pretty much the same as people of Paul's day? Why?

10. What are the ways our society worships the creation rather than the Creator? How has this affected you?

11. In verse 25, Paul digresses into a doxology in worship of God even in the midst of the bad news. Write a prayer of thanksgiving and worship.

Chapter 2

Romans 2:1—3:20

GOD'S RIGHTEOUSNESS IS REVEALED IN JUDGMENT

God's Principle of Judgment

Romans 2:1–16

The apostle Paul next advances his line of reasoning by addressing the religious person who is quick to judge the awful behavior seen in Romans chapter 1. This may be a righteous Jew interacting with Paul in a diatribe-style argument. In this, Paul sets up a discussion with an imaginary opponent who interacts with him at different points in the letter. The author's point of view is advanced through questions posed by the opponent.

Paul emphasizes God's standard and method of judgment for the sake of this religious person. Once this is understood, God's justice is upheld and His character is seen to be consistent with His righteous actions.

> Therefore you are inexcusable, O man, whoever you are who judge, for in whatever you judge another you condemn yourself; for you who judge practice the same things. (2:1)

The religious person, standing on the sidelines of the argument in 1:18–32, would certainly agree with Paul's assessment of these unreligious Gentiles. Their behavior is detestable and they are without excuse (1:20).

WORD STUDY
JUDGMENT

Judgment—*discernment or separation between good and evil*. The essence of the idea of judgment is that by this means God delivered—overthrowing evil. (This is why Israel's judges were called that, as they were instruments of God's judgment against oppression and evil, but deliverance for God's people of covenant.)

As Judge, God judges among people and their actions according to the standards of His law. Judgment can refer either to this process of discernment or to the punishment meted out to those who fall under His wrath and condemnation (John 5:24).

In the Bible the most important judgment is the final judgment, the ultimate separation of good and evil at the end of history. The precise time of this judgment is appointed by God (Acts 17:31), but it remains unknown to man (Matt. 24:36).

From earliest times it has been recognized that God Himself is the Judge of mankind (Gen. 18:25), and that He has the power and wisdom to judge with righteousness, truth, and justice (Ps. 96:13; 98:9). The final judgment is a task given specifically to God's Son (John 5:22; Acts 17:31) to conclude His work as mediator, deliver His people from sin, and destroy all God's enemies. God's people are associated with Christ in the exercise of this judgment (1 Cor. 6:2–3; Rev. 20:4).[6]

Certainly, God should judge them. But Paul disturbs his questioner with the assertion that the righteous Jew is equally without excuse. While such a one may wish to call down the wrath of God on the heinous activity of 1:18–32, he should think again. Such an attitude will not save him from his own deserved wrath.

God's judgment, as 2:1 states, extends to those who judge those who do such things. It does not matter if someone simply regards an act or attitude as evil or actually participates in those deeds. Judgment of others brings condemnation. This would certainly have brought a vehement denial on the part of the religious person. The righteous Jew flees from the camp of the judged and guilty. He simply is not, in his own mind, included in their number because he is part of the people of God, the

---

6   Jack W. Hayford, *Hayford's Bible Handbook* [computer file], electronic ed., Logos Library System, (Nashville: Thomas Nelson) 1997, © 1995.

Jews. So, Paul dramatically explains the flaws in this reasoning. Religious people are not necessarily righteous; it is those who do not do evil who are righteous. This is explained in chapter 2. The idea shocks Paul's questioner. How could he *not* stand apart from those evildoers in 1:18–32? The reason is clear.

Paul's questioner ought to adopt an entirely different attitude toward his own stance before God. Instead of religious hypocrisy, there should be drastic humility before God. Paul pleads his case based upon the need for repentance rather than haughtiness. The history of Israel presents God as merciful and patient. Many times Israel could rightly have been expelled from their favored status as a people. But God was generous and kind toward His people.

But we know that the judgment of God is according to truth against those who practice such things. (2:2)

Here Paul establishes a link between his questioner and himself. The truth of God provides the bond. The religious Jew will be very willing to rest upon God's truthfulness towards humanity. God is truth and must be relied upon for the final and righteous judgment. There is no question that this is bad news for the Gentiles of 1:18–32; but this is also, unfortunately, bad news for the religious hypocrite as well. No one escapes the judgment of God who practices the evil deeds listed in chapter 1.

The beauty of this is that the standard is truth as defined by God Himself. This can be relied upon fully by Jew and Gentile alike. All of humanity is measured by the truth of God's Word and not human notions.

And do you think this, O man, you who judge those practicing such things, and doing the same, that you will escape the judgment of God? Or do you despise the riches of His goodness, forbearance, and longsuffering, not knowing that the goodness of God leads you to repentance? (2:3, 4)

Hypocrisy is often blind to the obvious: God's judgment is coming on all who practice evil. It is so easy to assume that religious behavior or tradition will exempt one from the judgment of God. This is the attitude of the questioner of Paul. One wonders if Paul is not placing himself in his own letter as the questioner. Is this questioner actually the apostle before he became a follower of Christ? Paul was very familiar with the attitudes and arguments of the religious elite within Judaism. He himself was trained well in all its logic and traditions. But this did not relieve Paul from the guilt of his sin. Unfortunately the destination of such pursuit of religion was stubborn hypocrisy rather than soft-heartedness before God. In addition, religious attitudes, arguments cause hardness of heart towards other people, especially towards those not within one's own tradition.

Repentance must be embraced by all kinds of people, from those who come from religious traditions just as much as from those who are from secular backgrounds. An individual's tradition and pedigree does not negate the necessity of God's forgiveness.

Repentance is a large theme within Scripture. Many prophets of the Old Testament called Israel to repentance. But the prophet Jonah provides a dramatic reminder both of God's unfailing grace towards all people and an example of a godly man who wishes that judgment and wrath would come to those outside the faith. Jonah shows how God was pleased to respond to the heartfelt actions of the people of Nineveh. This made Jonah so angry that he nearly despised the kindness and grace of God. Like Jonah, believers in Christ are often apt to condemn people who are trapped in the downward spiral of life apart from God rather than to present to them the glorious opportunity of repentance. Often we are so blinded by the sinfulness of others we forget that they are

WORD STUDY
HYPOCRISY

Hypocrisy—*pretending to be what one is not.* The New Testament meaning of "hypocrisy" and "hypocrite" reflects its use in Greek drama. In the Greek theater, a hypocrite was one who wore a mask and played a part on the stage, imitating the speech, mannerisms, and conduct of the character portrayed.

Throughout His ministry, Jesus vigorously exposed and denounced the hypocrisy of many who opposed Him, especially the scribes and Pharisees. They paraded their charitable deeds, praying and fasting as a theatrical display to win the praise of people (Matt. 6:1–2, 5, 16). They sought to give the appearance of being godly, but they were actually blind to the truth of God (Luke 20:19–20).

The apostle Paul encountered hypocrisy among some Jewish Christians, who refused to eat with the Gentile converts. Paul pointed out that "sincere [literally, unhypocritical] love" is one of the marks of Christian ministry. And he exhorted his readers to behave like Christians: "Let love be without hypocrisy" (Rom. 12:9).[7]

---

[7] Ronald F. Youngblood, general editor; F. F. Bruce and R. K. Harrison, consulting editors, *Nelson's New Illustrated Bible Dictionary: An authoritative one-volume reference work on the Bible with full color illustrations* [computer file], electronic edition of the revised edition of *Nelson's Illustrated Bible Dictionary*, Logos Library System, (Nashville: Thomas Nelson) 1997, © 1995.

ACCENT ON APPLICATION
Romans 2:6

God "will render to each one according to his deeds."

People sometimes wonder about God's justice in dealing with people who have never heard the gospel. The beauty of God's justice shows itself in the way He judges humanity. No person will be judged unjustly. No one who isn't a sinner will be judged one! This may sound obvious, but it is assurance to the believer who is asked about the eternal fate of nice people who haven't responded to the gospel of grace. God will always do right toward people. We can count on this. It enables us to bring the gospel of grace to those who understand that they are sinners.

victims of the Evil One who has entrapped them in a spiral of despair and a cycle of destruction.

It is easy to sit at arms' length and accuse people of being sinful, as if we've forgotten our own sinfulness. Yet, like Jonah, we may have to repent for our own haughtiness towards others. It is fascinating that in Romans, the Spirit of God has caused Paul to call for repentance not from those who are obviously in error, but from those who are sitting in judgment upon such people. The religious elite is God's first target of rebuke. Of course, all who have sinned need to repent and reach out to God. Later Paul makes his case for this.

It must have been a shock to the religious reader to learn that not only those who are obviously sinful are destined for a day of wrath. Yet, this is the message to those who are religious but not redeemed. Paul's language is so strong here: The religious person is treasuring

up for himself a storehouse of wrath! The storehouse is full, not because the person is religious and moral, but because religiosity does not transform the life of the individual. Spirituality is not enough. There must be a focus to the devotion. There must be an accounting for the movement of God in history.

The crowning event of history is the work of God in Christ at the Cross. This must be reckoned with. This is the great leveler. At the Cross, every person is brought to the same position. God intends that the Cross be the focus of humanity's problem with sin. He also wishes to crown the Christ as King in Resurrection. This is seen by all through the proclamation of the Good News of the kingdom of God. Before a person embraces this New Covenant message, one only has God's demands and the condemnation that results from ignoring His Word. That is, God's righteous judgment upon all humanity is revealed.

This brings us back to that great theme: the absolute and wonderful justice of God.

There is no way to charge God with injustice. He remains above humanity in His purity and in His demands. Yet, He is totally consistent in His righteousness. He does not demand what He cannot bring about. So, those who resist and refuse God rightly receive the wrath of God. We do not want to store up this kind of treasure for ourselves. Paul gave a shock to the religious in their own smugness and self-righteousness. Thus, we move on to the purity of God's principle and method of judging such people.

---

who "will render to each one according to his deeds." (2:6)

Remember that Paul concerns himself with the justice of God throughout the Epistle to the Romans. In the section beginning at 1:18 and extending to 3:20, he is most concerned with God's justice in judgment. Is God right in the way He treats humanity in ultimate judgment? Another way of asking this question is: On what basis does God judge and is this basis just? Both the basis and the method of judgment are given in Romans 2:1–16. In 2:6, the Spirit of God reveals the basis for judgment: God gives to each person based on works. Here Paul quotes directly from Psalm 62:12. This is the only Old Testament text that is specifically quoted between

1:18 and 2:24. This verse provides the foundation for God's righteous action in judgment.

We must remember that Paul is not speaking of salvation here but of judgment. The two concepts are distinct. God looks at the actions of human beings and judges them accordingly, giving an appropriate reckoning for works done. Later in the letter he will speak of salvation. But judgment comes first in the flow of the apostle's argument. There is no need of salvation, of course, if there is no judgment upon individual guilt or innocence. One must be found guilty before salvation is necessary or even desired! The Old Testament text is very clear in this regard: Judgment is based upon a person's deeds. This is the underpinning for Paul's argument, which brings both Jew and Gentile to the same point before God and with each other. This is not a pleasant thought for a religious person. Religious tradition and practice can hide the verdict of the righteous judge. The word of guilt, spoken from God Himself, must be reckoned with.

---

eternal life to those who by patient continuance in doing good seek for glory, honor, and immortality; but to those who are self-seeking and do not obey the truth, but obey unrighteousness—indignation and wrath, tribulation and anguish, on every soul of man who does evil, of the Jew first and also of the Greek; but glory, honor, and peace to everyone who works what is good, to the Jew first and also to the Greek. (2:7-10)

These verses have puzzled interpreters for centuries. They seem to say that, if a person's good works are the basis of judgment, eternal life may be granted. The text actually says this! Note what is given to those who persistently and completely do well: They receive eternal life, glory, honor and immortality (v. 7) and glory, honor, and peace (v. 10). Note what is to be reckoned to those who do evil, are self-seeking, and do not obey the truth: They receive indignation and wrath (v. 8), and tribulation and anguish (v. 9). The order of judgment is likewise significant. The Jew is the first

WORD STUDY
ETERNAL LIFE

Eternal life—*a person's new and redeemed existence in Jesus Christ that is granted by God as a gift to all believers.* Eternal life refers to the quality or character of our new existence in Christ as well as the unending character of that life. The phrase, "everlasting life," is found in the Old Testament only once (Dan. 12:2). But the idea of eternal life is implied by the prophets in their pictures of the glorious future promised to God's people.

The majority of references to eternal life in the New Testament are oriented to the future. The emphasis, however, is upon the blessed character of the life that will be enjoyed endlessly in the future. Jesus made it clear that eternal life comes only to those who make a total commitment to Him (Matt. 19:16–21; Luke 18:18–22). Paul's letters refer to eternal life relatively seldom, and again primarily with a future rather than a present orientation (Rom. 5:21; 6:22; Gal. 6:8).

The phrase, "eternal life," appears most often in the Gospel of John and the Epistle of 1 John. John emphasizes eternal life as the present reality and possession of the Christian (John 3:36; 5:24; 1 John 5:13). John declares that the believer has already begun to experience the blessings of the future even before their fullest expression: "And this is eternal life, that they may know You, the only true God, and Jesus Christ whom You have sent" (John 17:3).[8]

---

[8] Ronald F. Youngblood, general editor; F. F. Bruce and R. K. Harrison, consulting editors, *Nelson's New Illustrated Bible Dictionary: An authoritative one-volume reference work on the Bible with full color illustrations* [computer file], electronic edition of the revised edition of *Nelson's Illustrated Bible Dictionary*, Logos Library System, (Nashville: Thomas Nelson) 1997, © 1995.

ROMANS 2 AND GOD'S JUST JUDGMENT

How does God judge people?
Based on their deeds
Romans 2:6

How does God measure deeds?
Based on the law they have
Romans 2:12

What law does a person have?
Jews have Mosaic Law
Gentiles have the law of conscience
Romans 2:13–16

to receive any reward from God. The type of reckoning is based on the behavior of each individual.

Absolute persistence in doing good works is rewarded. If anyone is an evildoer, this is rewarded as well. In other words, people receive their just desserts in the economy of God.

Interpreters try to bypass the obvious meaning of this text by saying that Paul must be speaking of the believer in Christ who is enabled to persist in doing good. This believer, therefore, is rewarded with eternal life. While certainly the believer is enabled by the Holy Spirit to persist in doing good, this is not what is in view here. We must note that the subject of a sinner's salvation is not brought up until 3:21. It is not yet time to present salvation because the righteous actions of God in judgment must first be established.

Indeed Paul does just this. God is so pure in His judgment that if someone were to totally, completely, and consistently do good works, that person would receive the designated rewards. There is no injustice with God here. He does not strike down the innocent. He rewards the innocent.

We may object to this, saying that it is impossible to obey God perfectly in order to merit eternal life. But Paul does not present a case for our ability or inability to perform to God's satisfaction. In fact, it may be better to simply let the text say what it does so that the argument can be maintained. God's judgment is based on works.

We must remember that the Holy Spirit, through Paul, is not addressing the sinner's salvation. This is a crucial point. People often present the objection to the above explanation of

Romans 2:7–9 by saying, "God is absolutely clear that salvation is not by works!" A hearty "Amen" must be said to that. But judgment, not salvation, is in view here and God is absolutely just in properly measuring the behavior of humanity. Let's allow the text to speak for what it is saying about judgment before we move on to consider the problem of the guilty: the need for salvation.

For there is no partiality with God. (2:11)

This verse provides the wonderful assurance to every human being that Almighty God does not play favorites in judgment. He does not have a group of people for whom He looks aside when they sin. Sin will be reckoned with. There is no partiality in providing rewards and there is no partiality when apportioning wrath and anger. While this is certainly a sobering thought, think of the beauty of these ideas. When we present to people the message of our holy God, we are able to stand completely on His justice and impartiality. He will consider the evidence of our behavior and judge accordingly. The religious have no special appeal to God. They are judged on the same basis, as are the irreligious—that is, their works. There is no difference. This profound good news for humanity turns out to also be bad news for humanity. The good news is that there is no injustice with God; the bad news is that this

doesn't help me as long as I am not in the camp of those who consistently do good. My own evaluation of myself brings a proper verdict of guilty before God.

The impartiality of God is wonderful because it levels all humanity. No one escapes His righteous evaluation of behavior. God will do right for every human being. Sometimes people argue about the state of those who have never heard the message of Christ. "Could God send those people to hell simply because they haven't heard about Jesus?" they ask. But this is the wrong question. God only pronounces the guilty verdict upon sinners. It is the righteous judgment of a holy God regarding our behavior that determines our destiny. God will righteously deal with all humanity. And the same must be said when considering what God has planned for the guilty. He has righteous ways with dealing with those who do wrong. Paul will speak to this issue later.

Here is another question: Don't we sin because we are sinners? Of course, the answer is, "Yes." Paul addresses this in chapter 7. But, again, that is not the question at hand. Paul is addressing the religious person's haughtiness in the face of the sinful people in 1:18–32 and the absolute perfect judgment of God in 2:1–11. The questions of our ability to obey God and the destiny of those who have never heard of Christ are not at all addressed in these verses. So, we will let the Spirit of God speak through Paul:

For as many as have sinned without law will also perish without law, and as many as have sinned in the law will be judged by the law (for not the hearers of the law are just in the sight of God, but the doers of the law will be justified; (2:12, 13)

Here Paul moves on to consider the method of judgment. Remember, the principle of judgment is based on works. In explaining the method of judgment, the apostle again presents us with two groups of people, Jews and Gentiles. The Gentiles do not have the law and the Jews do. This is the Mosaic Law, which was given to Moses as part of the covenant of God at Sinai just after the Exodus from Egypt and renewed just before the conquest of Canaan by Joshua. These verses from Romans show that both groups have a problem. Gentiles who

WORD STUDY
CONSCIENCE

Conscience—*a person's inner awareness of conforming to the will of God or departing from it, resulting in either a sense of approval or condemnation.*

The term does not appear in the Old Testament but the concept does. David, for example, was smitten in his heart because of his lack of trust in the power of God (2 Sam. 24:10). But his guilt turned to joy when he sought the Lord's forgiveness (Psalm 32). Such passages as Psalm 19 indicate that God is discernible to the human conscience, and is accountable therefore (Rom. 1:18–20).

In the New Testament "conscience" is found most frequently in Paul's epistles. However, the conscience is by no means the final standard of moral goodness (1 Cor. 4:4). Under both the old and new covenant the conscience is only trustworthy when formed by the Word and will of God. The law given to Israel was inscribed on the hearts of believers (Heb. 8:10; 10:16), so the sensitized conscience is able to discern God's judgment against sin (Rom. 2:14–15).

The conscience of the believer has been cleansed by the work of Jesus Christ; it no longer accuses and condemns (Heb. 9:14; 10:22). Believers are to maintain pure consciences or not encourage others to act against their consciences. To act contrary to the urging of one's conscience is wrong, for actions that go against the conscience cannot arise out of faith (1 Cor. 8; 10:23–33).[9]

---

9   Jack W. Hayford, *Hayford's Bible Handbook* [computer file], electronic ed., Logos Library System, (Nashville: Thomas Nelson) 1997, © 1995.

sin (even though they do not have the Mosaic Law) will perish and the law will judge Jews who disobey its commandments and ordinances. Only those who perfectly keep the law will be justified, regarded as righteous, by God. This means that only sinners are judged and this is good news. The innocent (if there are any) go free. The guilty are righteously judged. But what kind of law do the Gentiles have? That is Paul's next consideration.

For when Gentiles, who do not have the law, by nature do the things in the law, these, although not having the law, are a law to themselves, who show the work of the law written in their hearts, their conscience also bearing witness, and between themselves their thoughts accusing or else excusing them) in the day when God will judge the secrets of men by Jesus Christ, according to my gospel. (2:14–16)

God has done a remarkable thing for the Gentiles. He has written His law in their hearts and this is testified by their consciences. Certainly, the Mosaic Law is not entirely present there, but enough of the law of God is present in the Gentiles to witness of God's righteous ways. In fact, this is so powerful that the Gentiles are even excused from the judgment of God because they've kept the law! As Paul states, the conscience makes

accusation when the law is broken.

Whether the Jews have the law or the Gentiles have the law of the heart, which is revealed by the conscience, the judgment of God is sure. The gospel declares God will bring judgment upon all humanity, Jews and Gentiles, for sins done in secret or in public. Judgment according to the standard of God is as much a part of Paul's gospel as is the sinner's salvation. God is totally just and impartial when it comes to judgment. We count on this as we present the nature of God and the message of the Good News of the kingdom of God. God is holy, righteous, and just in His dealings with humanity.

So the method of judgment is clearly presented. If you are a Jew, the Mosaic Law will measure you. If you are a Gentile, the law of the heart, which is revealed by the conscience, will measure you. One might argue that Jews are worse off because of the detailed nature of the Mosaic Law. But this is a short view because Paul regards the law of the conscience to be equally condemning as the Law of Moses. The presence of law, whether explicit or implicit, is clearly recognized by individuals. Comparison of the two is immaterial for they both reflect the righteous expectations of God. It matters little whether one has disobeyed the Mosaic Law or the law of the conscience. Disobedience is disobedience. Both merit a guilty verdict from God. In this regard, Jew and Gentile both stand under God's righteous judgment.

QUESTIONS FOR PERSONAL REFLECTION AND GROUP DISCUSSION

Read Romans 2:1–16 and answer the following questions.

1. How could human judgment be properly called inconsistent, according to Romans 2:1–3?

2. How is God's judgment different from this?

3. What is God like and how should we respond to His character according to verse 4?

4. Paul suggests that each person will get what he deserves (2:5–11). Is this good news or bad news for mankind? Why?

5. Are those who hear the law in better shape than those who do not? Why or why not?

6. A person who has no written law still has a type of law. What is this law?

7. In Romans 2:6, Paul quotes Psalm 62. What does this Psalm teach us about a proper reaction to God?

8. How can you show a person of high moral standards that he or she is in need of Christ?

9. Since Paul says that God will give to each person according to what he has done, is he suggesting that people could attain eternal life through their actions? Why or why not?

10. Paul seems to be addressing the religious and moral people of his day. In what ways could a believer fall into the same errors that Paul describes?

God's Righteous Judgment
of the Jews

Romans 2:17—3:8

Indeed you are called a Jew,... (2:17)

Now Paul designates his questioner. The *you* in 2:1 is revealed in 2:17 to be a religious Jew with both the blessings and the failings of a religious person. Indeed, it is somewhat hard for Gentiles to understand the full impact of the words of Romans 1:17–20. Paul brings forth arguments that show the beauty and limitations of Jewishness. It is easy to regard this as an ethnic issue, but it is clear that Paul is considering religious people, not just the ethnically pure. Paul's questioner is not only in the Jewish family line, but also a beneficiary of the Jewish religion. So, the identity of Paul's diatribic questioner has become clear.

Indeed you are called a Jew, and rest on the law, and make your boast in God, and know His will, and approve the things that are excellent, being instructed out of the law, and are confident that you yourself are a guide to the blind, a light to those who are in darkness, an instructor of the foolish, a teacher of babes, having the form of knowledge and truth in the law. (2:17–20)

This Jew obviously places his trust in something more than blood heritage. He is in the embrace of the law as the embodiment of the knowledge of God. He boasts in God's special posture towards Israel, a well-known fact of history and clearly testified in the Old Testament. From the Jew's knowledge of the law comes knowledge of God's will. Through possessing the law he has quite a superior posture: he knows God's will; he approves the things that are excellent; he confidently guides the blind, gives light to those in darkness and instructs the foolish; and he teaches "babes."

Yet, this superior posture does not exempt this Jew from the same expectations he brings upon others. Here is where Paul's Jewish questioner becomes uncomfortable.

You, therefore, who teach another, do you not teach yourself? You who preach that a man should not steal, do you steal? You who say, "Do not commit adultery," do you commit adultery? You who abhor idols, do you rob temples? You who make your boast in the law, do you dishonor God through breaking the law? For "the name of God is blasphemed among the Gentiles because of you," as it is written. (2:21–24)

A so-called righteous, religious, teacher who arrogantly preaches the knowledge of God, must bring that

WORD STUDY
LAW

Law—*an orderly system of rules and regulations by which a society is governed.* In the Bible, particularly the Old Testament, a unique law code was established by direct revelation from God to direct His people in their worship, in their relationship to Him, and in their social relationships with one another.

Israel was not the only nation to have a law code. Such collections were common among the countries of the ancient world. These law codes generally began with an explanation that the gods gave the king the power to reign, along with a pronouncement about how good and capable he was. Then came the king's laws grouped by subject. The code generally closed with a series of curses and blessings.

The biblical law code, or the Mosaic Law, was different from other ancient Near Eastern law codes in several ways. Biblical law was different, first of all, in its origin. Throughout the ancient world, the laws of most nations were believed to originate with the gods, but they were considered intensely personal and subjective in the way they were applied. Even the gods were under the law, and they could suffer punishment if they violated it—unless, of course, they were powerful and able to conquer the punishers. The king ruled under the god whose temple and property he oversaw. Although he did not live under a written law code, he had a personal relationship to the god. Therefore, law was decided case by case and at the king's discretion. For most of a king's lifetime, his laws were kept secret.

By contrast, the biblical concept was that law comes from God, issues from His nature, and is holy, righteous, and good. Furthermore, at the outset of God's ruling over Israel at Sinai, God the great King gave His laws. These laws were binding on His people, and He upheld them. Furthermore, His laws were universal. Ancient oriental kings often tried to outdo their predecessors in image, economic power, and political influence. This was often their motivation in setting forth law codes. God, however, depicts His law as an expression of His love for His people (Ex. 19:5–6).

In Israel all crimes were crimes against God (1 Sam. 12:9–10). Consequently, He expected all His people to love and serve Him (Amos 5:21–24). As the final judge, He disciplined those who violated His law (Ex. 22:21–24; Deut. 10:18; 19:17). The nation or community was responsible for upholding the law and insuring that justice was done (Deut. 13:6–10; 17:7; Num. 15:32–36).[10]

---

[10] Ronald F. Youngblood, general editor; F. F. Bruce and R. K. Harrison, consulting editors, *Nelson's New Illustrated Bible Dictionary:* An authoritative one-volume reference work on the Bible with full color illustrations [computer file], electronic edition of the revised edition of *Nelson's Illustrated Bible Dictionary*, Logos Library System, (Nashville: Thomas Nelson) 1997, © 1995.

CROSS REFERENCE
Isaiah 52:5

"And my name is blasphemed continually every day." (See also Ezek. 16:23–30.)

The people of Israel engaged in idolatry, immorality, and other behaviors like those of people who did not know God. Even the Israelites' Philistine neighbors were ashamed of their behavior. So, Israel had no right to claim that their removal from the land and exile to another country was unjust. Indeed, God used the other nations to punish Israel.

We must be ever on guard for the encroachment of evil within the church. For, if God did not spare Israel, He will not spare the believing Gentiles. Paul indicates this in Romans 11. However, even the context of Isaiah 52:5 presents the hope of salvation. Sinners are never far from the saving hand of God because of Christ, the Suffering Servant.

same teaching to bear upon himself. Preaching against others does not exempt one from performing righteously and knowledge does not guarantee performance. The same standards apply to the religious, but more strictly since they know them explicitly.

The primary issue is: what does one do with the knowledge of God's righteous will? Is there obedience to the law or is there disobedience? No one will argue that the Jew is not blessed by having the law. Though it is a blessing to know God's will, such knowledge does not equal obedience, and only obedience to God provides a verdict of innocent. Any abrogation of this duty is enough to declare one guilty. If that were not enough, God's displeasure is clearly stated by the Old

Testament itself. Any time the law of God is broken, God is not simply displeased, but His Name is blasphemed in the presence of the Gentiles.

> For circumcision is indeed profitable if you keep the law; but if you are a breaker of the law, your circumcision has become uncircumcision. (2:25)

Paul's religious questioner may regard these words as "fighting words". The mark of the Jew was circumcision. This distinguished the Jew from all other people. Gentiles regarded this as heinous but Jews embraced it as beautiful. Yet, Paul brings total upheaval to the mark of God's covenant with the Jews, circumcision, by saying that it can be reversed by sin. This may be hard for twenty-first century believers to comprehend, but to Paul's questioner there is nothing more important than circumcision. It placed you among God's inner circle. Others are totally outside this most favored nation status.

It was almost incomprehensible to the religious Jew that this could be removed. One cannot replace the foreskin after it has been cut off. While the picture is both obvious and grotesque, Paul makes his point. Carrying the mark of circumcision does not guarantee a favored status with God. This is revolutionary. But Paul had to accept this for himself when he encountered Jesus on the road to Damascus. Although he was circumcised, he was outside the will of God, even opposing God. Nevertheless, Paul needed another work to take place—the recognition of the now obviously crowned King of kings.

> Therefore, if an uncircumcised man keeps the righteous requirements of the law, will not his uncircumcision be counted as circumcision? (2:26)

Here Paul provides the flipside of the issue of the Jew and his circumcision. The Gentile can be circumcised without the rite of circumcision. Is this blasphemy? No. It is simply the impartiality of God at work. Gentiles may perfectly keep the righteous requirements of the law because they are written upon the heart. This counts as circumcision. In other words, the Gentile is regarded as part of God's people because of righteous behavior, not because of a physical mark. This mark, upon which every male Jew staked the claim of being part of the family of God, became irrelevant. Circumcision has been re-defined. True circumcision is linked to absolute righteousness, not

ACCENT ON APPLICATION

Religious people are often quick to judge others and forgive themselves. Yet, we should note Paul's argument here. The name of God is blasphemed when the religious are found to be hypocrites. Such a stern word is presented here for all those who boast in God and who know His will. Certainly, this is a believer's heartbeat. But the question for all of us is presented clearly: Are we bringing the name of God disrepute by our behavior? It matters little if we say what we regard as right and good if our lives do not reflect these things. Often the religious people are labeled hypocrites, sometimes unjustly. But often the label is apt.

WORD STUDY
CIRCUMCISION

Circumcision—*the surgical removal of the foreskin of the male sex organ.* This action served as a sign of God's covenant with His people.

Circumcision, as practiced in some parts of the ancient world, was performed at the beginning of puberty (about age twelve) as an initiation into manhood. In contrast, the Hebrews performed circumcision on infants. This rite had an important ethical meaning. It signified the Jews' responsibility as the holy people whom God had called as His special servants in the midst of a pagan world.

The Bible first mentions circumcision when God instructs Abraham to circumcise every male in his household (Gen. 17:11). After this, the ritual was to be performed on every male child on the eighth day after birth (Gen. 17:12), at the time that child was named (Luke 1:59; 2:21).

Circumcision of the Jewish male was a visible, physical sign of the covenant between the Lord and His people. Any male not circumcised was to be "cut off from his people" (Gen. 17:14) and regarded as a covenant-breaker (Ex. 12:48).

Moses and the prophets used the term circumcised as a symbol for purity of heart and readiness to hear and obey. Through Moses, the Lord challenged the Israelites to submit to "circumcision of the heart," a reference to their need for repentance. "If their uncircumcised hearts are humbled, and they accept their guilt," God declared, "then I will remember My covenant" (Lev. 26:41, 42, also Deut. 10:16). Jeremiah characterized rebellious Israel as having uncircumcised ears (6:10) and being "uncircumcised in the heart" (9:26).

In the New Testament, devout Jews faithfully practiced circumcision as recognition of God's continuing covenant with Israel. Both John the Baptist (Luke 1:59) and Jesus (Luke 2:21) were circumcised.

A problem erupted in New Testament times because the tradition had become a badge of spiritual superiority, and some early Jewish believers in Jesus as the Messiah had difficulty relating to Gentile believers who had received Christ but were not circumcised. Gentile believers regarded their Jewish brethren as eccentric because of their dietary laws, Sabbath rules, and circumcision practices. Jewish believers tended to view their uncircumcised Gentile brothers as unenlightened and disobedient to the Law of Moses.

A crisis arose in the church at Antioch when some believers from Judea (known as Judaizers) taught the brethren, "Unless you are circumcised according to the custom of Moses, you cannot be saved" (Acts 15:1, 2). In effect, the Judaizers insisted that a believer from a non-Jewish background (Gentile) must first become a Jew ceremonially (by being circumcised) before he could be admitted to the Christian brotherhood.

A council of apostles and elders was convened in Jerusalem to resolve the issue (Acts 15:6–29). Among those attending were Paul, Barnabas, Simon Peter, and James, pastor of the Jerusalem church. To insist on circumcision for the Gentiles, Peter argued, would amount to a burdensome yoke (Acts 15:10). This was the decision handed down by the council, and the church broke away from the binding legalism of Judaism.

Years later, reinforcing this decision, the apostle Paul wrote to the believers of Rome saying that Abraham, "the father of circumcision" (Rom. 4:12), was saved by faith rather than by circumcision (Rom. 4:9–12). He declared circumcision to be of no value unless accompanied by an obedient spirit (Rom. 2:25, 26).

Paul also spoke of the "circumcision of Christ" (Col. 2:11), a reference to Christ's atoning death, which "condemned sin in the flesh" (Rom. 8:3) and nailed legalism "to the cross" (Col. 2:14). In essence, Paul declared that the New Covenant of Christ's shed blood had provided forgiveness to both Jew and Gentile and had made circumcision totally unnecessary. All that ultimately matters for both Jew and Gentile, Paul says, is a changed nature—a new creation that makes them one in Jesus Christ (Eph. 2:14–18).[11]

to an outward physical manifestation that is bestowed by ceremony.

And will not the physically uncircumcised, if he fulfills the law, judge you who, even with your written code and circumcision, are a transgressor of the law? (2:27)

This again may test the temper of the religious Jew. Paul now turns his argument on its head. The Jew who is the "instructor of the foolish [Gentile]" is now put under the judgment of the Gentile who is obedient to God and is thus righteous. Has Paul lost his mind? No. He simply places the emphasis where it should be. The one who righteously fulfills the law has a right to judge anyone who does not fulfill the law. This means that even a

11 Jack W. Hayford, *Hayford's Bible Handbook* [computer file], electronic ed., Logos Library System (Nashville: Thomas Nelson) 1997, ©1995.

Gentile may do so if that Gentile is upright in all his ways. Behavior trumps religious symbol. Obedience speaks louder than profession. God judges sin as if there were no religious symbol. Symbol is meaningless without consequent behavioral testimony.

For he is not a Jew who is one outwardly, nor is circumcision that which is outward in the flesh; but he is a Jew who is one inwardly; and circumcision is that of the heart, in the Spirit, not in the letter; whose praise

CROSS REFERENCE
2 Corinthians 5:16

"Therefore, from now on, we regard no one according to the flesh. Even though we have known Christ according to the flesh, yet now we know Him thus no longer."

God has established a new order in the kingdom of God. Those who have embraced the Lord Jesus by faith enjoy the benefits of a new society: the society of the people of God. In this society there are new standards to live by. Perhaps one of the most important is that "from now on, we regard no one according to the flesh." This means that we embrace the truth that earthly distinctions that mean so much in the world mean little in the kingdom of God. There is now "neither Jew nor Greek ... slave nor free ... male nor female; for you are all one in Christ Jesus." Racial distinctions are removed. Class distinctions are nullified. And the limitations or advantages based upon gender are also eliminated. This provided the church with a radical opportunity to have impact in all sectors of the Roman Empire as people realized they were brought to an equal level through the work of God. We are admonished to make sure that such worldly distinctions don't enter our own perspective of other people.

People evaluated Jesus by a purely human perspective while He was on earth. Even those who should have known better, the Jewish religious leaders, focused upon how Jesus did not live up to their own expectations of a leader who was to liberate them from bondage to Rome or on how Jesus did not fulfill their own understanding of the Mosaic law. Jesus was also crucified, which, to the Jewish leaders, brought Jesus under a curse (Gal. 3:13; Deut. 21:23). But Jesus is transformed through His resurrection to be the obviously victorious King, fully vindicated from any notion of being "cursed." Just as Jesus is seen in a new way as the resurrected Messiah, freed from simply earthly evaluation, so also believers are to regard no one from an earthly perspective.

ACCENT ON APPLICATION

Believers often designate various outward signs that indicate one is part of the family of God. These can include lifestyles and political affiliations. But we should carefully regard Paul's teachings. Outward signs do not guarantee anything. Inward reality evidenced by outward behavior is the sure sign of being part of the family of God. It is always a tendency of religious people to adopt certain symbols to designate who is in and who is out with God. This is contrary to the will of God. We must adopt the posture of those who appeal to the heart of the matter: that true religion is a matter of one's heart toward God and the fruitful behaviors that result from this and not of outward symbols which create exclusivity.

is not from men but from God. (2:28, 29)

In these verses, Paul travels to the heart of the matter. Outward manifestations are irrelevant in the New Covenant. The essence of the New Covenant is found in the inward realities of God Himself. It is no longer important whether one is circumcised or not. That is part of the Old Covenant, which is passing away. The New Covenant, found in Jeremiah 31 and Ezekiel 36, speaks of a new working of God who, by His Spirit, brings His purifying work to humanity through direct working on the heart. In words echoing these beautiful Old Testament texts, the Holy Spirit presents Himself here as the essential element in righteousness. The outflow that is pleasing to God requires an inward reality that is the work of God Himself by His Spirit. This is the true circumcision. Rather than boasting in God (2:17) as

the Jew did because of circumcision, now all people redeemed and renewed by the Holy Spirit find that God brings praises to them! What a concept. God totally accepts those who have such an inward circumcision and He commends them. There is no condemnation here, just commendation.

The New Covenant far outshines the Old Covenant. Yet, the righteous Jew may still argue that the status of the Jew is superior to that of the Gentile. This is seen in Romans 3:1.

What advantage then has the Jew, or what is the profit of circumcision? Much in every way! Chiefly because to them were committed the oracles of God. (3:1, 2)

It is no small thing that God has made His Word available through the Jews. The question presented by Paul's questioner regards the favored status of

Jews as seen in the dealings of God with His people. There is advantage of being within this family through whom God has presented His Word. There is no question that, God has chosen, by His own will, to work through Israel. This is a fact of history not to be disputed. The benefits of this, however, do not guarantee that a person is acceptable to God. The national status of Israel does not guarantee the righteousness of an individual within that group. The definition of what righteousness is explicit in the law given to Israel, but the actual gaining of righteousness is far from assured. In fact, Paul's testimony leaves in doubt the possibility that anyone could be declared righteous based on law keeping.

For what if some did not believe? Will their unbelief make the faithfulness of God without effect? Certainly not! Indeed, let God be true but

WORD STUDY
ORACLE

Oracle—*a prophetic speech, utterance, or declaration.*

The word "oracle" is used in several ways in the Bible. In the Book of Numbers it is used to describe the prophecies of Balaam the son of Beor, the soothsayer (Numbers 23–24; Josh. 13:22). The Hebrew word translated "oracle" means a "similitude, parable, or proverb." In 2 Samuel 16:23 the word "oracle" is a translation of a Hebrew word that means "word" or "utterance." It refers to a communication from God given for man's guidance.

A different Hebrew word is translated "oracle" in Jeremiah 23:33–38 (burden, KJV). This word means "a thing lifted up"; it can refer to a prophetic utterance as well as a physical burden. Jeremiah plays upon this double meaning and speaks of the prophetic oracle as a burden that is difficult to bear.

When the New Testament speaks of oracles, it sometimes refers to the Old Testament or some portion of it (Acts 7:38; Rom. 3:2). Hebrews 5:12 uses the term to speak of both the Old Testament revelation and the Word made flesh, Jesus Christ. First Peter 4:11 warns that the teacher of Christian truths must speak as one who utters oracles of God—a message from God and not his own opinions.[12]

---

[12] Ronald F. Youngblood, general editor; F. F. Bruce and R. K. Harrison, consulting editors, *Nelson's New Illustrated Bible Dictionary: An authoritative one-volume reference work on the Bible with full color illustrations* [computer file], electronic edition of the revised edition of *Nelson's Illustrated Bible Dictionary*, Logos Library System, (Nashville: Thomas Nelson) 1997, © 1995.

every man a liar. As it is written: "That You may be justified in Your words, and may overcome when You are judged." (3:3, 4)

The questions continue to flow from the questioner. Now, the faithfulness of God is called into question. While the question in verse one concerned the consequence of the favored status of Israel, this question regards the continuing posture of God towards Israel, even though some within Israel did not believe.

God's faithfulness to Himself and His Word is seen in God's judgment. Righteous, impartial judgment is as much a part of the faithfulness of God as is the redemption of the sinner. But this aspect of the faithfulness of God is least liked. People prefer to think that God's eye is simply turned away from their sins or that their religious tradition or family ties exempt them from judgment. But the oracles of God declare the righteousness of God's judgment. The Old Testament text that is quoted in Romans 3:3 confirms that faithfulness and justice are not separated from God any more than grace and truth are separated from Jesus Himself.

But if our unrighteousness demonstrates the righteousness of God, what shall we say? Is God unjust who inflicts wrath? (I speak as a man.) Certainly not! For then how will God judge the world? (3:5, 6)

The questions are now becoming more absurd. Put simply, the faulty logic of Paul's questioner flows something like this:

When God judges, His righteousness is obvious. Therefore, when I sin, I provide an opportunity for God's righteousness to be seen clearly. So, I am doing God a favor in providing Him an opportunity to see how great God is by my sin! If I am doing Him a favor, then why would I deserve wrath?

The essence of what it is to be God—to stand outside the world and judge it—is not to be compromised. We must remember that God is totally just to set whatever standards He wishes. God will judge the earth, and this requires Him to measure every human being. No ridiculous appeal to how one is doing God a favor by sinning will bring any leniency. God's justice requires that there is no leniency for sin. Sin is so heinous that to treat it with any less vigor is to offend reason.

For if the truth of God has increased through my lie to His glory, why am I also still judged as a sinner? (3:7)

The answer to this question relates not to the kindness and patience of God, which has been evident in God's dealings with Israel, but to the essential ability of God to set His standards and judge accordingly. God's principle of judgment is works as measured by law. This is a glorious truth, but not one that releases the sinner from culpability.

And why not say, "Let us do evil that good may come"?—as we are slanderously reported and as some affirm that we say. Their condemnation is just. (3:8)

There certainly were people in Paul's day that were pushing his gospel to extremes that he did not intend. Later in Romans Paul shows God ushering in the New Covenant. But this does not mean that Paul was without law or principle. Lawlessness is not the mark of the believer. Doing evil is never an option for the follower of Christ. While God is seen to be totally above sin in His very nature and is seen in His graciousness towards humanity, a cavalier attitude toward evil is never warranted. In no way will there be tacit toleration of sin. It is clear from this verse that some people were proclaiming a gospel of license and not a gospel of grace. There is a distinction between the two. A gospel of license presents many opportunities to stray far from God's intended way of life. A gospel of grace provides the inner work of the Holy Spirit as the way of life. Such a way of life is totally consistent with God's perfect will. Those who proclaim a gospel of license to sin are properly to be regarded as guilty of evil.

QUESTIONS FOR PERSONAL REFLECTION
AND GROUP DISCUSSION

Read Romans 2:17—3:8 and answer the following questions.

1. List at least five characteristics of a person who considers himself a Jew according to Romans 2:17–20.

2. If you had these characteristics, what kind of attitude would you have toward the Gentiles?

3. What was Paul's criticism of Jews who had this attitude?

4. What kind of circumcision does Paul say is best? Why does he say this?

5. Does a Jew have any advantage over a non-Jew according to Romans 3:1, 2? Why or why not?

6. If God's righteousness is shown through our own unrighteousness, aren't we doing God a favor by being evil? Why or why not?

7. According to Genesis 12:3, when God made His covenant with Abraham which people did He intend to reach with His blessings?

8. Some unbelievers reject Christianity because there are so many hypocrites among us. How would you speak to someone about this objection?

9. What are you doing to make sure that your Christian profession matches your performance?

10. How would Paul describe you if he were writing about you? Would he speak about ritual? Would there be reality in that ritual or not? Would he speak about a sense of privilege? Would this be a proper perception of yourself? In what ways is it necessary for you to change?

God's Righteous Judgment of
All Humanity

Romans 3:9–20

What then? Are we better than they?
Not at all. For we have previously
charged both Jews and Greeks that
they are all under sin. (3:9)

We are getting to the culmination
of the first major part of Paul's argument. Now Paul links himself with
his imaginary opponent. Paul and
his questioner are both within the
favored nation of Israel. But does
this guarantee anything with reference to righteousness before God?
Certainly not! Paul had lived the lifestyle of the chosen people. He was
blessed to have lived in a household
where the oracles of God were held
in high esteem. But this did not pre-
vent sin nor did it bring righteousness to him. Paul, as well as his
imaginary opponent, both found sin
quite appealing. One step into sin
brought forth a lifestyle tuned quite
well to sin's music. Thus, the lifestyle
of the religious looks quite a bit like
that of the pagan. And such is reality.

ACCENT ON APPLICATION
Evangelism and Romans 3:9

"For we have previously charged both Jews and Greeks that they are all under sin."

God's intends, through the apostle Paul, to bring all of humanity to the
place of equal standing as the "guilty" before Almighty God. He does this mas-
terfully through the examination of people's deeds in light of the law of God as
it is revealed through the Mosaic Law and the law of the conscience. As believers interact with a society at odds with God and His law, we are able to help people discern whether or not they are in right standing with Him. This need not be
done in a shaming way of self-righteously declaring how sinful others are. We
are able to call attention, even gently, to whether people have always done
what God would have had them do. In such a way we identify with people in
that we, too, have fallen short of what God expects. We also are able to help
people identify the way conscience is helping people understand what is true of
God's character and expectations. We can trust that people will have a God-re-
vealed picture of their own sinfulness. We do not need to create that on our
own. God has left a witness even to the most hardened person of his or her need
to repent. In this we can rest and be confident.

Old Covenant/New Covenant

Note the dramatic comparison of the Old Covenant with the New Covenant in 2 Corinthians 3. The benefits and characteristics of the Old Covenant are contrasted with those of the New Covenant:

Characteristics of the Old Covenant	*Characteristics of the New Covenant*
• Of the letter (2 Cor. 3:6)	• Of the Spirit (2 Cor. 3:6)
• Which kills (2 Cor. 3:6)	• Which brings life (2 Cor. 3:6)
• Written on stone (2 Cor. 3:3, 7)	• Written on hearts (2 Cor. 3:3)
• Came with glory, though fading (2 Cor. 3:7)	• Came with surpassing glory (2 Cor. 3:8, 10)
• Brought condemnation (2 Cor. 3:9)	• Brought righteousness (2 Cor. 3:9)
• Temporary (2 Cor. 3:11)	• Permanent (2 Cor. 3:11)

Religiosity guarantees nothing in regard to righteousness. Once sin has entered the scene, then judgment is the sure result. No amount of obedience can reverse the verdict. In addition, those who have sinned are now regarded as under sin in all its power.

As it is written:
"There is none righteous, no, not one;
There is none who understands;
There is none who seeks after God.
They have all turned aside;
They have together become unprofitable;
There is none who does good, no, not one."
"Their throat is an open tomb;
With their tongues they have practiced deceit";
"The poison of asps is under their lips";
"Whose mouth is full of cursing and bitterness."
"Their feet are swift to shed blood;
Destruction and misery are in their ways;
And the way of peace they have not known."
"There is no fear of God before their eyes." (3:10–18)

Paul connects several different Old Testament passages with exquisite skill to show the extent of sinful humanity. The first five verses here, vv. 10–14, show the desperate state of the Gentile world. These verses are widely regarded to refer primarily to those outside of the context of the people of Israel. As such, then, Paul is declaring from the Word of God, the testimony of Gentile guilt. There is no question, when referring to the behavior of these Gentiles, that their condemnation is just. God is right to bring forth His absolute judgment upon such people. But, in order to present the full picture, Paul turns to the behavior of the Israelites. Verses 15–17 are taken from Isaiah 59:7, 8 which declare the transgression of those within the Israelite community, which bring God's just punishment. Paul proves through the "oracles of God" that both Jew and Gentile are rightly under the judgment of God. We can see that virtually all aspects of sin are included in this description. Actions, attitudes and speech are all included. Those who do such things, that is, all of us, deserve judgment. Such is God's own testimony as Judge of the world.

———————

Now we know that whatever the law says, it says to those who are under the law, that every mouth may be stopped, and all the world may become guilty before God. Therefore by the deeds of the law no flesh will be justified in His sight, for by the law is the knowledge of sin. (3:19, 20)

The law of God, contained in these Old Testament texts, speaks to all of humanity. No one is found outside the confines of these passages of Scripture. Every human being is exposed in the light of the Word of God and is found wanting. The whole world, by its own behavior, is clearly outside of the will of God as revealed in His Word. Thus, by God's own proclamation as Judge, all humanity is brought under the same guilty verdict. Following the law of God will not cause a person to be justified, that is, be made right with God. Sinners have no hope at this point in Paul's argument. If we look to law as the way of hope, we are sorely disappointed. We only receive an intimate knowledge of sin, which leads to God's righteous judgment. God justly brings wrath, anger, destruction, and condemnation upon those who do evil according to the law. Sinners find no relief in a law-oriented life. This is true of those who are not yet believers in Christ as much as believers. Of course, the former is in view here. The weakness of the law-oriented life for the believer will be addressed in chapter 7. The intimate knowledge of sin and the intellectual knowledge of sin are assured through the law. The Gentile has the law of the heart and the Jew the explicit Mosaic Law. Neither brings freedom from sin.

QUESTIONS FOR PERSONAL REFLECTION
AND GROUP DISCUSSION

Read Romans 3:9–20 and answer the following questions.

1. Romans 3:9–20 begins the conclusion of the section beginning in 1:18. What is that conclusion?

2. When Paul uses the pronoun *we* in 3:9, who is he referring to?

3. Paul quotes from the Old Testament to make his point about the sinfulness of man. The quotations can be divided into three sets, verses 10–12, verses 13, 14, and verses 15–18. Summarize each set in one sentence.

4. What must our response be to the law of God according to verse 19?

5. Doesn't this passage seem a bit negative? Why does Paul discuss the "bad news" before getting to the positive?

6. Do you think that people need to be aware of this bad news? Why or why not?

7. Notice that Paul refers to proper speech. Review what James has to say in James 1:19, 26; 3:1–12 about the importance of appropriate speech.

8. How is it possible to communicate the bad news to nonbelievers in a way that does not turn them off?

Chapter 3

Romans 3:21—5:21

God's Righteousness Is Revealed
in Salvation

God's Work of Justice and Grace
Through Christ Jesus

Romans 3:21–31

In the previous section (1:18—3:20), the apostle Paul has established an essential building block in his argument about the absolute justice of God. It was crucial to level the ground for all of humanity. Whether Jew or Gentile, it makes no difference. God's absolute just judgment based on works yields the same verdict: Guilty. The Gentile, who had the law of the conscience, which at times coincided with the Mosaic Law (2:14, 15), did not follow that law and was found to be a lawbreaker.

The Jew, even in religious observance, has not followed the Mosaic Law to the absolute perfection required by that Law (2:12, 13). Religious observance alone has not brought forth the righteousness required by God. The conscience of the Gentile has raised his or her level of morality but has not brought forth the righteousness God expects either.

Jews and Gentiles appear amazingly similar. And that is Paul's point. There is no difference when it comes to religious observance even with all the rules attached to the Mosaic code. Religious practice and regulations secure the hypocrisy and condemnation of the practitioner apart from the gracious work of Christ applied by the Holy Spirit. That is why at the end of the section of 3:9–20, Paul proved through the collection of Old Testament quotations that the Old Testament itself brings forth a proper word of condemnation on the Jew and the Gentile alike. Law brings condemnation and a realization of sinfulness. It cannot be said enough: Law does not bring forth the righteousness of God in a person.

God worked under a law system as described in 1:18—3:20. People lived under that system of religious observance, and still do. The only appropriate end of this is that they are regarded as lawbreakers under that system. That was true for the religious and for those who were not so religious but were morally and intuitively mindful of God's law. Guilt and condemnation are assured under that system.

But if Paul had left us at this point, deep despair would have been the appropriate response. But he has not. One of the great turning points in the letter to the Romans occurs between 3:20 and 3:21. Paul has marked this out with the phrase "But now."

But now the righteousness of God apart from the law is revealed, being witnessed by the Law and the Prophets, (3:21)

The word "now" (Greek, *nuni*) points out the important new era that has dawned upon the world. Everything is different because God has worked in a totally just and gracious way through Jesus Christ. This is the era of the kingdom of God. Having been inaugurated by Christ when He walked this earth, this kingdom is now present by the Holy Spirit's continuing work on earth through His servants in the Christian church. This is why the apostle has such conviction of soul regarding the work of God as he stated in 1:16, 17. Indeed, Paul's whole life changed based upon the revelation that the new era has come in all its fullness. The New Covenant brings with it the end of empty religious observance and inaugurates the season when the Spirit of God circumcises the heart and transforms human behavior from within.

The present work of God is not through law. The text itself indicates that God's work is apart from the law. Paul's argument hinges on recognition of the total inability of making sinful people righteous through religious observance and law-keeping. It then moves on to the new and gracious provision of God to a bankrupt people. This is the Good News! Humanity does not need to strive through law-keeping in the attempt to gain the favor of God. Now the way of God is apart from the law. But this does not mean that the Word of God is silent about this new way of working. Indeed, in chapter 4 Paul argues that this is not a new way of working at all; this

WORD STUDY
"NOW"—Greek *nuni*

Note how the apostle designated the new life in the letter to the Romans:
God *now* provides atonement (3:25, 26)
God *now* justifies by the blood of Jesus (5:9)
But *now* we are set free from sin (6:22)
There is *now* no condemnation for those in Christ (8:1)
We are *now* delivered from the law (7:6)
Our present sufferings aren't worth comparing to future glory (8:18)
It is clear that Paul uses this little word to indicate the dramatic turn of events. The word first appears in Romans in 3:21 and provides a beautiful marker to a new era.

has always been God's way of reconciling sinners.

---

even the righteousness of God,
through faith in Jesus Christ, to all
and on all who believe. For there is
no difference; (3:22)

A new way of being righteous has been brought into the arena of the human experience. Since human beings have not followed the righteous commands of the law (whether implicit or explicit) condemnation resulted and God was just in bringing forth the guilty verdict. But God decided that justice could be maintained while graciously providing for those who have chosen the way of sin. The work of Jesus Christ perfectly upholds the demand for justice while at the same time brings relief for the beleaguered sinner.

The righteous God through the unique faithfulness and purity of Jesus Christ graciously brings the required righteousness to people. Paul describes both the objective means of this work, which satisfies God's holiness and the subjective means, which applies this work to individuals. The righteous actions of God are further described in 3:23–26. We find the riches of God's grace in many of the terms Paul uses in those verses such as redemption, propitiation, justification, and demonstration. Jesus acts with perfect faithfulness in carrying out God's plan for bringing sinful humanity back to Him.

This begins with Jesus coming to earth to live a sinless life. The perfection of His life is evident in the four Gospels, where Jesus is shown to be fully human, yet without sin. People exercise faith in a Jesus Christ who is totally faithful. Thus, salvation is secured for humanity

WORD STUDY
PROPITIATION

Propitiation [*pro* PISH *ih a shun*]—*the atoning death of Jesus on the Cross, through which He paid the penalty justice required because of man's sin, thus setting mankind free from sin and death.*

The word comes from an old English word, propitiate, which means "to atone" or "to appease"—to establish grounds for reconciliation. Propitiation (*hilasmos*) in the New Testament finds its meaning illustrated in the Old Testament mercy seat (the lid of the ark of the covenant). Just as the blood was poured on the mercy seat, covering the sins of the people, Jesus' blood has redeemed us: "He Himself is the propitiation for our sins, and not for ours only but also for the whole world" (1 John 2:2). *Hilasmos* is used in the New Testament only in 1 John 2:2 and 4:10; the word describes Christ, through His sacrificial death, as appeasing the wrath of God on account of sin. It also pictures His death as expiatory, providing a covering for sin. By means of the atoning death of Christ, God can be merciful to the sinner who believes in Him, and reconciliation is effected.[13]

through Christ's faithfulness. This is the objective means of salvation. The perfect life and death of Jesus is the ground from which salvation grows. Without the faithfulness of Jesus Christ, there would be no salvation. When people exercise faith to believe in Christ, they grasp the total faithfulness that Christ exercised on their behalf. There is plenty of faithfulness for all, so all who believe are eligible for redemption. Our subjective need is to believe. This brings salvation home to our own lives.

---

for all have sinned and fall short of

the glory of God, being justified freely by His grace through the redemption that is in Christ Jesus, (3:22b–24)

We are brought to one of Paul's favorite concepts: the impartiality of God. There is no difference in humanity when it comes to salvation. Whether a person is a Jew or a Gentile matters little. Both Jews and Gentiles are urged to believe in the same faithful God who in complete righteousness provides a way of escape from the predicament of sin. Thus, note the leveling statement of 3:23—"all have sinned and fall short of

---

[13] Jack W. Hayford, *Hayford's Bible Handbook* [computer file], electronic ed., Logos Library System (Nashville: Thomas Nelson) 1997, ©1995.

the glory of God." But the leveling continues in 3:24 as every person who finds redemption does so by God's grace, which is only through Christ Jesus.

Adam and Eve, before the tragic choice of disobedience, enjoyed a full relationship with God and even shared in His glory by virtue of their innocence. Their perfection mirrored that of the Creator who had invested Himself in humanity by making man and woman in His own image. But when disobedience came, their perfection was removed. As a result the fall of humanity occurred. Humanity tumbled from the beauty of unhindered fellowship with God to the place of shame and slavery to sin. Their choice to rebel was also a choice to become distanced from God's glory.

This glory was manifest in those who had encountered God. This visible manifestation is consistent with God's perfection. Moses shared in that brilliance after he met with God on Sinai. Jesus revealed His glory to the disciples on the Mount of Transfiguration. So, when our text says all have fallen short of God's glory, it points to the great chasm that is fixed between the perfect nature of God and the imperfection which sin brought to humanity. We do not have the visible brilliance of God; rather, we have the darkness of sin as part of our nature. But believers expect that the brilliance shall return as a part of God's redeeming, sanctifying work. While such brilliance will not be complete in this lifetime, in the age to come it will be full.

One wonders here if Paul's choice of a certain term to describe an aspect of salvation is meant to underline the concept that there is no difference between people where salvation is

CROSS REFERENCE
Ephesians 2:8, 9

"For by grace you have been saved through faith, and that not of yourselves; it is the gift of God, not of works, lest anyone should boast."

Paul uses different words to define the saving work of God through Jesus Christ. In Romans 3:24, Paul focuses on being justified. Here in Ephesians 2, the emphasis is on being saved. Paul covers the realm of God's redemptive work in declaring that one is saved through faith. Salvation from the wrath of God brings us to God. So, God saves us *from* and He saves us *to*. Concepts like redemption, justification, sanctification, reconciliation, and glorification all speak of God's great work of salvation. Of course, we must believe in Christ to appropriate this salvation.

WORD STUDY
REDEMPTION

Redemption—*deliverance by payment of a price.* In the New Testament, redemption refers to salvation's provision, which "buys back" what has been lost. In the Old Testament, the word redemption refers to redemption by a kinsman (Lev. 25:24, 51, 52; Ruth 4:6; Jer. 32:7, 8), rescue or deliverance (Num. 3:49), and ransom (Ps. 111:9; 130:7). In the New Testament it refers to loosing (Luke 2:38; Heb. 9:12; Luke 21:28; Rom. 3:24; Eph. 1:14).

In the Old Testament redemption was applied to the recovery of property, animals, persons, and the whole nation. These things typify the dimensions of recovery and release New Testament believers' experience in life through the price Jesus paid. So the Old Testament evidences New Testament promise—God's ability in Christ to redeem from the slavery of sin (Ps. 130:7, 8), from enemy oppressors (Deut. 15:15), and from the power of death (Job 19:25, 26; Ps. 49:8, 9).

The New Testament describes the exact cost of redemption: "the precious blood of Christ" (1 Pet. 1:19; Eph. 1:7), which believers are exhorted to remember as they pursue obedient service, faithful ministry, and personal holiness (1 Cor. 6:19, 20; 1 Pet. 1:13–19).[14]

concerned; this is a term that was often used in the slave markets: *redemption* was used when one was buying back a slave. This is not a particularly glamorous image. Not many people would wish to be a slave. But, like the slaves of old, we are bought back by God to belong to Him. Thusly, God brings out the beauty of this very earthy word.

We must also understand the word *justified* to fully grasp the idea of salvation. This word is closely related to the theme of the letter to the Romans—the absolute justice and righteousness of God. *Righteousness, justice, justified,* and *justification* all share the same root word in the original Greek language. The basic definition of the word "justified" (Greek, *dikaioun*) is to acquit. This definition fits perfectly in the context of the letter as a whole. Paul has successfully placed all of humanity underneath the condemnation of God. All deserve God's wrath. All can look forward to wrath, anger, and distress. But that is not the end of the story. For in Christ there is acquittal. Those who have the

---

14 Jack W. Hayford, *Hayford's Bible Handbook* [computer file], electronic ed., Logos Library System (Nashville: Thomas Nelson) 1997, ©1995.

WORD STUDY
FORGIVENESS

Forgiveness—*the act of excusing or pardoning another in spite of his slights, shortcomings, and errors.* As a theological term, forgiveness refers to God's pardoning or passing away of the sins of human beings and His releasing them from the implications and effect of those deeds.

No religious book except the Bible teaches that God completely forgives sin (Ps. 51:1, 9; Is. 38:17; Heb. 10:17). The initiative comes from Him (John 3:16; Col. 2:13) because He is ready to forgive (Luke 15:11–32). He is a God of grace and pardon (Neh. 9:17; Dan. 9:9).

Sin deserves divine punishment because it is a violation of God's holy character (Gen. 2:17; Rom. 1:18–32; 1 Pet. 1:16), but His pardon is gracious (Ps. 130:4; Rom. 5:6–8). In order for God to forgive sin, two conditions are necessary. A life must be taken as a substitute for that of the sinner (Lev. 17:11, 14; Heb. 9:22), and the sinner must come to God's sacrifice in a spirit of repentance and faith (Mark 1:4; Acts 10:43; James 5:15).

Forgiveness in the New Testament is directly linked to Christ (Acts 5:31; Col. 1:14), His sacrificial death on the Cross (Rom. 4:24), and His Resurrection (2 Cor. 5:15). He was the morally perfect sacrifice (Rom. 8:3), the final and ultimate fulfillment of all Old Testament sacrifices (Heb. 9:11—10:18). Since He bore the law's death penalty against sinners (Gal. 3:10–13), those who trust in His sacrifice are freed from that penalty. By faith sinners are forgiven—"justified" (Rom. 3:28; Gal. 3:8, 9). Those who are forgiven sin's penalty are also freed to live beyond its controlling power in their lives (Rom. 6:1–23).

Christ's Resurrection was more than proof of His deity or innocence; it was related in a special way to His forgiveness. Christ's Resurrection was the act by which God demonstrated to all the incapability of sin to triumph over Him, or for the guilt He bore in our place to remain. It was God's declaration of the perfect righteousness of His Son, the Second Adam, representing us—declaring His acceptance of Christ's sacrifice (1 Tim. 3:16). Thus, in Him all who believe are acquitted and declared righteous, and thus, Christ's Resurrection was a necessary action to the forgiveness of man's sins (1 Cor. 15:12–28), for it not only verified His dominion over sin and death, but certified the same to all His redeemed. To be forgiven is to be identified with Christ in the full triumph of His Crucifixion and Resurrection.

Christ has the authority to forgive sins (Matt. 1:21; Heb. 9:11—10:18). This forgiveness is an essential part of the gospel message (Acts 2:38; 5:31). But blasphemy against the Holy Spirit (attributing to Satan a deed done by Jesus through the power of God's Spirit) is an unpardonable sin (Mark 3:28, 29)—not because God cannot or will not forgive such a sin but because such a hardhearted person has put himself beyond the possibility of repentance and faith.

God's forgiveness of us demands that we forgive others, because grace brings responsibility and obligation (Matt. 18:23–35; Luke 6:37). Jesus placed no limits on the extent to which Christians are to forgive their fellowmen (Matt. 18:22, 35; Luke 17:4). A ceaselessly forgiving spirit shows that we are truly living as followers of Jesus the Lord (Matt. 5:43–48; Mark 11:25).[15]

righteousness of God through the faithfulness of Jesus are able to say that, though God once condemned them, He has now acquitted them. But the acquittal is not obtained by their merit, rather through the work of the righteous and holy God. God did all this freely, without any compulsion. It is totally God's gracious decision. Grace, by definition, is given without merit; one does not demand grace; one only receives it as a free gift from God.

---

whom God set forth as a propitiation by His blood, through faith, (3:25)

Those who have fallen short of God's glory must provide payment for their own sins. All sin must be punished and paid for. God's wrath justly falls upon the sinful. He rightly punishes sin. It is part of God's justice in the economy of creation that sin receives its due.

In this verse, God takes action for the redemption of the lost. God's wrath fell upon Jesus because He is the propitiation for sin. Some have translated this word as *expiation*, pointing to the release or forgiveness of sin. But the idea of propitiation, which carries with it the thought of turning away the wrath of God, is ideally suited to the overall context of this letter. It is clear in 1:18—3:20 that wrath will rightly fall upon the sinner, whether Jew or Gentile. People sometimes struggle

---

[15] Jack W. Hayford, *Hayford's Bible Handbook* [computer file], electronic ed., Logos Library System (Nashville: Thomas Nelson) 1997, ©1995.

with the idea that God capriciously, vindictively, or irrationally brings forth wrath. Notions regarding pagan deities included such irrational exercise of wrath, but not so with the God of our Lord Jesus Christ.

There is no caprice, vindictiveness, nor irrationality in God's actions of bringing wrath on humanity. In fact, logical, reasonable justice demands wrath. There can be no other way. The extraordinary truth is that Jesus took the wrath of God upon Himself. The man who knew no sin took on the sins of humanity and received the payment for those sins. The wrath of God came in full force upon the person of Jesus Christ at the Cross. The payment is "by His blood, through faith." It is possible that the word *faith* here should to be translated *faithfulness*. Thus, the reference is to the faithfulness of Jesus Christ to His Holy God and to the righteous demands of God's law. He is able to offer Himself as the pure sacrifice for humanity because of His faithfulness.

---

whom God set forth as a propitiation by His blood, through faith, to demonstrate His righteousness, because in His forbearance God had passed

WORD STUDY
ATONEMENT

Atonement—*The law required that the sacrificial victims must be free from defect, and buying them always involved some cost to the sinner. But an animal's death did not automatically make people right with God in some simple, mechanical way. The hostility between God and people because of sin is a personal matter. God for His part personally gave the means of atonement in the sacrificial system; men and women for their part personally are expected to recognize the seriousness of their sin (Lev. 16:29, 30; Mic. 6:6–8). They must also identify themselves personally with the victim that dies: "Then he shall put his hand on the head of the burnt offering, and it will be accepted on his behalf to make atonement for him" (Lev. 1:4).*

In the Old Testament, God Himself brought about Atonement by graciously providing the appointed sacrifices. The priests represented Him in the Atonement ritual, and the sinner received the benefits of being reconciled to God in forgiveness and harmony.[16]

---

[16] Jack W. Hayford, *Hayford's Bible Handbook* [computer file], electronic ed., Logos Library System (Nashville: Thomas Nelson) 1997, ©1995.

WORD STUDY
FAITH

Faith (Mark 11:22), *pistis (pis-tis)—conviction, confidence, trust, belief, reliance, trustworthiness, and persuasion.*
In the New Testament setting, faith is the divinely implanted principle of inward confidence, assurance, trust, and reliance in God and all that He says. The word sometimes denotes the object or content of belief (Acts 6:7; 14:22; Gal. 1:23).[17]

over the sins that were previously committed, (3:25)

The atoning work of Christ is the declaration of the righteousness of God. Sin, by its disastrous effects, requires God to act. The public spectacle of the Cross of Jesus Christ, where sin is ultimately addressed, shows God's commitment to justice. Thus, Jesus Christ was put to death before the world, received the wrath of God destined for sinners, and so showcased the righteousness of God. Ultimately the sin problem was dealt with before all. Whether or not people embrace this remains to be seen. The divine judge will bring the required wrath nonetheless. Though God has assigned that the "wages of sin is death" (6:23) He has not required payment to this time. But a time is coming when God will bring forth all of humanity for judgment. Up until the time of Jesus' public sacrifice, sin was not yet dealt with. Judgment was in the future and still is. But for those who embrace the work of Christ, judgment has already come. Their judgment fell upon the perfect man who gave Himself for their sins. He was offered for justice's sake—God's justice. So, we either have the justice of God for sin meted out upon Jesus who died in our stead or we wait for it to come upon us personally.

God's forbearance, His patience, has allowed the deferral of ultimate justice for humanity. But one should not consider that His patience indicates a lack of commitment to justice. Patience with sinners is not the same as tolerance of sin. The Cross of Christ proves God's demand for justice. In the future, when everyone is presented at the throne of God, it will be clear that God's patience will not last forever.

Although Old Testament believers were truly forgiven and received genuine atonement through animal sacrifice,

---

[17] Jack W. Hayford, *Hayford's Bible Handbook* [computer file], electronic ed., Logos Library System (Nashville: Thomas Nelson) 1997, ©1995.

the New Testament states that during the Old Testament period, God's justice was not served: "For it is not possible that the blood of bulls and goats could take away sins" (Heb. 10:4). Atonement was possible "because in His forbearance God had passed over the sins that were previously committed" (Rom. 3:25). However, God's justice was served in the death of Jesus Christ as a substitute: "Not with the blood of goats and calves, but with His own blood He entered the Most Holy Place once for all, having obtained eternal redemption … And for this reason He is the Mediator of the new covenant" (Heb. 9:12, 15).[18]

to demonstrate at the present time His righteousness, that He might be just and the justifier of the one who has faith in Jesus. (3:26)

We, of course, must remember that the "present time" Paul speaks of is not just the time of the first century. This is the present "age" (Greek, *kairos*). The new season, a fresh era has arrived. The moving of God in the New Covenant marks this era. The old is gone and God's righteousness is seen in all of its fullness. Here we see the justice that required the punishment for sin; we see the justice that allows the acquittal of

CROSS REFERENCE
Genesis 15:6

"And he believed in the LORD, and He accounted it to him for righteousness."

Genesis 15 begins the story of God's covenant that included justification by faith. In essence, God promised to do something for Abraham that he did not deserve. There was no goodness in Abraham that caused God to begin the redemptive plan for him. God verified this covenant in a peculiar way that was perfectly consistent with Abraham's world. God Himself passed between pieces of a sacrifice prepared by Abraham. In Abraham's time, people ratified covenants by preparing a sacrifice of animal pieces and then walking together in between those pieces. God passed through the pieces alone. This was His oath that the covenant depended upon Him alone. Abraham's only responsibility was to believe.

---

[18] Ronald F. Youngblood, general editor; F.F. Bruce and R.K. Harrison, consulting editors, *Nelson's New Illustrated Bible Dictionary: An authoritative one-volume reference work on the Bible with full color illustrations* [computer file], electronic edition of the revised edition of *Nelson's Illustrated Bible Dictionary*, Logos Library System (Nashville: Thomas Nelson) 1997, ©1995.

individuals by the faithful work of Jesus Christ on their behalf; we see the justice of God's righteous actions to bring redemption through the blood of Jesus, the perfect sacrifice, upon whom the wrath of God rests. We also see God as the justifier who both punishes based on His absolute pure, perfect character and acquits based upon His absolutely pure and perfect character. The God of forgiveness and grace differs in no way from the God of wrath and ultimate punishment. In fact, the total righteousness of God is seen in both sides. To understand God one must embrace the God of grace and the God of righteous judgment, who is one and the same. Paul has already demonstrated with complete and convincing logic that God deals justly with humanity.

Those who have faith in Jesus understand both the just judgment of God as well as the just acquittal—God's justification. The faithfulness of Jesus brings this to pass. Romans 2:6–11 requires that God reward the absolute, total obedience of Jesus Christ with glory, honor, and immortality. Indeed, Jesus is the only one to whom God could freely grant the promise of merited glory. Jesus' holy life provided the opportunity for a perfect, atoning death. If it were not for the perfection of Jesus' daily life on earth, His death would only have been for His own sin. Because He had no sin, the wrath that fell on Jesus was for others; because He was God, He could choose to become the justifier.

God the Father brought wrath upon God the Son who freely gave Himself for the redemption of humanity. At the Cross, Jesus' life of perfection became our life of perfection. We exchanged our daily sinfulness for the absolute perfection of Jesus' daily life. The death that would have rightly fallen upon the religious and the irreligious fell instead upon Jesus *by His own choice*. This makes His Atonement a part of the divine plan so the wrath that fell upon Him was not capricious or improper, but was gladly received by the Son. Justice and mercy were linked inextricably in the atoning work of God through Christ. Thus, the benefits of Christ's holy life are to our benefit: Christ's redeeming death is to our benefit; the justice God requires regarding our sin have been fully met; the demand to keep the law perfectly is also met in Christ Himself. His life is our life and His death is our death. This comes to us when we exercise faith in Him.

In this, perhaps the most compact theological section in Scripture, Paul has put forth the very essence of how grace, justice, mercy, love, and wrath all mingle perfectly in the work of Christ.

Where is boasting then? It is excluded. By what law? Of works? No, but by the law of faith. (3:27)

With this verse, we return to the theme of boasting which was introduced in 2:17. There the Jew boasted

WORD STUDY
ACCOUNTED

Accounted—(Gen. 15:6) *chashab* (kah-*shahv*)—*To think, reckon, put to-gether, calculate, imagine, impute, make account; to lay one's thoughts to-gether, to form a judgment; to devise, to plan, to produce something in the mind, to invent.*

This verb is normally the equivalent of the English word "to think," but also contains a strong suggestion of "counting." *Chashab* is the consideration of a great number of elements, which results in a conclusion based on a wide over-view. In this verse, God added up everything that Abraham's belief meant to Him, and computing it all together, determined that it was equal to righteous-ness. *Also* (Rom. 4:3) *logidzomai* (log-*id*-zom-ahee); Compare "logistic" and "logarithm." Numerically, to count, compute, calculate, sum up. Meta-phorically, to consider, reckon, reason, deem, evaluate, value. *Logidzomai* final-izes thought, judges matters, draws logical conclusions, decides outcomes, and puts every action into a debit or credit position.[19]

in his relationship with God, in the knowledge of His will, and in the pos-session of the law. But Paul undercut the foundation of any boasting before God. There is no possibility for people to say God owes them something. Boasting in religious tradition is like-wise excluded. Also, the law did not bring cause for boasting but cause for wrath to freely flow. So boasting in performance is excluded. The faith-fulness of God and our embrace of Christ yield humility, not boasting.

The law of faith is versus the law of works. The former demands gratitude not haughtiness. Pride in works, i.e. religious performance or tradition, is excluded because we can only operate with the principles of the new era of the kingdom of God where the law of faith trumps the law of works. In this New Covenant era, all those who em-brace Christ by faith are at the same level. Religious performance means nothing in terms of God's justification and all those who know God through Christ are the very same—redeemed sinners—nothing more and nothing less. There is no partiality with God.

Therefore we conclude that a man is justified by faith apart from the deeds of the law. (3:28)

---

[19] Jack W. Hayford, *Hayford's Bible Handbook* [computer file], electronic ed., Logos Library System (Nashville: Thomas Nel-son) 1997, ©1995.

This conclusion is succinct. Justification, or acquittal before a holy God, in spite of our sins, proceeds from faith and not from doing the deeds of the law. The believer's faith brings reality of God's faithfulness to bear upon all who call upon Him. The faithfulness of God guarantees the effectiveness of personal faith in Him. God extends new life in the new era totally on the basis of His own faithful actions and character to those who receive Christ. A person's faith in Christ links that person inextricably to the faithfulness of God. This is necessarily separate from the deeds of the law since the law only brought death, wrath, and destruction. Sinners cannot count on the law for a hopeful future.

Or is He the God of the Jews only? Is He not also the God of the Gentiles?

WORD STUDY
HOPE

Hope—*confident expectancy.* In the Bible, the word hope stands for both the act of hoping (Rom. 4:18; 1 Cor. 9:10) and the thing hoped for (Col. 1:5; 1 Pet. 1:3).

Hope does not arise from the individual's desires or wishes but from God, who is Himself the believer's hope: "My hope is in You" (Ps. 39:7). Genuine hope is not wishful thinking, but a firm assurance about things that are unseen and still in the future (Rom. 8:24, 25; Heb. 11:1, 7).

Hope distinguishes the believer from the unbeliever, who has no hope (Eph. 2:12; 1 Thess. 4:13). Indeed, a believer is one in whom hope resides (1 Pet. 3:15; 1 John 3:3). In contrast to Old Testament hope, the believer's hope is superior (Heb. 7:19).

Christian hope comes from God (Rom. 15:13) and especially His calling (Eph. 1:18; 4:4), His grace (2 Thess. 2:16), His Word (Rom. 15:4), and His gospel (Col. 1:23). Hope is directed toward God (Acts 24:15; 1 Pet. 1:21) and Christ (1 Thess. 1:3; 1 Tim. 1:1). Its appropriate objects are eternal life (Titus 1:2; 3:7), salvation (1 Thess. 5:8), righteousness (Gal. 5:5), the glory of God (Rom. 5:2; Col. 1:27), the appearing of Christ (Titus 2:13), and the resurrection from the dead (Acts 23:6; 26:6, 7).[20]

---

[20] Jack W. Hayford, *Hayford's Bible Handbook* [computer file], electronic ed., Logos Library System (Nashville: Thomas Nelson) 1997, ©1995.

Yes, of the Gentiles also, since there is one God who will justify the circumcised by faith and the uncircumcised through faith. (3:29, 30)

Verse 29 is tied to verse 28. Since any Jew or Gentile is justified by faith apart from works, then God must be the God of both Jew and Gentile. Every person who observes the Jewish religion acknowledges that God is God of all creation and that God will judge all human beings. But the Jews reserve the special place of redemption for themselves. After all, didn't God call them out of Egypt, out of slavery, and into a covenant relationship with Himself? Of course He did. But this does not guarantee that redemption will flow to individuals. Redemption requires that a person take the step of faith. So, in the new era of the kingdom of God where the Spirit of God is writing God's laws upon the human heart, God is seen as the *saving* God of both Jew and Gentile. The affirmation of God's place among Gentiles revolutionizes the parochial thoughts of the Jew.

The method of salvation is the same for both Jew and Gentile. Both must rely upon faith for justification. Acquittal from guilt and the subsequent sentence of death only comes through the embrace of Christ by faith. In either case, for Jew or Gentile, God displays His justice in the death of Christ so that all humanity might embrace His Son by faith. Now everyone who calls upon the Lord Jesus Christ, no matter what his or her ethnic or religious background, finds justification. This is fitting, since, as every Jew knows, there is but one God. This is their fundamental creed (Deut. 6:4). Since there is but one God, then both Jews and Gentiles fall under His dominion and into His plan of salvation.

Do we then make void the law through faith? Certainly not! On the contrary, we establish the law. (3:31)

It is reasonable to ask about the role of the law in the new era of the kingdom of God. Every Jew reveres the place of the law. But now what? Is there a nullification of this important communication from God? No. In fact Paul intensifies the relation of the law to the Jewish and Gentile individual—all come under the law of God, whether written or unwritten. In addition, as Paul argues in chapter 8, the power to perform in accordance with God's will rests in the empowering work of the Holy Spirit who brings forth righteousness from the believer. Also, the law itself testifies of the New Covenant era. So, the law remains intact. Later Paul addresses the specific relationship that believers have with the Mosaic Law because the New Covenant does not eliminate the need for God's law in the world. So Paul must argue the supremacy of the way of faith over the works of the law. Paul covers this topic in chapter 4.

QUESTIONS FOR PERSONAL REFLECTION AND GROUP DISCUSSION

Read Romans 3:21–31 and then answer the following questions.:

1. How, according to Romans 3:21, has righteousness been revealed?

2. How do people attain this righteousness according to Romans 3:22?

3. To whom will this righteousness be given (3:22)?

4. Why is boasting not a proper attitude for the believer in Christ?

5. Can a man be justified by upholding the law of God? Why or why not?

6. What is the distinction between the Gentile and the Jew in God's eyes? (Rom. 3:29, 30.)

7. Several words in this passage have rich and deep theological significance. Define these words: redemption, justification, propitiation.

8. In what ways do God's actions demonstrate the justice of God as Romans 3:25, 26 state?

9. How does righteousness by faith "establish the law" as Paul suggests in 3:31?

WORD STUDY
JUSTIFIED

Justified (Matt. 12:37) *dikaioo*—*a legal term signifying to acquit, declare righteous, show to be righteous.* In this passage Jesus refers to the Day of Judgment as the day of His determining condemnation or justification, based on our hearts' response to the Spirit.[21]

Both the New Way and the Old Way Are Based on Faith

Romans 4:1–25

What then shall we say that Abraham our father has found according to the flesh? For if Abraham was justified by works, he has something to boast about, but not before God. (4:1, 2)

The case of Abraham is the first illustrative example to prove Paul's point about the primacy of faith over the works of the law. Paul says, "Let's look at the life of Abraham as he lived it." Is he able to boast that he merits the good pleasure of God? Not from God's point of view. Sure, Abraham could boast if works justified him. But this is not the Scriptural attestation, Paul demands. Boasting, therefore, is excluded from Abraham's life. Indeed, Abraham nowhere boasts in his own righteousness. The Scriptures say so.

For what does the Scripture say? "Abraham believed God, and it was accounted to him for righteousness." (4:3)

The accounting that mattered in Abraham's case rested on the principles of grace and faith, not merit and works. This important biblical citation provides absolute grounds to prove the primacy of the way of faith over works. Abraham, the father of the Jews, could not point to his own righteousness either for the call of God on his life or for the grace extended to him. He believed God. He exercised faith in the God who sees all. He reaped the benefits of grace through faith. God reckoned in Abraham's favor: Righteousness was granted. In no way did Abraham earn the goodness of God. God simply justified him based upon his faith. Grace and faith flowed to Abraham because of his response to a merciful and mighty God.

---

[21] Jack W. Hayford, *Hayford's Bible Handbook* [computer file], electronic ed., Logos Library System (Nashville: Thomas Nelson) 1997, ©1995.

Paul provided this test case to build his argument that law-oriented living is not capable of bringing righteousness to the sinner. Just as wrath and anger are due the sinner, so grace and mercy freely flow to the one who believes in Christ. But this is not just the new way of the kingdom of God. It is also the old way. It is the ancient principle of God and the way He has worked all along. In no way can Paul be charged with making up a new and strange teaching. The way of grace through faith is the way of God's revelation to Abraham.

Now to him who works, the wages are not counted as grace but as debt. (4:4)

Sometimes people will exclaim that they simply want what is due to them. That may be a good philosophy in some aspects of life. But it is not a wise way to work with God. Paul has already powerfully argued that our "due" or our "debt" as Romans 4:4 calls it, is wrath, anger and destruction. So, if one wants to count on works for what is due, so be it. But what accrued to Abraham had nothing to do with works. Abraham was not due the blessings from God. But Abraham believed and entered into a relationship with God by faith that counted on God's grace. We all have to choose a way of reckoning. Do we want it to be based on our performance or upon His grace? Of course, when it is expressed this way, the answer comes easily, doesn't it?

CROSS REFERENCE
Ezekiel 18:30–32

"Therefore I will judge you, O house of Israel, every one according to his ways," says the Lord GOD. "Repent, and turn from all your transgressions, so that iniquity will not be your ruin. Cast away from you all the transgressions which you have committed, and get yourselves a new heart and a new spirit. For why should you die, O house of Israel. ... Therefore turn and live."

Ezekiel 18 mirrors the development of Paul in Romans 1:18—5:11, which is summarized in 5:12–21. Ezekiel 18 shows the people of Israel complaining that they were exiled for no fault of their own. They thought their fathers were to blame. God's reply: "No! It is for your own sin that you remain in exile." God's justice is upheld by this reply. But God's mercy is shown in the appeal that the Israelites get a new heart and a new spirit through repentance, humility, and faith.

> But to him who does not work but believes on Him who justifies the ungodly, his faith is accounted for righteousness, (4:5)

This verse contrasts with verse 4. If you don't wish to reckon with God based on works, then a reckoning based on faith is a great option. We are far better off to reckon with a God who acquits (justifies) the ungodly than to try to perform in a totally righteous way (which is impossible). This is an accounting based upon God's grace through our faith and not based upon our feeble attempts to keep God's law. Of course, when Paul speaks of "him who does not work ..." it does not mean that a believer does nothing. He addresses this in chapter 6. At this point in Paul's argument, he is contrasting human performance and God's grace.

> just as David also describes the blessedness of the man to whom God imputes righteousness apart from works: "Blessed are those whose lawless deeds are forgiven, And whose sins are covered; Blessed is the man to whom the LORD shall not impute sin." (4:6–8)

Paul now turns to David's description of a life under the blessing of the living God. It is unfortunate that here the word "impute" is used to translate the Greek word *logizetai*. Previously, this word was translated "accounted." In other translations, the word is translated "reckon." Most people do not use impute in daily conversation. But the concept is important: it establishes the fundamental way of operation in God's graceful economy. Here, reckoning, or accounting, is accomplished based on faith and apart from works. A life in God's blessing, like David's, depended on such a reckoning. The life that is accounted as righteous is given the legal status of "not guilty." Such a person is acquitted of sin. Paul previously called this "justification." The guilty, he said are acquitted simply by the work of the righteous and just God who justifies the ungodly.

Paul quotes from Psalm 32:1, 2 in verse 6 to provide proof of David's experience. This establishes the primacy of grace through faith; God simply forgives based upon His gracious choice in response to believing faith. "Lawless deeds are forgiven" and "sins are covered." God Himself covers the shameful nakedness of sin. When God chooses to not reckon for sin, as 4:8 states, truly the man is blessed by God.

> Does this blessedness then come upon the circumcised only, or upon the uncircumcised also? For we say that faith was accounted to Abraham for righteousness. (4:9)

CROSS REFERENCE
Jeremiah 31:31–34

"Behold, the days are coming, says the LORD, when I will make a new covenant with the house of Israel and with the house of Judah—not according to the covenant that I made with their fathers in the day that I took them out of the land of Egypt. My covenant which they broke, though I was a husband to them, says the LORD. But this is the covenant that I will make with the house of Israel after those days, says the LORD: I will put My law in their minds, and write it on their hearts; and I will be their God and they shall be My people. No more shall a man teach his neighbor, and every man his brother, saying,' Know the LORD,' for they all shall know Me, from the least of them to the greatest of them, says the LORD. For I will forgive their iniquity, and their sin I will remember no more."

More than six hundred years before the death and Resurrection of Christ, Jeremiah prophesied that God would make a New Covenant. This covenant is based upon the grace of God that is found in the Messiah. A person's standing before God is guaranteed, not by the performance of law and ritual, but by the presence of God's Holy Spirit. In this covenant, God ushers in a new era of peace with God through the Lord Jesus Christ, the obedient One who provides humanity with access to the Father.

Is this principle applicable only to Jews or also to Gentiles? This is a fundamental question. The Israelites counted on their special, corporate relationship with God to cancel out personal sin. Paul has already argued that this accounting was not valid. But the question from Paul's opponent in verse 9 relates to the "favored nation status" that God granted Israel. Does this favor extend to the issue of a reckoning based on grace through faith? "No," says Paul. The reasons are found in Abraham's relationship with God. The mark of Israel's special covenant with God was circumcision, a mark first given to Abraham. But was the reckoning based on grace through faith a part of the meaning of circumcision? If it was, then one may argue that the reckoning based on grace through faith was only applicable to Israel. But Paul proves that it applies to the uncircumcised Gentiles as well as the circumcised Jews.

Since "faith was accounted to Abraham for righteousness," it is important to establish whether this was "circumcised faith" or "uncircumcised faith." If it can be established Abraham's faith was linked closely with circumcision, the case can be made that God reckons righteousness based on Israel's favored nation status. But if no such link can be established, then the Gentiles are included.

How then was it accounted? While he was circumcised, or uncircumcised? Not while circumcised, but while uncircumcised. (4:10)

This is the answer. God accounted righteousness to Abraham while Abraham was still uncircumcised. Paul uses the historical record of Scripture to establish a legal precedent. One cannot argue that God is playing favorites in accounting based on faith. God grants righteousness to all who abandon themselves and express personal faith in Him. They are assured the blessings of Abraham.

And he received the sign of circumcision, a seal of the righteousness of the faith which he had while still uncircumcised, that he might be the father of all those who believe, though they are uncircumcised, that righteousness might be imputed to them also, (4:11)

Paul here says that the sign of circumcision was not based on law but based on the righteousness of Abraham's faith. The Jews were holding

on to circumcision as a sign of their righteousness as God's most favored nation. It actually was meant to announce the blessings of righteousness by faith; that Gentiles as well as Jews may have the blessedness of faith-based, not law-based, reckoning. So, Abraham is the "father of all those who believe." This did not sit well with those who considered Abraham to be exclusively the father of the Jews. But Paul extends the fatherhood of Abraham to all who have faith. This is not ethnic fatherhood, but faith-based fatherhood. God presents His relationship with Abraham as the first faith-based, justifying relationship, which is to be embraced by all. Even circumcision is not an exclusive mark announcing that only Jews are righteous. It announced the availability of righteousness by faith to all, even the uncircumcised Gentiles. God accepts all people who embrace the Lord by faith.

---

and the father of circumcision to those who not only are of the circumcision, but who also walk in the steps of the faith which our father Abraham had while still uncircumcised. (4:12)

This is a remarkable statement regarding Paul's own countrymen. God is the Father, not of all who are circumcised, but of all those who walk in the same steps of faith that

ABRAHAM AND THE COVENANT OF GOD

In Romans 4:11-12 Paul refers to the agreement between Abraham and God called the Abrahamic covenant, which was verified by circumcision. A covenant is "an agreement between two people or two groups that involves promises on the part of each to the other." The concept of covenant between God and His people is one of the most important theological truths of the Bible. By making a covenant with Abraham, God promised to bless His descendants and to make them His special people. Abraham, in return, was to remain faithful to God and to serve as a channel through whom God's blessings could flow to the rest of the world (Gen. 12:1–3).

Before Abraham, God made a covenant with Noah, assuring him that He would not again destroy the world by flood (Genesis 9). Another covenant was between God and David, in which David and his descendants were established as the royal heirs to the throne of the nation of Israel (2 Sam. 7:12; 22:51). This covenant agreement realized its complete fulfillment when Jesus the Messiah, a descendant of the line of David, was born in Bethlehem about a thousand years after God made this promise to David the king.

A covenant, in the biblical sense, implies much more than a contract or simple agreement. A contract always has an end date, while a covenant is a permanent arrangement. Further, a contract generally involves only one aspect of a person's life, such as a skill, or a portion of one's money. However, a covenant covers a person's total being, and embraces all features of their life, purpose, and destiny.

The Old Testament word for covenant gives insight into this important word. It is derived from a Hebrew root meaning "to cut." This explains the ancient practice of two people passing between the cut portions of slain animals to seal an agreement with each other (Jer. 34:18). Some ritual or ceremony such as this always accompanied the making of a covenant in the Old Testament: (a) some entered into a covenant sharing a holy meal (Gen. 31:54); (b) Abraham and his children were commanded to be circumcised as a sign of their covenant with God (Gen. 17:10–11); (c) Moses sprinkled the blood of animals on the altar and upon the people who entered into covenant with God at Mount Sinai (Ex. 24:3–8).

The Old Testament contains many examples of covenants between people who related to each other as equals. For example, David and Jonathan entered into a covenant because of their love for each other. This agreement bound each of them to certain responsibilities (1 Sam. 18:3). The striking thing about God's covenant with His people is that God is holy, all-knowing, and all power-ful, but He consents to enter into covenant with man, who is weak, sinful, and imperfect.

In the Old Testament, God's chosen people confirmed their covenant with God with oaths or promises to keep the agreement. At Mount Sinai, the nation of Israel promised to perform "all the words which the Lord has said" (Ex. 24:3). When the people later broke this promise, they were called by their leaders to renew their oath (2 Kin. 23:3). By contrast, God does not break promises. His oath to raise up believing children to Abraham (Gen. 22:16–17) is an "everlast-ing" covenant (Gen. 17:7).

The New Testament makes a clear distinction between covenants of Law and covenants of Promise. The apostle Paul spoke of these "two covenants," one originating "from Mount Sinai," the other from "the Jerusalem above" (Gal. 4:24–26). Paul also argued that the covenant established at Mount Sinai, the Law, is a "ministry of death" and "condemnation" (2 Cor. 3:7, 9)—a covenant that cannot be fulfilled from man's side because of human weakness and sin (Rom. 8:3).

But the "covenants of promise" (Eph. 2:12) are God's guarantees that He will provide salvation in spite of mankind's inability to keep our side of the agree-ment because of our sin. The provision of a chosen people through whom the Messiah would be born is the promise of the covenants with Adam and David (Gen. 3:15; 2 Sam. 7:14-15). The covenant with Noah is God's promise to with-hold judgment on nature while salvation is occurring (Gen. 8:21–22; 2 Pet. 3:7, 15). In the covenant with Abraham, God promised to bless Abraham's descen-dants because of his faith.

These many covenants of promise may be considered as tributaries to one grand covenant of grace, which was fulfilled in the life and ministry of Jesus. His death ushered in the new covenant under which we are justified by God's grace and mercy rather than our human attempts to keep the law. And Jesus Himself is the Mediator of this better covenant between God and humanity (Heb. 9:15).[22]

---

[22] Jack W. Hayford, *Hayford's Bible Handbook* [computer file], electronic ed., Logos Library System, (Nashville: Thomas Nel-son) 1997, © 1995.

Abraham did. This revolutionized the common view of the relationship of ethnic Israel to God. It was assumed among the Jews that if you were a part of ethnic Israel and had the mark of circumcision that your relationship with God as Father was secure. Paul here limits such a view, adding the element of walking by faith. Ethnic background and religious observance are not enough to ensure God's favor. A walk of faith, just as Abraham had, is necessary. In some ways, Paul was asking the Jews to live like Gentiles! This was an abhorrent thought to some Jews to be sure! But those Jews who recognized God's way of grace through faith understood that this magnified rather that depreciated God's greatness. God's inclusion of the Gentiles in the way of righteousness is the mark of His greatness and love. At the same time it does not reduce God's preference for the nation of Israel as the vehicle that brought so many benefits accrue to the world.

For the promise that he would be the heir of the world was not to Abraham or to his seed through the law, but through the righteousness of faith. For if those who are of the law are heirs, faith is made void and the promise made of no effect, because the law brings about wrath; for where there is no law there is no transgression. (4:13–15)

In Romans 4:13–25 Paul explains why the promises given to Abraham and his heirs are given because of faith, not law. The law came with built-in deficiencies. But faith has unlimited possibilities for those who live therein. Paul states that God promised Abraham that he would be heir of the world. The context of this promise shows to whom the promise pertains. If the promise is law-based, then the heirs of the promise are only those who perfectly keep the law. But since the promises are given based on faith, all who live by faith are Abraham's heirs.

The blessings of Abraham are extended through the righteousness of faith, which is both objective and subjective in nature. Righteousness comes to the heirs of Abraham because of their faith in the faithful God. Faith in a faithful God provides the solution for human weakness. Abraham knew he was totally unable to do what God said would occur. But Abraham believed, nonetheless. He was convinced of God's ability to bring, through him, blessing to the world. Thus, the righteousness of faith is both the righteousness that extends to all who believe in God and the righteousness that is guaranteed by God who is perfectly able, powerful, consistent, and faithful to keep His promises. In some cases, faith is simply wishful thinking. But the Spirit of God through Paul emphasizes the sureness of faith in a faithful God. The ground of faith is secure for it rests in God Almighty. We apply that to ourselves when we trust in His ability to bring His promises to pass.

His righteousness by punishing sin. Humanity's sin problem stops the promise dead in its tracks.

For if those who are of the law are heirs, faith is made void and the promise made of no effect, because the law brings about wrath; (4:14, 15a)

Here the inability of the law to bring about the fulfillment of the promises to Abraham is stated plainly. The way of the law brought about wrath. This is not the case with the promise to Abraham. We have already seen how Paul argued effectively that the law-era had only one sure end for humanity: God's wrath. So if one is expecting the blessings of Abraham to come based on law, there will be severe disappointment. If this were the case, faith would be made void and become empty and the promise made of no effect, cancelled. Faith becomes empty because of the demand of the law, which requires justice. The promise is cancelled because of the faithlessness of humanity. It is impossible to keep the law; therefore, any promise connected with the law is null and void. For blessings to come based on the law, one would need to perfectly perform the law. But since the testimony of human behavior shows lawlessness and transgression, any possibility of promise extending to people is impossible and God must uphold

for where there is no law there is no transgression (4:15b)

This is a peculiar thought if not understood properly. But it ties the bankruptcy of the law with the full blessing of faith. For if one wishes to continue under the law the end is transgression. And if the end is transgression, then wrath appropriately extends to all who transgress. On the other hand, if one is living with no law, then there is likewise no transgression. While this was a novel thought to Paul's readers, and especially to his imaginary questioner, the plight of humanity requires God to work in a different way in order for blessing to extend to them. Faith implies the absence of law. Therefore, transgression is not measured. This is exactly what human beings need—a way in which our transgressions are not measured in order to bring forth wrath.

Therefore it is of faith that it might be according to grace, so that the promise might be sure to all the seed, not only to those who are of the law, but also to those who are of the faith of Abraham, who is the father of us all (4:16)

This verse recalls Paul's statement in Ephesians 2:8, 9: "For by grace are you saved, through faith, and that not of yourselves. It is the gift of God, not the result of works, in order that we might not boast." The way of grace through faith is the only opportunity of blessing for both Jews and Gentiles. The story of Abraham proves that he is the hope of blessedness for all peoples. This makes him father of all, not just of the Jews. Of course, the *all* here refers to those of his seed. In this case, being of his seed pertains to all who have faith in God just as Abraham did. The promise is "sure" (Greek, bebaian), steadfast, and is guaranteed to come about. If the promise were by the law, then the fulfillment would surely be in doubt for it would depend upon our performance of the law. This is why God planned that the fulfillment of the promise would be based on faith and be according to grace. That way its fulfillment is guaranteed for it depends on a faithful God and not on human obedience. What a blessing this is!

(as it is written, "I have made you a father of many nations") (4:17a)

This quotation of the Old Testament provides proof that God includes all people in the seed of Abraham, not just those who keep the law. ("Nations"—Greek, *ethnon*—is sometimes translated "Gentiles.")

in the presence of Him whom he [Abraham] believed—God (4:17b)

The wording of this verse is confusing unless the thought that comes before the previous Old Testament quotation is repeated to emphasize the transnational fatherhood of Abraham. So it reads, "Abraham, the father of all who have faith, stands in the presence of God." This takes us back to Genesis where Abraham is confronted with his own weakness in light of the God's improbable promise. Nonetheless, he believed. The Holy Spirit makes it abundantly clear that Abraham's focus was not upon his own faith; it was God Himself. The faith of Abraham depends upon the faithfulness of God. Abraham had no ability to bring the promise to pass. Nonetheless, he exercised faith in the God before whom he stood.

God, who gives life to the dead and calls those things which do not exist as though they did; (4:17c)

This verse points to the power of God to bring about anything He wishes. The fact that He brings life to the dead refers to Abraham's impotence and the barrenness of Sarah's womb. God would have to perform a miracle if life were to come from such deadness. But Abraham believed in this God who "calls those things which do not exist as

THE ESSENTIAL PLACE AND POWER OF GOD'S WORD

Just as we owe our natural existence to the Creator's spoken word and life-giving breath, so we owe our New Birth to the power of God's Word and the Holy Spirit's activation of its power. God's intent for our created being is only completely fulfilled when our spirits are alive toward Him. As sin has produced spiritual death in people (Eph. 2:1–3), so salvation in Jesus Christ has provided spiritual life. This text tells us that the "seed" that has produced new life in us is the *Word* of God, which has begotten us again by the Holy Spirit's power (Titus 3:5) and made us members of God's new creation (2 Cor. 5:17). The power of God's Word—the Holy Scriptures—is in no way more manifest than in this: its power to bring spiritual life to all who open to its truth. James 1:18 elaborates the fact that God's "word of truth" is the means by which He brought us new life, emphasizing that He has done this as a direction of His own will. God's will to save us (2 Pet. 3:9) has been effectively expressed in His Word, which accomplishes that work (John 1:13).[23]

though they did." Undoubtedly this is a reference to God's creative abilities. He called the world into existence out of nothing. God's word is enough. He is powerful and effective even when simply speaking. Thus, the spoken promise to Abraham brings to mind God the Creator who spoke and it was done; it highlights the faithfulness and power of God in whom we believe.

---

who, contrary to hope, in hope believed, so that he became the father of many nations, according to what was spoken, "So shall your descendants be." (4:18)

Abraham was a realist. He knew the condition of his body and that of Sarah's as well. Unless God acted, there was no reason to hope. What God promised was way beyond the scope of human ability. Thus, when Abraham believed, it was "contrary to hope." The realist in him knew the chances for a child to be naturally conceived was nil. Nonetheless, Abraham "in hope believed." For he knew that the God who raises the dead and creates out of nothing is able to make all things new, even contrary to natural human abilities. For the promise does not depend upon the condition of Abraham's body or Sarah's womb, but upon God, who is not constrained by

---

[23] Jack W. Hayford, *Hayford's Bible Handbook* [computer file], electronic ed., Logos Library System, (Nashville: Thomas Nelson) 1997, © 1995.

these minor impediments. The promise of innumerable heirs is the spoken promise of God. It is in the same category of the spoken words of the Creator when He brought the world into being. Only His words are needed.

The Spirit of God reminds us of the simple necessity of the spoken word of God. What else is important when it comes to promises? Certainly, when God speaks, the created realm listens! Out of nothing and deadness springs life. Abraham believed in this. Thus, when incredulity was the natural response, he had a sure and certain hope.

_____

> And not being weak in faith, he did not consider his own body, already dead (since he was about a hundred years old), and the deadness of Sarah's womb. (4:19)

Abraham's full-faith evaluation of himself distinguishes him from so many of us. He saw very clearly the limitations of his own body and that of Sarah's womb. But Abraham's full-faith response to the promise of God made these limitations minor. He did not consider these issues very important in light of God's abilities. His faith in God's promises was steadfast.

_____

> He did not waver at the promise of God through unbelief, but was

> strengthened in faith, giving glory to God, and being fully convinced that what He had promised He was also able to perform. (4:20, 21)

Abraham's life testifies to the beauty of the faith-filled life. He "did not waver." This steadfastness over a long period of time marked his life. Even when it seemed like the promise was going to be lost, he stayed secure in the belief that God would act. Here unbelief is more than the occasional questioning of God. "It denotes the active rejection of faith, the positive refusal to give credence to God's offered promise."[24] But Abraham found strength in his faith. This is the way of the Spirit. We gain strength by the Holy Spirit to operate in the midst of overwhelming obstacles. Such strength allowed Abraham to bring "glory to God." Abraham exercised faith in Him who is able to bring forth what is promised. This brought his strengthening from God. Abraham was convinced of the certainty of God's promise and of His wonder-working ability. So he remained steadfast and found strength to go on.

_____

> And therefore "it was accounted to him for righteousness." (4:22)

Paul brings us back to the heart of the matter: Righteousness is by faith.

_____

24 Cranfield, *Romans*, p. 248. Here he cites Michel, p. 126.

It is amazing that Paul gives us this long explanation of the faith of Abraham. Yet, it is the same with us. When we believe in the Lord for salvation, we believe that God can bring life out of our deadness. This is just like the quickening that Abraham expected. Sure and certain hope depends not on our faith but upon the promise of God to bring such things to pass. Thus, when it came time to bring Abraham's life to ultimate account, God declared him righteous based upon his faith. Abraham believed and found God's righteousness applied to his account.

Now it was not written for his sake alone that it was imputed to him, but also for us. (4:23, 24)

God gives us the Scriptures not simply to present a history lesson. He provides His Word to give us life. For the same reckoning of righteousness that Abraham received is ours as well. Certainly Abraham is a wonderful picture of faith; but God intends his story to be our story. It was for our sake the Abraham's story was given. He paved the way of faith, not of works, in order that we might

ACCENT ON APPLICATION
The Kingdom of God in the Writings of Paul

"In Christ" is the expression Paul most frequently uses to designate new life through the gospel. This term places the believer in the circle of all that is represented and contained in Christ including His salvation conquest and personal rule. The essential truth is that the Savior-King has come, and in Him, the rule of God has altered the limits sin has heretofore placed on individuals. People no longer need be ruled by their carnality (flesh) or controlled by evil (the devil). Being freed, that is, transferred to a new kingdom, they can know the joy of a relationship with God through the power of the Cross and can realize the reinstatement of their rule under God through the power of the Holy Spirit. Living in the kingdom brings a dual hope: the present promise of grace to reign in life and eternity with Christ.

The term *In Christ* designates the new life that may be lived in the benefits of, and by the power of, the King Jesus, "who has brought life (the present reign in life through Christ—Rom. 5:17) and immortality (the eternal reign forever with Christ—Rev. 22:5) to light through the gospel" (2 Tim. 1:10).[25]

---

[25] Jack W. Hayford, *Hayford's Bible Handbook* [computer file], electronic ed., Logos Library System (Nashville: Thomas Nelson) 1997, ©1995.

have the hope of faith and not the dread of the law-oriented life.

_____

but also for us. It shall be imputed to us who believe in Him who raised up Jesus our Lord from the dead, who was delivered up because of our offenses, and was raised because of our justification. (4:24, 25)

We return to the efficacy of faith for those who believe in Jesus. Paul now brings the point of chapter 4 to bear on our own experience. The same accounting of righteousness by faith that Abraham experienced becomes ours when we exercise faith in God. For the God who brought forth life out of deadness in Abraham's case also brings forth life from the deadness of our Lord's body. The Resurrection of Christ becomes the capstone for the reconciling work of God through the Cross.

The answer to sin and our need for righteousness is found in the work of Christ. Note that Paul highlights the problem of sin in that Christ was "delivered up because of our offenses." Sin rightly demands wrath. So someone is going to have to pay for our offenses against the holy God. But in addition, we need to find the righteousness that is required by God. So, while at the Cross the sin problem is dealt with, so also is there the conferring of righteousness upon us by the Resurrection of Christ. The Resurrection is the guarantee that God accepted the payment for sin and has recognized the work of Jesus in conferring a righteous status on those who believe in Him. Sin's debt is cancelled and our need for righteousness is found in the Righteous One, Jesus Christ. His sinless life becomes ours; His atoning death is ours as well.

QUESTIONS FOR PERSONAL REFLECTION
AND GROUP DISCUSSION

Read Romans 4:1–25 and then answer the following questions.

1. What are we to learn from Abraham's example according to Romans 4:1–3?

2. What kind of blessedness does Paul speak of in describing David's writings in Romans 4:6–9?

3. Why is it important that Abraham was justified before he was circumcised according to Romans 4:10–12?

4. Why is it not possible to look to the law for our inheritance as saints? See Romans 4:13–15.

5. How does one receive the promise of God and to whom does that promise apply according to Romans 4:16, 17?

6. According to Romans 4:18–21, how is Abraham an example of a person of hope and belief? What obstacles were in his way? What can we learn from Abraham?

7. From this chapter, what are the three or four main lessons, which we can learn?

8. How does the Bible describe Abraham in the following passages: Genesis 26:5; Isaiah 41:8; Hebrews 11:11, 12?

The Benefits of Righteousness by Faith

Romans 5:1–11

Therefore, having been justified by faith, we have peace with God through our Lord Jesus Christ, through whom also we have access by faith into this grace in which we stand, and rejoice in hope of the glory of God. And not only that, but we also glory in tribulations, knowing that tribulation produces perseverance; and perseverance, character; and character, hope. Now hope does not disappoint, because the love of God has been poured out in our hearts by the Holy Spirit who was given to us. (5:1–5)

The word *therefore* in Romans 5:1 forces us to look back to what Paul had just written. At the end of chapter 4, Paul declared that by faith we have the benefits that ensue from the death and Resurrection of Christ. The work of Christ provides atonement and justification for us. Righteousness can be embraced by the sinner, not due to his own works, but because faith in Christ brings him into that blessing. This is just as Abraham's faith was credited to him as righteousness. Thus, "having been justified by faith," we gain all the benefits of the righteous. These benefits are here cited.

But let us again note that our being justified by faith results from the faith of the individual in the Lord Jesus Christ and the faithfulness of God who is able to bring about what is promised. Both of these aspects are in view when "faith" is mentioned here. Our faith is in the faithful God who is able to do what He said He would do.

This verse is often isolated as a memory verse (and it is a great one). But we must remember to tie it to its context. In a dramatic turn of events God has changed the destiny of the individual sinner. Romans chapter 2 says that all who break the law, whether the written law or the unwritten law of conscience, deserve the wrath of God. For there will be "indignation and wrath, tribulation and anguish, on every soul of man who does evil, of the Jew first and also of the Greek" (2:8, 9). But through the saving work of Christ and the response of faith on the part of the sinner this destiny is changed. Instead of wrath we receive peace "through our Lord Jesus Christ." Apart from Christ no peace is possible, only wrath.

---

through whom also we have access by faith into this grace in which we stand, and rejoice in hope of the glory of God. (5:2)

God made a conduit for His grace;

WORD STUDY
ACCESS

Access—the privilege of having an audience with one's superior. Access to God is that positive, friendly relationship with the Father in which we have confidence that we are pleasing and acceptable to Him. Jesus is the "new and living way" (Heb. 10:20) who gives us access to God.[26]

this conduit is Christ Himself. For there is only one name by which we are saved, Jesus Christ. God is able to make us stand because we stand not in our sin, but in the protective provision of Christ's work. This is a gracious standing. God's grace allows us to stand before Him without trembling in terror.

Terror would be appropriate in the sinner standing before God. But those who have been made righteous have no terror because we know we stand by God's redeeming work and not by our own merit. Through sin we had "fallen short of the glory of God" but we now have "hope of the glory of God." This hope is not just wishful thinking because hope in God's promises will come to pass. Just as Abraham testifies, hope does not depend on us but upon God who brings about what He has declared. God has promised that we will find the ultimate perfection when the fullness of the kingdom is revealed.

The hope of perfection ("the glory of God") is guaranteed for the believer. Current peace with God and the future perfection of God belong to the ones who are righteous by faith.

And not only that, but we also glory in tribulations, knowing that tribulation produces perseverance; and perseverance, character; and character, hope. (5:3, 4)

The Spirit of God, through Paul, here says that while we are guaranteed perfection in the future, currently we glory in tribulations. Believers are quite aware of the divide between their present experience and their desire to be totally freed from sin's consequences. Present tribulations are not a sign of God's displeasure. No, they are a guarantee of future blessedness. In these tribulations we glory (literally, "boast" or "exult," Greek, *kauchometha*) just as

---

[26] Ronald F. Youngblood, general editor; F. F. Bruce and R. K. Harrison, consulting editors, *Nelson's New Illustrated Bible Dictionary: An authoritative one-volume reference work on the Bible with full color illustrations* [computer file], electronic edition of the revised edition of *Nelson's Illustrated Bible Dictionary*, Logos Library System, (Nashville: Thomas Nelson) 1997, © 1995.

we rejoice (same Greek word) in the "hope of the glory of God." Just as believers are guaranteed the inheritance of future blessedness when perfection comes, so also we are guaranteed to receive the perfect result of our current tribulations. For they, too, bring something good and godly. They bring forth perseverance, character, and hope.

The word "perseverance" carries with it the idea of patient endurance. While no one wishes to endure simple fate, with God in control even tribulations are subject to God's ultimate direction. So, when tribulations become a part of our lives we can either grumble, as the Israelites did (and we are prone to do) or we can walk through them patiently, for they bring the blessedness of a faith tested. This is called "character." Faith tested in the proving ground of

God, which is part and parcel of human experience, leads to strong character. As a result of these tribulations, hope is strong. Those who are full of faith in the midst of the storms of life reap the deep assurance of the future and ultimate blessedness of God. In no way will the believer be disappointed. Again, the experience of Abraham becomes ours. He hoped in the promises of God, not because he was worthy, but because of the worth of God.

Now hope does not disappoint, because the love of God has been poured out in our hearts by the Holy Spirit who was given to us. (5:5)

Hope in God does not bring us to shame. In no sense will we b e

---

WORD STUDY
TRIBULATION

Tribulation—*great adversity and anguish; intense oppression or persecution.* Tribulation is linked to God's process for making the world right again. His Son underwent great suffering, just as His people undergo a great deal of tribulation from the world (Rom. 5:3; Acts 14:22). This tribulation has its source in the conflict between God and the devil (Gen. 3:15), which will end with the devil being cast into the lake of fire to suffer eternal tribulation (Rev. 20:10).[27]

---

[27] Ronald F. Youngblood, general editor; F. F. Bruce and R. K. Harrison, consulting editors, *Nelson's New Illustrated Bible Dictionary: An authoritative one-volume reference work on the Bible with full color illustrations* [computer file], electronic edition of the revised edition of *Nelson's Illustrated Bible Dictionary*, Logos Library System, (Nashville: Thomas Nelson) 1997, © 1995.

PAUL AND THE GIFT OF THE HOLY SPIRIT

Paul's teaching about the Holy Spirit harmonizes with the accounts of the Spirit's activity in the Gospels and Acts. According to Paul, it is by the Holy Spirit that one confesses that Jesus is Lord (1 Cor. 12:3). Through the same Spirit varieties of gifts are given to the body of Christ to ensure its richness and unity (1 Cor. 12:4–27). The Holy Spirit is the way to Jesus Christ the Son (Rom. 8:11) and to the Father (Rom. 8:14–15). He is the Person who bears witness to us that we are children of God (8:16–17). He "makes intercession for us with groanings which cannot be uttered" (Rom. 8:26–27).

The Holy Spirit also reveals to Christians the deep things of God (1 Cor. 2:10–12) and the mystery of Christ (Eph. 3:3–5). The Holy Spirit acts with God and Christ as the pledge or guarantee by which believers are sealed for the day of salvation (2 Cor. 1:21–22), and by which they walk and live (Rom. 8:3–6) and abound in hope with power (Rom. 15:13). Against the lust and enmity of the flesh Paul contrasts the fruit of the Spirit: "Love, joy, peace, longsuffering, kindness, goodness, faithfulness, gentleness, self-control" (Gal. 5:22–23).

Since the Holy Spirit is the present avenue on earth of expressed power of the Godhead, it is imperative that one not grieve the Spirit, since no further appeal to the Father and the Son on the day of redemption is available (Eph. 4:30). Jesus made this clear in His dispute with the religious authorities, who attributed His ministry to Satan rather than the Spirit and committed the unforgivable sin (Matt. 12:22–32, John 8:37–59).

In Paul's letters Christian liberty stems from the work of the Holy Spirit: "Where the Spirit of the Lord is, there is liberty" (2 Cor. 3:17). This is a process of "beholding as in a mirror the glory of the Lord," and "being transformed into the same image from glory to glory, just as by the Spirit of the Lord" (2 Cor. 3:18). The personal work of the Holy Spirit is accordingly one with that of the Father and the Son, so Paul can relate the grace, love, and communion of the Godhead in a trinitarian benediction: "The grace of the Lord Jesus Christ and the love of God, and the communion of the Holy Spirit be with you all. Amen" (2 Cor. 13:14).[28]

---

[28] Jack W. Hayford, *Hayford's Bible Handbook* [computer file], electronic ed., Logos Library System, (Nashville: Thomas Nelson) 1997, © 1995.

disappointed in God's promises. Not only is He able to bring about what He has promised, but also He has given us a taste of this in the love that has been poured out in our hearts. In fact, a "pouring out" is not just a taste, it is abundant.

The lavish love of God has burst into the human experience through the Holy Spirit's presence and fullness in our lives. This is the firstfruit of our belief. But God is not stingy here. Abundant love mediated to us by the Holy Spirit is God's perfect way of assuring us that we have entered the state of blessedness in which future glory is certain.

For when we were still without strength, in due time Christ died for the ungodly. (5:6)

This sentence appears to begin another paragraph, but the context ties it to the preceding verse. Part of the love that God lavished upon us came when we were without strength; even in that ungodly state, at precisely the right time (Greek *kairos*, "season"), Christ died for us. Just as Abraham's body was weak and hopeless in regard to bringing forth physical life, so also our weakness excludes us from bringing forth righteousness. We rightly deserve wrath, anger, and distress. The public death of Christ and demonstration of His power in His Resurrection guarantees the love of God

for the weak and ungodly. There is no earthly reason for Christ to do this. The heavenly reason is God's love for us. Thus, the Cross is God's love letter sent freely to us, sealed in blood. Our proper response is all that is necessary.

For scarcely for a righteous man will one die; yet perhaps for a good man someone would even dare to die. But God demonstrates His own love toward us, in that while we were still sinners, Christ died for us. (5:7, 8)

The logic of these two verses may escape us. On closer examination we see that Paul is tying what was said about the "righteous" and the "good" in chapters 2 and 3 with the movement of the love of God here in chapter 5. Here is his logic:

One would not die for a righteous man. Such a person does not need anyone to die for him since he is pure and merits life on his own.

One perhaps would die for a good person who is not sufficiently righteous to merit life but is sufficiently good to evoke another person's self-sacrificial death.

But Paul has made it clear that there is "none righteous, no not one" (3:10) and "none good, no, not one"

(3:12). So, these first two possibilities do not exist in reality. Only the third possibility is reality:

God's overwhelming love toward ungodly sinners is thoroughly demonstrated in Christ's death. In the human realm this is absurd. In the heavenly realm, it proves God's love.

The phrase *but God demonstrated His own love* is the turning point in the argument. Human sentiment cannot compare to God's love. It is love for the weak, the ungodly, and the sinner. One can only say, "Wow, what love!" That is the correct response. We have no merit that gains status for us before God. We only have His unfailing love. It is no wonder Paul on so many occasions in his letters breaks into doxologies, that is, expressive praise, for God's wonderful works and pure character.

Much more then, having now been justified by His blood, we shall be saved from wrath through Him. (5:9)

Here again Paul's argument may be a little hard to follow. But once we understand his method, the thought unpacks easily. In verse 9, Paul is building his case from the previous verse. The logic goes something like this:

While we were enemies, Christ died for us. Yet, He made us righteous through His blood. Then we will certainly be saved from God's wrath because we are no longer enemies, but friends of God!

The hard work is done through the death of Christ. Saving us from wrath is the easy work. Those who are righteous, either by perfect performance like Jesus, or by God's decree through faith in Christ, shall easily escape God's righteous punishment. This form of thought is typical in Paul's rabbinic training. If it can be shown that the hard work is done, then the easy work will more certainly be accomplished. The hard work is the guarantee that the easy work will come about. Whenever we see the phrase *how much more* or *much more* in Paul's writings, we should be on the lookout for such a form of argumentation. In fact, this is employed again in the next verse.

For if when we were enemies we were reconciled to God through the death of His Son, much more, having been reconciled, we shall be saved by His life. (5:10)

Paul, by the Holy Spirit, introduces us to another powerful concept: reconciliation. Reconciliation brings two estranged parties together to form a peaceful relationship where they can engage with each other without fear. The death of Christ accomplished this work on our behalf. The wrath of God came down on Him rather than on us. God's righteous punishment for sin, as our due wages, rests upon Jesus. Since that hard work is already accomplished, then it is easy for God to save us from wrath by the perfect and resurrected life of His Son. The perfection of Jesus is our guarantee that wrath will not come to us.

When we are joined to Christ through faith, His death pays for our sins and we are reconciled to God. Then Christ's Resurrection life gives us the power to live a life that pleases God. God through Christ does all the work. That is our guarantee of salvation from the righteous wrath of God. Notice, it is all His work, not our own. Our own merit is not involved. Worship is the appropriate response to this astonishing gift.

And not only that, but we also rejoice in God through our Lord Jesus Christ, through whom we have now received the reconciliation. (5:11)

WORD STUDY
RECONCILIATION

Reconciliation—*the process by which God and man are brought together again.* The Bible teaches that God and man are alienated from one another because of God's holiness and man's sinfulness. Although God loves the sinner (Rom. 5:8), it is impossible for Him not to judge sin (Heb. 10:27). Therefore, the initiative in reconciliation was taken by God—while we were still sinners and "enemies," Christ died for us (Rom. 5:8, 10; Col. 1:21). Reconciliation is thus God's own completed act, something that takes place before human actions such as confession, repentance, and restitution. God Himself "has reconciled us to Himself through Jesus Christ" (2 Cor. 5:18).

Paul regarded the gospel as "the word of reconciliation" (2 Cor. 5:19), and pleaded, "as though God were pleading through us:...Be reconciled to God" (2 Cor. 5:20).[29]

---

[29] Jack W. Hayford, *Hayford's Bible Handbook* [computer file], electronic ed., Logos Library System, (Nashville: Thomas Nelson) 1997, © 1995.

Adam and the Entrance of Sin into the World

Genesis 3 tells how Adam failed to keep God's command not to eat of the tree of the knowledge of good and evil. The consequence of this disobedience was death (Gen. 2:17), both physical (Gen. 5:5) and spiritual (Eph. 2:1). Eve disobeyed first, lured by pride and the desire for pleasure (Gen. 3:5–6; 1 Tim. 2:14). Then Adam, with full knowledge of the consequences, joined Eve in rebellion against God (Gen. 3:6).

The consequences of disobedience were: (1) loss of innocence (Gen. 3:7); (2) continued enmity between the seed of the woman [Christ] (Gen. 3:15; Gal. 3:16) and the seed of the serpent [SATAN and his followers] (John 8:44); (3) the cursing of the ground and the resultant hard labor for man (Gen. 3:17–19); (4) the hard labor of childbirth (Gen. 3:16); (5) the submission of woman to her husband (Gen. 3:16; Eph. 5:22–23); and (6) separation from God (Gen. 3:23–24; 2 Thess. 1:9).[30]

Thus, Paul focuses our attention toward the worship of Jesus Christ. He is our Savior. It is only through Him that we gain access to the righteous God. So, we glory and boast in Him, not in our own religious tradition or performance.

---

30 Ronald F. Youngblood, general editor; F. F. Bruce and R. K. Harrison, consulting editors, *Nelson's New Illustrated Bible Dictionary: An authoritative one-volume reference work on the Bible with full color illustrations* [computer file], electronic edition of the revised edition of *Nelson's Illustrated Bible Dictionary*, Logos Library System, (Nashville: Thomas Nelson) 1997, © 1995.

QUESTIONS FOR PERSONAL REFLECTION AND GROUP DISCUSSION

Read Romans 5:1–11 and then answer the following questions.

1. Why can we say that we have peace with God through our Lord Jesus Christ according to Romans 5:1?

2. For what should the believer in Christ rejoice as Romans 5:2, 3 indicate?

3. What kind of a hope does God give us (v. 5)?

4. How does Christ's death demonstrate God's love for us according to Romans 5:6–8?

5. What has God done for us and what should our response to God be as Romans 5:9–11 dictates?

6. Reflecting upon what Paul spoke about earlier in this epistle, why is having "peace with God" so significant to him?

7. What are the character qualities which Paul mentions will come as a result of suffering?

8. What obstacles get in our way of allowing God to work out His purposes in the midst of our trials and sufferings?

The Superiority of the Era of Grace Over the Era of Law

Romans 5:12–21

Therefore, just as through one man sin entered the world, and death through sin, and thus death spread to all men, because all sinned—(5:12)

We are granted in Romans 5:12–21 a summary of what has been a part of Paul's argument in 1:18—5:11. Practically all of what Paul stated in the preceding chapters are compressed into these ten verses. The way of the law is contrasted with the way of grace; these two are typified in the persons of Adam and Christ; death, condemnation, and wrath follow the way of Adam; and life, righteousness, and glory follow the way of Christ and all those who by faith appropriate His benefits.

Now we are taken back to Genesis for a history lesson. There sin found its entry point through the disobedience of Adam. For humanity, disaster followed. Where sin reigned, so did death, condemnation, and the assurance of wrath to come. This death then spread to all people, as the text says, "Because all sinned." Adam began the fatal episode and we human beings participate in it by choosing to sin. The first part of the argument in Romans 1:18—3:20 chronicles our

choice to be with Adam in this regard. When we choose Adam's path, we verify in ourselves that we prefer sin to the way of righteousness. As a result, death continues its deadly reign. Death is a part of the human experience in this fallen world through the entry of sin. We cooperate with sin, so we bring condemnation justly upon ourselves. The created realm feels the affects of the sinful choice of Adam just as we do. The world is in the bondage of corruption (Rom. 8:21) and we in our fallen bodies sense the same bondage to the destruction that befell Adam.

(For until the law sin was in the world, but sin is not imputed when there is no law. Nevertheless death reigned from Adam to Moses, even over those who had not sinned according to the likeness of the transgression of Adam, who is a type of Him who was to come. (5:13, 14)

These two verses digress to show that God's law was in existence prior to the giving of the written law to Moses on Sinai. The fact that death reigned from Adam until Moses proves that a law existed during this time period. Sin, God says, cannot be reckoned unless there is law. Since we know the wages of sin is death, the reign of death requires the presence of law to measure sin. This is the law of the conscience and the heart, not the

Mosaic code. The sins during the time of Adam until Moses were breaches of the unwritten law, the law that is written on the heart and testified of in the conscience. Then sin and death reigned to testify to the breach of God's law. When wrath comes, it is justified punishment for sin upon all humanity, whether during the time between Adam and Moses or after the written code was given.

Adam here is called a "type of Him who was to come." While there is nearly universal agreement that Adam is a type of Jesus, there is also nearly universal agreement that Adam is quite unlike Jesus. Some have called Adam the antitype of Jesus. It may be that Adam is more a type of Moses than Jesus since Adam was given an explicit law like Moses'.

As we follow the argument of this section, the contrast (not comparison) is between the way of the law and the way of grace. Adam and Jesus are the key figures in the contrast, but not because they themselves are comparable. The contrast is between the life under law inaugurated by Adam and the life under grace inaugurated by Christ. The two could not be more dissimilar!

But the free gift is not like the offense. (5:15a)

The way of the free gift is not like the way of offense. These are the two eras that are being contrasted in these verses. We must be careful here to stick with the Holy Spirit's way of expression. What is contrasted is the way of gift and grace brought by Jesus against the way of offense and law brought by Adam and his heirs. Adam and Christ, *per se*, are not compared, but what they represent certainly is in sharp contrast.

For if by the one man's offense many died, much more the grace of God and the gift by the grace of the one Man, Jesus Christ, abounded to many. (5:15b)

The flow of this verse is simplified if we ask one question: Which work is greater, the work of Adam or the work of Christ? Since we already know of the great work of Jesus Christ as the fulfillment of the law on our behalf, this is not a difficult question at all. Certainly the tragic work of Adam set in motion the sinful legacy for all to see and in which we freely participate. But the work of Christ is so much more powerful than this. In it we can experience the grace that abounds to many. The contrast is dramatic. The way of Adam brings death and the way of Christ brings the grace of God, which abounds to all who believe.

And the gift is not like that which came through the one who sinned.

For the judgment which came from one offense resulted in condemnation, but the free gift which came from many offenses resulted in justification. (5:16)

Adam, and all who sprang from him, followed the path of violating both the written and unwritten law of God. Not one person (apart from Jesus) can claim to be free from sin. As a result, God's righteous judgment rests on sinners and results in condemnation. The legacy of Adam is perpetuated by each generation. So, they freely and willingly bring judgment justly upon themselves. Of course, the fallen quality of Adam is also perpetuated since we are born into a universe that carries the scars of sin's lethal reign.

Jesus broke this deadly chain of judgment and condemnation. His gift, in contrast with the way of the law, resulted in justification. So, if you wish to follow the way of the law, then judgment and condemnation are the result. If you wish to follow the way of grace, justification is sure.

For if by the one man's offense death reigned through the one, much more those who receive abundance of grace and of the gift of righteousness will reign in life through the One, Jesus Christ.) (5:17)

Again, we see the beautiful contrast between the offense under law and righteousness under grace. Remember, when Paul uses the phrase *much more*, he is using a form of argument typical of the rabbis of his day. The question is, which is greater, the work of Adam or the work of Christ? Since the work of Jesus Christ is so wonderfully superior to Adam's deadly work, the result of Christ's work is extraordinarily, superabundantly, superior! Life reigns for the righteous by faith as opposed to death's ugly claim over those living under law.

Therefore, as through one man's offense judgment came to all men, resulting in condemnation, even so through one Man's righteous act the free gift came to all men, resulting in justification of life. (5:18)

The entrance of sin into the world through Adam carries its sure result: judgment that leads to condemnation for all who sin. But fortunately, the story does not end there. For sin is no match for the actions of the righteous one. The righteous act of providing grace while still upholding the essential character of God, which demands that sin be punished, leads to astonishment and praise.

The Cross of Christ focuses on the grace and justice of God. This proceeds to justification in our lives through Christ's work. Surely we can see that this is no contrast of equals; we see the smallness of sin in the shadow of immense grace and justice working perfectly together through the work of our God and Savior.

For as by one man's disobedience many were made sinners, so also by one Man's obedience many will be made righteous. (5:19)

Adam's disobedience opened the door for sin and death to enter into the world. Since then all has changed for humanity. Our frail existence is the consequence of our embrace of Adam's path. There we gather to ourselves the rewards of Adam's sin. His choice becomes our choice for, as Romans 5:12 states, death comes to all because all have sinned. But just as slavery to sin and death are the destinies of the descendants of Adam, so also is righteousness the destiny of those who embrace the Christ's obedience. Paul has already indicated that this is ours through our belief in the Lord Jesus Christ.

Sin's impact is sure since Adam chose to sin but the obedience of Christ, in contrast, eliminates this problem for the person who has Christ's righteousness.

Moreover the law entered that the offense might abound. But where sin abounded, grace abounded much more, so that as sin reigned in death, even so grace might reign through righteousness to eternal life through Jesus Christ our Lord. (5:20, 21)

We must be careful here in our understanding of the role of the law for humanity. Paul's assertion that the "law entered that the offense might abound" does not explain the whole purpose of the law. This is but one aspect of the role of the law. While this may not seem gracious, the presence of the law allows people to see sin's utterly sinful attributes. Indeed, the law even promotes further sinfulness for those who have already chosen that path. But that simply provides the contrast for people to see God's righteousness in distinction from their own waywardness.

The law invites abundant sinfulness by making such choices blatantly obvious. But this is no match for abounding grace. Grace superabounds to bring hope for the sinner. *Superabounds* is the literal reading of the Greek word here

We know of the reign of death for we see it all the time in the world. Yet, grace reigns through righteousness. As we noted before, this righteousness is both the righteous actions of the Father in providing a just way of forgiveness as well as the righteousness of Jesus' living. Only through the actions of the righteous God applied by the Holy Spirit to the believer will grace reign. The only way for this to occur is through Jesus Christ our Lord. Liberty is found through the righteous actions of God, which are embraced by faith in Christ.

So, the way of the law, as typified by Adam and all who follow in his footsteps, leads to one outcome: Judgment, death, and condemnation. The way of grace leads to righteousness for the sinner, justification and eternal life. Those who embrace this righteousness by faith are released from the era of the law into the era of grace. No longer does one fear death for Christ has been victorious over death. Those who are in Christ also enjoy this victory. All the rewards of Christ's righteous actions are now ours. Some are fully realized now and some will be embraced later. The Resurrection guarantees our future and the presence of the Holy Spirit is the seal for us now.

QUESTIONS FOR PERSONAL REFLECTION
AND GROUP DISCUSSION

Read Romans 5:12–21 and answer the following questions.

1. According to Romans 5:12, what are the results of sin in human life?

2. Why did death spread to all men (Rom. 5:12)?

3. How can it be said that death reigned?

4. In what sense can it be said, "grace reigned" (Rom. 5:20, 21)?

5. In Romans 5:15–19, the relative qualities of the sin of Adam are contrasted with the actions of Christ. List the qualities of each of these: the sin of Adam, the work of Christ.

6. How does Ezekiel 18 (particularly vv. 1–4, 20) relate to this section?

Chapter 4

Romans 6:1—8:39

God's Provision for Practical Righteousness Is By His Spirit

Ushering In the New Era of Grace in Life

Romans 6:1–23

Many people consider chapters 6 through 8 as the climax of the Book of Romans. While there is much to treasure here we must make sure that we understand these chapters in their context.

Here we continue to consider how God's actions in Christ are fully just. So, Paul addresses ideas that may call into question the righteousness of the provision of grace. For in this section the Spirit of God reminds us that it is only through Him

as the empowering presence that true practical righteousness may be attained on this earth. Paul is very practical in these chapters, but he also provides a deep theological base for understanding the plight of humanity—both those who have been justified by faith and those who try to attain righteousness on their own.

Chapters 6 through 8 bring the issues of salvation home to each individual. Here Paul turns to questions that are common among Christians, such as: If grace is truly God's way of dealing with sin, then what are we to do with our tendencies to sin? How do we make righteousness real in everyday life?

What shall we say then? Shall we continue in sin that grace may abound? Certainly not! How shall we who died to sin live any longer in it? Or do you not know that as many of us as were baptized into Christ Jesus were baptized into His death? (6:1–3)

The objection brought up by our imaginary opponent is perfectly reasonable. If where sin abounds, grace abounds even more, then it makes sense that we should increase sin so that grace may increase! Of course, Paul opposes this notion in the strongest possible terms. "Certainly not!" he exclaims.

Here is where human logic fails to grasp the economy of God, for the reign of righteousness is meant to break the stronghold of sin and death. A person's identity is no longer wrapped up in his or her sinful past. We gained a new identity when we embraced Christ by faith. We embraced all that Christ stands for and endured for us. His righteous life becomes ours. His death on account of sin becomes ours. His holy, resurrected life is ours also. Since we have been baptized into all of this, it is absurd that we should even think of going back and living in the old era of sin. Our baptism into Christ is identification with Jesus' death to sin—our sin! Since He dealt with the problem of our sin at the Cross, then we are to no longer associate with that form of living. His death to sin is our death to sin. Our literal baptism in water vividly symbolizes the reality of our identification with Christ's death on the Cross. Why, when sin has already been dealt a lethal blow, would we even entertain going back to its ugly, terrifying reign in our lives? This is absurd.

ACCENT ON APPLICATION
The Declaration of Independence from Sin

Baptism declares identity with Christ, and so our freedom from sin. The New Testament tells nothing of an unbaptized Christian. People believed and were baptized. Baptism highlighted the decision on the part of the believer to part ways with a sinful past. Thus, if newness is not emanating from our lives, perhaps we have forgotten our declaration of independence from sin and our embrace of the power of the Holy Spirit to bring a radical kingdom way of living into being. Sin shall not have dominion over you! It is a promise. Sin may rule as an outlaw in the life of a believer, but it can never reign as king. It has no right.

WORD STUDY
BAPTISM

Baptism—*Increasing numbers of Christians find their focus on the power inherent in the Holy Spirit's presence at baptism. While repentance and faith must precede the moment, and new birth has been experienced, water baptism is seen as a moment (1) at which past bonds to sin may be severed, as Israel's oppressors were defeated—1 Cor. 10:2; (2) when a commitment to separate from the past life of carnal indulgence is made, as circumcision symbolized—Col. 2:11–15; and (3) when the fullness or overflowing of the Holy Spirit's power may be added to enhance the believer's power for witness and ministering (Acts 2:38, 39). This position sees baptism as both a witness and as an encounter. It is symbolic (burial to the past—Rom. 6:3, 4) but it is also releasing and empowering for the future.*[31]

Therefore we were buried with Him through baptism into death, that just as Christ was raised from the dead by the glory of the Father, even so we also should walk in newness of life. (6:4)

Baptism by immersion dramatically symbolizes the work of Christ as it is applied to us. When people enter the waters of baptism, they do so upon declaring their own sinfulness and faith in the Lord Jesus. They proclaim verbally that Christ's work is now applied to them. When people enter the water, their bodily action symbolizes their lives reclining in death. Yet, it is not their own deaths that they embrace, but Christ's death on their behalf. As people are raised up out of the waters of baptism to breathe again they have an altogether different look about them. Their appearance has changed visibly thus corresponding to the change which occurs spiritually when they embraced Christ by faith. Jesus' death is theirs. Jesus' resurrected life is also theirs. That resurrected life, the life that has died to sin just as Christ died to sin once and for all, is the way of the normal Christian life.

For if we have been united together in the likeness of His death, certainly we also shall be in the likeness of His resurrection, knowing this, that our old man was crucified with Him, that the body of sin might be done

---

[31] Jack W. Hayford, *Hayford's Bible Handbook* [computer file], electronic ed., Logos Library System (Nashville: Thomas Nelson) 1997, ©1995.

away with, that we should no longer be slaves of sin. (6:5, 6)

The term *in Christ* is one of Paul's favorite phrases. It means that what Christ has done on our behalf is also our possession. In the above verse, the Spirit of God describes this as being united together with Christ's work. To have the death of Christ on our behalf assures that we have the resurrected life as well. We must be careful here not to simply identify this resurrection with our future bodily resurrection after physical death. That limits the concept far too much.

For Paul, resurrection is complete freedom from sin's deadly tentacles, not only in the life to come but in our current existence as well. Resurrection life is ours now through the work of Christ. This resurrection life guarantees freedom from sin for human beings who have embraced Christ by faith. Yet, as we all know, this is not always realized. Paul will address this shortly. But here the fact of the matter is plainly stated: Freedom from sin's reign is guaranteed through the righteous work of Christ and is applied to the believer. Whether we embrace this is another question.

Our nature has changed profoundly through the work of Christ which we embrace by faith. The body of sin is eradicated. Freedom from sin is a present reality by the work of the Holy Spirit and sin is banished from everyday living for the believer. When Christ went to the Cross, our old man was right there being crucified with Him. There God eradicated the bondage to sin and its chains were obliterated. Slavery to sin is in the past tense for us. The practical issue for each believer is whether we will live in this reality or not. Unfortunately, too many believers know sin as the outlaw king rather than the banished despot.

For he who has died has been freed from sin. (6:7)

This is a simple yet profound statement. Obviously, people in caskets do not respond to sin any longer! Sin has no hold over dead people. The spiritual reality for all believers is that Christ's death is ours. We embrace His stone cold death to sin so that we can be unresponsive to sin's allure. Every believer, in fact, exists in this spiritual reality. This is freedom. The question is, will we live in that freedom?.

Now if we died with Christ, we believe that we shall also live with Him, knowing that Christ, having been raised from the dead, dies no more. Death no longer has dominion over Him. (6:8, 9)

Our future resurrection is also guaranteed in our union with Christ. Christ in His resurrected glory need not consider having to be crucified again. His death is once and for all. His Resurrection is likewise once and for all. Death has no hold over the King; death has no hold over the King's children who embrace Him by faith.

We live with Him in at least two ways. First, we have the assurance of future existence in total and absolute perfection. Presently, we have been empowered by the Holy Spirit to be unresponsive to sin and totally responsive to Christ's resurrected life.

For the death that He died, He died to sin once for all; but the life that He lives, He lives to God. (6:10)

We might say that the Holy Spirit here gives us a christological reality. That is, we are told something about the eternal existence of Jesus Christ, the resurrected One. This carries through to affect our own lives. But as with most statements about God, the point is not to file more knowledge, but to allow the truth to change our lifestyles and activities.

Likewise you also, reckon yourselves to be dead indeed to sin, but alive to God in Christ Jesus our Lord. (6:11)

This is the punch line of verse 10. Our reality is to be like Jesus' resurrected reality. A work is to go on in each of our lives that mirrors the life of Jesus the resurrected One. In this verse, the Holy Spirit gives us one of the few commands in this section of Romans. To do so He uses a term that is reminiscent of the earlier flow of thought. We are to reckon (*logizomai*) ourselves dead to sin.

We have seen this word used before. Paul has explained how God reckons our faith as righteousness and how God judges through a reckoning of works according to law. But now our reckoning relates to every day life because we have already been made righteous by faith. We now are to bring that reality into existence moment by moment. We might think of this as bringing into the physical realm what is true in the spiritual realm. Thus, the first step is to reckon, consider, and fix in our minds that, indeed, God's work of release from slavery to sin is complete. The flip side to this is to reckon ourselves "alive to God in Christ Jesus our Lord." We do not move from slavery to sin to simply do whatever we wish. No, we belong to another. We belong to the one who makes us alive to God. Thus, the lordship of sin is replaced with the lordship of Christ. Once the reckoning is complete, we then can move on to the will and the body.

Therefore do not let sin reign in your mortal body, that you should obey it in its lusts. (6:12)

Since the reign of Christ is secure in our lives by faith, we now move into the area of our will. We have the ability by the Holy Spirit to say, "No" to sin's desire to rule us. We have a long history of sin's deadly reign with all of the havoc it wreaks. Our bodies are still mortal due to the pervasive effects of the fall of humanity. But that does not mean we are doomed to live in continual misery. Sin still wishes to rule in us, however, even though its chains are broken. Its reign as a despotic ruler has been broken, but it still wishes to rule as an outlaw. We feel this in the pull sin still has in our lives. Nonetheless, the power, as the Spirit of God, rests in us, not in sin. So, we have moved from the reckoning of the mind to the decision of the will to not let sin reign. The individual parts of the body are addressed in the next verse.

And do not present your members as instruments of unrighteousness to sin, but present yourselves to God as being alive from the dead, and your members as instruments of righteousness to God. (6:13)

The essence of the phrase *do not present* is better captured with the command *stop presenting*. Stop presenting the members of your body as instruments of unrighteousness. Paul intends that the believers stop something that is heavily ingrained in their very being. But sin's reign is over, so what we do with our physical members is now up to us! No longer will sin carry deadly force so that we inevitably do evil with our bodies. In fact, just as Christ is alive from the dead, we too must carry ourselves in that same power. We have Christ's resurrection power through the Holy Spirit to make a difference in the physical realm through the reign of righteousness in our bodies. So, we take our feet, our hands, our fingers, and every part of our body and present them to God as His instruments for

CROSS REFERENCE
Galatians 5:22, 23

"But if you are led by the Spirit, you are not under the law. But the fruit of the Spirit is love, joy, peace, longsuffering, kindness, goodness, faithfulness gentleness, self control. Against such there is no law."

Law is unnecessary for those led by the Holy Spirit because the Holy Spirit only leads in the direction of righteousness. Each of the items listed in Galatians 5:22, 23 cuts against the grain of sin. The religious person enacts regulations to produce ethical behavior; the person of the Spirit lives by the Holy Spirit and righteousness is assured. Thus, law is irrelevant.

ACCENT ON APPLICATION
The Danger of Legalism

God, in Christ, terminates our relationship with the law. Yet, many people erect religious rules and obligations to control behavior. Thus, rules that have little to do with moral righteousness and nothing to do with Spirit-filled living creep into the church. We must resist the temptation to make rules that create the appearance of a Holy Spirit. Definitions of good and bad behavior are given in Scripture (as in Gal. 5:19–23), but only the Holy Spirit empowers such fruitful behavior. Religious authorities in Jesus' day were fond of rules that they thought defined righteousness. We must trust the Holy Spirit to give guidance through the Word that will strip away all non-biblical regulations.

righteousness' sake. This is immensely practical. Every morning we present our bodies as offerings for righteous duty by the power of the Holy Spirit.

We may easily see the progression of thought in this way:

1. *Reckon* is a movement in the mind of the believer (v. 11).
2. *Don't let sin reign* is an action of the will of the believer (v. 12).
3. *Stop presenting* and *present* are done with the body of the believer (v. 13).

Thus, mind, will, and body are the focus of Paul's concern to bring righteousness into life every day by the Holy Spirit.

For sin shall not have dominion over you, for you are not under law but under grace. (6:14)

We are once again brought face to face with the contrast of the two eras. The era of law brought only death, judgment, condemnation, and wrath to the sinner. But the era of grace is of life, peace, justification, and eternal life. Since the believer is not at all in the era of the law any longer but is now in the era of grace, any domination by sin is totally out of place. The domination (Greek, *kuriusei*, from which we get the word *lord*) of sin is part of an old, bygone era. It no longer pertains to the believer who lives in the era of grace. We live in the good of this truth in every way through the proper reckoning of the mind, the right determination of the will, and the presentation of every part of our bodies. All of this is in the era of grace and not the terror of the law.

This leaves open the concern that, since we are not under law's dominion any longer, then what is to guard us

ACCENT ON APPLICATION
Displacement of the Law

After his conversion Paul said, "To me, to live is Christ" (Phil. 1:21). Before his conversion he might well have said, "To me, to live is law." In his mind he had judged Christ according to the Jewish law, finding Him condemned by it. Since the law pronounced a curse on one who was impaled on a stake (Deut. 21:23; Gal. 3:13), Paul took the side of the law and agreed that both Christ and His people were accursed.

After his conversion, Paul recognized the continuing validity of the Scripture that declared the impaled man to be accursed by God, but now he understood it differently. If Christ, the Son of God, subjected Himself to the curse pronounced by the law, another look at the law was called for. The law could not provide anyone with righteous standing before God, however carefully he kept it. Paul knew that his life under the law stood condemned in the light of his Damascus Road experience. It was not the law in itself that was defective, because it was God's law. It was instead the people with whom the law had to work who were defective.

The righteous standing that the law could not provide was conferred on believers through their faith in Christ. That righteous standing was followed by a righteous life. In one tightly packed sentence Paul declared that God has done what the law, weakened by the flesh, could not do, "sending His own Son in the likeness of sinful flesh, on account of sin: He condemned sin in the flesh, that the righteous requirement of the law might be fulfilled in us who do not walk according to the flesh but according to the Spirit" (Rom. 8:3–4).

The law could lead neither to a righteous standing before God nor to a righteous life. Paul, while faithfully keeping the law, was condemned before God rather than justified. His life was not righteous but was sinful because he "persecuted the church of God" (1 Cor. 15:9). This situation radically changed when Paul believed in Christ and knew himself to "be found in Him, not having my own righteousness, which is from the law, but that which is through faith in Christ, the righteousness which is from God by faith" (Phil. 3:9).

Christ, then, "is the end of the law for righteousness to everyone who believes" (Rom. 10:4). The word "end" is ambiguous: it may mean "goal" or "completion." As the law revealed the character and will of God, it pointed to Christ as the goal. He was the fulfillment of all the divine revelation that had preceded Him: "All the promises of God in Him are Yes" (2 Cor. 1:20). But when the law came to be regarded as the way of salvation or the rule of life, Christ put an end to it. The law pronounced a curse on those who failed to keep it; Christ redeemed His people from that curse by undergoing it Himself. He exhausted the curse in His own person through His death.

According to Paul, the law was a temporary provision introduced by God to bring latent sin into the open. When they broke its individual commands, men and women would realize their utter dependence on divine grace. Centuries before the law was given, God promised Abraham that through him and his offspring all nations would be blessed. This promise was granted in response to Abraham's faith in God. The later giving of the law did not affect the validity of the promise. Instead, the promise was fulfilled in Christ, who replaced the law.

The law had been given to the nation of Israel only, providing a privilege that set it apart from other nations. God's original promise embraced all nations and justified Paul's presentation of the gospel to Gentiles as well as Jews. The promise had wide implications: "Christ has redeemed us from the curse of the law ... that the blessing of Abraham might come upon the Gentiles in Christ Jesus, that we might receive the promise of the Spirit through faith" (Gal. 3:13–14).[32]

from simply sinning because there is no law-given consequence for those under grace. This objection is raised next.

think this way. Just because the believer lives in the era of grace is not an excuse to sin. Sin is never the right option for the righteous.

What then? Shall we sin because we are not under law but under grace? Certainly not! (6:15)

Paul meets this concern with his forceful, categorical denial, "Certainly not!" It is absurd for a believer to

---

Do you not know that to whom you present yourselves slaves to obey, you are that one's slaves whom you obey, whether of sin leading to death, or of obedience leading to righteousness? (6:16)

---

[32] Ronald F. Youngblood, general editor; F. F. Bruce and R. K. Harrison, consulting editors, *Nelson's New Illustrated Bible Dictionary*: An authoritative one-volume reference work on the Bible with full color illustrations [computer file], electronic edition of the revised edition of *Nelson's Illustrated Bible Dictionary*, Logos Library System, (Nashville: Thomas Nelson) 1997, © 1995.

Sin's rightful claim to rule over the sinner is totally negated when that person comes to faith in Christ. This truly breaks sin's reign and leaves the person free to obey. The key here is that freedom from sin's reign provides us the opportunity to voluntarily become slaves to another. As a free person, a believer can certainly choose to obey sin and the lusts of the flesh. That is a possibility. The testimony of the church illustrates this only too well. But God desires something much better for the believer: slavery to righteousness through obedience which is voluntary and empowered by the Holy Spirit. This brings a life of peace and joy.

We live our lives under the lordship of Christ rather than the lordship of sin which results in death. The nature of sin does not change when we become followers of Christ. Sin's deadly nature continues. Thus, while one may choose to live under sin's rule even as a believer, the pervasiveness of death's sting permeates all that is done under that rule. Thus, why would anyone freely choose sin's way? Romans chapter 7 answers these concerns.

But God be thanked that though you were slaves of sin, yet you obeyed from the heart that form of doctrine to which you were delivered. And having been set free from sin, you became slaves of righteousness. (6:17, 18)

We have here one of the few references in 1:18—11:36 to the believers in Rome. It is clear that Paul rejoices in what he knows of these believers. They "obeyed from the heart" the teaching they received. The reference to heart indicates the very center of one's being. Paul does not here refer specifically or only to the emotions as we may think of when the term *heart* is used. The heart for Paul represents the essence of who people are. So Paul commends these believers for receiving the pattern of teaching completely so that their whole way of living is transformed. These Roman believers seem to understand the antithesis presented in verses 17 and 18. The way of the follower of Christ leads from the slavery to sin to the slavery to righteousness.

I speak in human terms because of the weakness of your flesh. For just as you presented your members as slaves of uncleanness, and of lawlessness leading to more lawlessness, so now present your members as slaves of righteousness for holiness. (6:19)

Paul fully recognizes the inadequacy of equating slavery to sin with slavery to righteousness. Slavery itself was a heinous practice with built-in injustices and cruelty. But the analogy is meant to communicate certain elements of truth about the Christian life. The full measure of the blessing of being a slave to righteousness is lost in the analogy.

WORD STUDY
HEART

Heart—*the inner self that thinks, feels, and decides.* In the Bible the word heart has a much broader meaning than it does to the modern mind. The heart is that which is central to a person. Nearly all the references to the heart in the Bible refer to some aspect of human personality.

In the Bible all emotions are experienced by the heart: love and hate (Ps. 105:25; 1 Pet. 1:22); joy and sorrow (Eccl. 2:10; John 16:6); peace and bitterness (Ezek. 27:31; Col. 3:15); courage and fear (Gen. 42:28; Amos 2:16).

The thinking processes of man are said to be carried out by the heart. This intellectual activity corresponds to what would be called mind in English. Thus, the heart may think (Esth. 6:6), understand (Job 38:36), imagine (Jer. 9:14), remember (Deut. 4:9), be wise (Prov. 2:10), and speak to itself (Deut. 7:17). Decision-making is also carried out by the heart. Purpose (Acts 11:23), intention (Heb. 4:12), and will (Eph. 6:6) are all activities of the heart.

Finally, heart often means someone's true character or personality. Purity or evil (Jer. 3:17; Matt. 5:8); sincerity or hardness (Ex. 4:21; Col. 3:22); and maturity or rebelliousness (Ps. 101:2; Jer. 5:23)—all these describe the heart or true character of individuals. God knows the heart of each person (1 Sam. 16:7). Since a person speaks and acts from his heart, he is to guard it well (Prov. 4:23; Matt. 15:18–19). The most important duty of man is to love God with the whole heart (Matt. 22:37). With the heart man believes in Christ and so experiences both love from God and the presence of Christ in his heart (Rom. 5:5; 10:9–10; Eph. 3:17).[33]

Nonetheless, Paul accepts our inability to fully comprehend what slavery to righteousness is all about and takes the analogy as far as he can.

Believers can understand how they presented themselves to uncleanness. They are mindful of their old way of life and how it led to further rebellion against God. Just as the work of sin led to greater lawlessness, so the embrace of righteousness leads to greater holiness. Paul has in mind here not the status of being holy, which is conferred upon the believer by faith, but the process of becoming holy in everyday life. Believers are called to this holiness.

---

[33] Jack W. Hayford, *Hayford's Bible Handbook* [computer file], electronic ed., Logos Library System, (Nashville: Thomas Nelson) 1997, © 1995.

> For when you were slaves of sin, you were free in regard to righteousness. What fruit did you have then in the things of which you are now ashamed? For the end of those things is death. (6:20, 21)

Slavery to sin means no obligation to righteousness. The reverse is true as well. Slavery to righteousness means no obligation to sin.

Slavery to sin bears its appropriate fruit. It is a wonder that anyone would wish to choose the fruit of such slavery. Believers can look back in thankfulness at having been released from the fruit of sin. The list of vices at the end of chapter 1 reminds us of the decadence of a life in slavery to sin. The end of this is death with all its stench and sorrow. Yet sin's allure is due to the continuing link believers have to the flesh.

> But now having been set free from sin, and having become slaves of God, you have your fruit to holiness, and the end, everlasting life. For the wages of sin is death, but the gift of God is eternal life in Christ Jesus our Lord. (6:22, 23)

When saying, "But now," Paul reminds the believers of the new era in which they now live. No longer does death reign in their daily lives. They are now part of the kingdom of God, set free from sin. And the way of the kingdom of God is the continual eradication of daily sin from an individual's life and the life of the community of the people of God. God introduces a totally new way of living that is to be marked by freedom from sin and sin's deathly stench, which affects so much in daily life.

Paul also moves from the concept of slavery to righteousness to that of slavery to God. Being enslaved to the Almighty God can only bring blessing and goodness in total contrast to the believer's former master, sin. The Spirit of God contrasts the fruit of sin's ugly domination (death) with the fruit of God's dominion (holiness). This leads to everlasting life totally free from the stain of sin and the mark of death.

Next Paul revisits the choices that are offered here. Under which era do we wish to live? Shall we live under the era of law where people receive their due wages after a proper reckoning? Or is the era of grace preferable, where God extends His blessed gift of eternal life not on the basis of what is deserved, but by a different reckoning? This reckoning is based upon the faithfulness of Jesus Christ and the justice of God the Father. The work of the Holy Spirit applies this truth to our lives and brings eternal life to those who believe in Christ Jesus our Lord. With this stark contrast, it is a wonder why anyone would choose slavery to sin, death, and judgment over righteousness, life, and peace with God.

QUESTIONS FOR PERSONAL REFLECTION AND GROUP DISCUSSION

Read Romans 6:1–23 and answer the following questions.

1. What is the problem with the following attitude: Since we are forgiven, it does not matter how we live? How would Paul have answered this according to Romans 6:1–4?

2. Why is it important to realize that we not only identify with Christ in His death, but also in His Resurrection? How does this have an effect on our lives? (Rom. 6:5–7)

3. In Romans 6:11–14 Paul gives us a set of five commands. What are they?

4. Each of the above commands relates to a reason that is given in verse 14. What is that reason?

5. In what sense are we slaves and in what sense are we not slaves according to Romans 6:15–18?

6. What were the benefits of slavery to sin and the benefits of slavery to God in Romans 6:19–23?

7. What would you say to a believer who has a certain habitual sin? This believer says, "I can't stop sinning." Base your answer on this chapter.

8. How does Colossians 3:1–5 compare to this section of Romans?

The Limitations of a Law-Oriented Life

Romans 7:1–25

Paul gives further explanation of the role of law and its end for believers in 7:1–6 and then moves to consider the problem of the continuing presence of the flesh. It is a mistaken assumption that law will restrict the flesh. Religious formalism and rigid legalism have no power over the flesh. Indeed, Paul speaks of his struggle with the flesh in the presence of law. This section beautifully sets up the apex of Paul's argument found in chapter 8. But we must first consider the presence of law, its legacy, and impotence.

Or do you not know, brethren (for I speak to those who know the law), that the law has dominion over a man as long as he lives? (7:1)

The Roman believers knew issues of law, for they were in the very center of the Empire where the rule of law was supreme. It is no wonder that Paul would choose the analogy of Roman law to explain God's law. It is possible that he used Old Testament law as his example but the historical context makes Roman law more probable. In either case the point is the same: The law has dominion (Greek, *kurieuei*), is lord over a person as long as he lives. As long as someone is alive, law pertains to that person. Apart from dying, there is no way to get out from under law.

For the woman who has a husband is bound by the law to her husband as long as he lives. But if the husband dies, she is released from the law of her husband. (7:2)

While we may be able to look at this text and make pronouncements

---

CROSS REFERENCE
Galatians 5:1

"Stand fast therefore in the liberty by which Christ has made us free, and do not be entangled again with a yoke of bondage."

Galatians, along with Romans, declares the glorious freedom of the children of God. It is a freedom from law. The death of Christ liberates the believer from the law. Christ has provided all the obedience God justly demands. His absolute obedience is ours by faith. His atoning death is ours by faith. His Resurrection life is ours by faith. So, we live, not according to the letter, but according to the Spirit of God.

about the permanence of marriage, that is not the point of the text. Certainly, marriage is meant to be permanent, broken only when a husband or wife passes away. To leave a spouse in order to commit adultery is clearly wrong. But the Holy Spirit provides an illustration that confirms the decisive change that occurs when there is death. Death provides radical change with reference to the law. According to the law, a woman is bound to her husband while he is alive. But when his death occurs, "she is released from the law of her husband." It is very important to see that she is released from the law of her husband. She is obviously released from her husband, but the law pertaining to this relationship is terminated. It no longer applies to her.

So then if, while her husband lives, she marries another man, she will be called an adulteress; but if her husband dies, she is free from that law, so that she is no adulteress, though she has married another man. (7:3)

It is appropriate, under law, that a woman who leaves her husband and marries another man be called an adulteress. This is perfectly consistent with the law of the husband. No one would object to this legal designation. She is bound to that law. But if the husband dies, she is free from that law. Again, the Scripture is referring to

the woman's terminated relationship with the law. The emphasis is not on the relationship with the husband, but the relationship with the law. The law of the husband is totally passé if the husband dies. She, therefore, is free to marry another man and not be called an adulteress. This illustration indicates that death terminates the relationship with the law. It is important to understand this point.

Therefore, my brethren, you also have become dead to the law through the body of Christ, that you may be married to another—to Him who was raised from the dead, that we should bear fruit to God. (7:4)

Just as the death of the husband ended the law of the husband, so also the death of Christ terminates humanity's relationship with the law. Since believers participate in Christ's death by faith, law orientation is not the believer's way. We no longer relate to God on the basis of law as we did in the old era.

The new era, marked by the Cross of Christ, terminates law orientation as a way of life. We are released from the law in order to belong to Christ Himself. Law-oriented living is part of the old era. The way of the new era is to embrace Christ by faith and follow Him. This new way assures that believers will bear Godly fruit. The death of Christ terminated the law-oriented

FLESH AS PART OF HUMAN EXPERIENCE

Flesh here in Romans 7 is "the earthly part of a person, representing lusts and desires (Eph. 2:3). The flesh is contrary to the Spirit (Gal. 5:17). Those who are in the flesh cannot please God (Rom. 8:8). Galatians 5:19–23 contrasts works of the flesh with the fruit of the Spirit. The flesh is not completely condemned, however, for Christ Himself was described as being 'in the flesh' (1 John 4:2). Christ alone is our salvation, since by the works of the law 'no flesh shall be justified' (Gal. 2:16)."[34]

life; the Resurrection of Christ makes possible a new relationship to God through Christ.

> For when we were in the flesh, the sinful passions which were aroused by the law were at work in our members to bear fruit to death. (7:5)

Paul introduces us to the downside of the law. It arouses the passions that are in a person to further perpetuate sin. This strengthens sin's reign in that person's life.

We must be careful here. As Paul states later, the law itself is good. But the law, which should have led to life through our obedience to it, brought death and a compounding of sin. The problem is not the law, but the flesh, which exists in every person. For the

sinner, life under law guarantees the perpetuation of sin. Sin's guaranteed end is fatal fruit. The stench of death is part of the sinner's law-oriented life. The same bodily members that are meant to be offered for righteousness (6:13) become purveyors of death in a law-oriented life.

> But now we have been delivered from the law, having died to what we were held by, so that we should serve in the newness of the Spirit and not in the oldness of the letter. (7:6)

The word "delivered" (Greek *katargeo*) here is the same as that used in the illustration of the woman who is released from the law of the husband. This is the end of the illustration and its point is made here. The law-

---

[34] Ronald F. Youngblood, general editor; F. F. Bruce and R. K. Harrison, consulting editors, *Nelson's New Illustrated Bible Dictionary: An authoritative one-volume reference work on the Bible with full color illustrations* [computer file], electronic edition of the revised edition of *Nelson's Illustrated Bible Dictionary*, Logos Library System, (Nashville: Thomas Nelson) 1997, © 1995.

oriented life, which brought the perpetuation of sin for the sinner and
bore deadly fruit, is terminated. This
stranglehold that the law had over the
sinner is abolished. Freedom is declared due to the death of Christ. He
has freed us from that which dominated us. But this freedom is now to
be lived out in the newness of the
Spirit and apart from the law. The oldness of the letter, which is another way
of saying "law orientation," cannot be
the way of true life. Life, in the pattern
of the resurrected one is to be lived by
the Holy Spirit. No other way bears
living fruit. Religious traditions and
legality are totally incompatible with a
life lived by the Holy Spirit. Paul will
further explain such a life in chapter 8,
but first he must answer an objection
regarding his view of the law.

What shall we say then? Is the law
sin? Certainly not! On the contrary, I
would not have known sin except
through the law. For I would not
have known covetousness unless the
law had said, "You shall not covet."
(7:7)

One can understand why this
question might be asked. Paul paints a
less than beautiful portrait of the law.
But the ugly part of the portrait is not
the law but the sinner. The law, standing on its own indicating the will of
God, is truly beautiful. But when sinful human beings relate to the law,

something ugly results: death.

The law itself is not sin, but sinful
human beings often use the law to evil
ends. So, Paul points out the beauty of
the law even for the sinner. Knowledge
of sin comes through the law. This is
true of the Mosaic Law, which specifies
the transgression in no uncertain terms,
as well as the law of the heart as testified
by the conscience. In either case, law
brings forth the understanding that
God's righteous law has been breached.
The example given here is covetousness.
The commandment prohibiting covetousness made such a transgression obvious.

But sin, taking opportunity by the
commandment, produced in me all
manner of evil desire. For apart from
the law sin was dead. (7:8)

Here Paul elucidates another facet
of the law. The law of God is intended
to protect and to bring life. But it is
used by sin to raise objections in a sinner's mind. The introduction of the
law, which would bring glorious freedom, is interpreted by humanity as a
terrible restriction of our freedom.
Thus, people bristle at the arrogance
of God in trying to restrict our
so-called freedom to do whatever we
wish. So, people desire the very things
that will be destructive to them. Apart
from the presence of law, sin may lie
dormant. Law provides opportunity
for sin to spring to life.

> I was alive once without the law, but
> when the commandment came, sin
> revived and I died. (7:9)

Again, in a relative sense, apart from law, Paul was alive and free. He could do what he wished without constraints. But he brought forth more sin by using the law, which is right and good. The problem is with the sinner and the sin, not the law. Sin uses law as a tool for further sinfulness bringing more death into the life of the sinner. Paul is using a play on words here. He is alive apart from the law, but when the law came, sin came to life and he died. Death is the sure end for the sinner under law.

> And the commandment, which was
> to bring life, I found to bring death.
> (7:10)

We must continually remember that Paul's experience mirrors that of all humanity, except Christ. God's holy law would have brought life had he obeyed. But like everyone else, he disobeyed and the law delivered death. This was true for Paul even though, as a Pharisee, he was fully devoted to the law. He, of all people, understood the law. Yet it did not restrain sin in him. In fact, it brought death to him and to all who are under law. The only one for whom the law truly brought life was Jesus, the righteous one. He receives honor, glory,

and immortality based upon His perfect obedience to the law.

> For sin, taking occasion by the com-
> mandment, deceived me, and by it
> killed me. (7:11)

Paul continues. The commandment was fertile ground in which sin could grow with awesome destruction. Sin is deceptive; it tries to convince people that God is unfair in the restrictions of the law. This provokes reactions of rebellion against the Holy One. Such rebellion rightly brings death. Paul graphically says that sin killed him.

> Therefore the law is holy, and the
> commandment holy and just and
> good. (7:12)

Paul has shown that the law is not the problem. Its origins are in God Himself. In Him is no evil thing. The law, in its general sense, as well as the commandments, the more specific renderings of the law, is found to be pure. At no time can we blame God for evil. Sin dwells in us and uses even good things for its own evil schemes. But the law of God is absolutely perfect.

> Has then what is good become death
> to me? Certainly not! But sin, that it
> might appear sin, was producing

WORD STUDY
SIN

Mankind originally fell into sin at the temptation of Satan. As the tempter, he continues to lure people into sin (1 Pet. 5:8); nevertheless, people remain fully responsible for what they do. God is not the author of sin, but His plan for world redemption does include His dealing with the reality of sin (2 Sam. 24:1; 1 Chr. 21:1). This truth is dramatically witnessed in the death of Jesus Christ. The crucifixion happened according to God's will; but at the same time, it was the worst crime of human history (Acts 2:23).

Sin is not represented in the Bible as the absence of good, or as an illusion that stems from our human limitations. Sin is portrayed as a real and positive evil. Sin is more than unwise, inexpedient, calamitous behavior that produces sorrow and distress. It is rebellion against God's law—the standard of righteousness (Ps. 119:160).

Since God demands righteousness, sin must be defined in terms of mankind's relation to God. Sin is thus the faithless rebellion of creatures against the just authority of their Creator. For this reason, breaking God's law at any point involves transgression at every point (James 2:10).

Violation of the law of God in thought, word, and deed shows the sinfulness of the human heart. Sin is actually a contradiction to the holiness of God, whose image mankind bears. This depraved condition is called "original sin" because it comes from Adam and characterizes all persons from the moment of their birth.

The moral depravity of mankind is total in that "the carnal mind is enmity against God; for it is not subject to the law of God, nor indeed can be" (Rom. 8:7). Apart from Christ, all are "dead in trespasses and sins" (Eph. 2:1). But this does not mean that people behave as wickedly as they might, for God restrains the outworkings of the sinful heart. At times He even helps sinners to do things that conform to the law (Gen. 20:6). The corruption of sin is not developed or expressed to the same degree in every person. Neither is it expressed in the same way in any person at all times.

Sin involves the denial of the living God from whom human beings draw their life and existence (Acts 17:28); the consequence of this revolt is death and the torment of hell. Death is the ultimate penalty imposed by God for sin (Rom. 6:23).[35]

---

[35] Ronald F. Youngblood, general editor; F. F. Bruce and R. K. Harrison, consulting editors, *Nelson's New Illustrated Bible Dictionary: An authoritative one-volume reference work on the Bible with full color illustrations* [computer file], electronic edition of the revised edition of *Nelson's Illustrated Bible Dictionary*, Logos Library System, (Nashville: Thomas Nelson) 1997, © 1995.

Paul now argues against the conclusion that God's good gift of the law is the problem. Here we see the graciousness of the law, even if it is used by sin for its own ends. For even when the law is used by sin to produce further lawlessness, the law wins by making sin appear utterly sinful. The spotlight makes the transgressions obvious. Even the wrong use of the law by sin is turned to something good. Certainly sin is never good. But when sin is seen to be exceedingly sinful then one role of the law, planned by a holy God, has been fulfilled. While the original intention for the law was to bring life, a secondary intention for the law was to make sin totally visible to the sinner. The law does this admirably.

There has been great controversy and extensive discussion as to whether or not Paul is here speaking as a believer or as a person prior to conversion. The use of the present tense and his reference to himself in the first person leads us to think of this as a description of Paul's experience as a believer. But the rather negative view of the quality of his life and the bondage to sin seem to be too severe for a believer's experience.

The two options are not mutually exclusive. Perhaps Paul is simply speaking of life under law for anyone, believer or unbeliever. This would certainly make sense in the context of the letter. Paul focuses most of his attention in chapter 7 upon the law and not on whether a person is a follower of Christ. The pervasive problem is sin's presence in the individual, which perverts the true intention of the law. It is true that believers have died to the law, but this does not necessarily mean that the law orientation has departed. Indeed, it seems that a law-oriented way of life is a distinct tendency for the believer. Paul wishes to show the powerlessness of such orientation. It cannot bring freedom from sin. It was not intended to do so either for a believer or for one who has not yet believed. With such a view, we simply take the text as an indictment of law orientation rather than using it to discern whether Paul was speaking as a believer or unbeliever.

For we know that the law is spiritual, but I am carnal, sold under sin. (7:14)

Our translation here is lacking a bit in clarity. The law is spiritual (Greek, *pneumatikos*). With the emphasis on spiritual things in the beginning of the twenty-first century, such a designation is fuzzy. Paul uses the term *pneumatikos* to indicate something that is of the Holy Spirit. This distinguishes what Paul is saying from what many in our day say is spiritual. Because the law is of the Holy Spirit, then apart from the working of the Holy Spirit, it cannot be followed. Thus, when Paul asserts his own carnality, that is, that he is of the flesh, he asserts the basic problem. He, as a fleshly person sold under sin, cannot obey the law. Something other than the law will release Paul. This is true for the believer and unbeliever alike.

> For what I am doing, I do not understand. For what I will to do, that I do not practice; but what I hate, that I do. If, then, I do what I will not to do, I agree with the law that it is good. (7:15, 16)

There is a fundamental disconnect between what Paul wishes to do in accordance with law and what he in actuality does. He recognizes the incongruity between his actions and his will and is powerless to do anything about it. He cannot simply enlist his will to obey God's law. He agrees with the law that it is good but this only confirms the justice of the law in the midst of his own powerlessness to obey it. He hates what he does because he knows it is against God's wishes. This confirms that the law gives testimony to what is right and good in God's eyes.

> But now, it is no longer I who do it, but sin that dwells in me. (7:17)

The problem is not the will, or the law, but the sin that is rooted in Paul (and in all people). To focus on the law brings into one's heart a loathing

of disobedient behavior. This is true even when we understand that justification by faith brings us into a right standing before God even when sin has practical root in us.

> For I know that in me (that is, in my flesh) nothing good dwells; for to will is present with me, but how to perform what is good I do not find. (7:18)

The way of the flesh cannot bring forth good fruit for God. Such fruit is in a totally different dimension. No matter how much Paul tries to will obedience to the law, he finds that the power of sin is right there to confound him. By himself, even with a sensitive conscience, he cannot please God in the flesh. He does not know how to perform what is good. This highlights the bankruptcy of the flesh, the power of sin, and the impotence of a law-oriented life.

> For the good that I will to do, I do not do; but the evil I will not to do, that I practice. (7:19)

Here Paul restates his real-life dilemma. With all his heart, he wishes to please God, but he simply cannot do so because of the presence of sin working through his flesh.

ACCENT ON APPLICATION
The Bankruptcy of the Flesh

A believer must not rely on the flesh—even to obey God! Some think that sheer will power will create God-pleasing obedience. Flesh-oriented law keeping marked the Old Covenant. It has no place in the New Covenant. Preachers even admonish believers to pray more, witness more, or read more Scripture in order to please God. These are wonderful activities, but God enables us to do such things by His Spirit. It is no use to do them because someone told us we must do so. Flesh-oriented obedience does not produce the fruit of the Holy Spirit.

Now if I do what I will not to do, it is no longer I who do it, but sin that dwells in me. (7:20)

Paul is not abrogating responsibility here. He is not trying to get himself off the hook. He is simply stating the reality of the power of sin that resides within him. In his own mind, he wishes to do good works but willpower is not enough to bring this about.

I find then a law, that evil is present with me, the one who wills to do good. For I delight in the law of God according to the inward man. But I see another law in my members, warring against the law of my mind, and bringing me into captivity to the law of sin which is in my members. (7:21–23)

The problem is not Paul's desires,

for he wishes to do good. The problem is the law! He delights in God's law, certainly, but his law orientation brings forth other laws that are operative in his life. There is the law of sin that takes advantage of the law of God. There are the desires that overpower his members, the parts of his body, to bring forth all kinds of wickedness. Evil is present with him and no amount of focus on the law can bring forth freedom from such evil. Paul says that even the law of his mind is not strong enough to bring forth the good that he wishes to do. One can conclude that the law is powerless in all its aspects to bring true freedom from sin. Left on its own, the life of the law-oriented person will bring utter despair.

O wretched man that I am! Who will deliver me from this body of death? I thank God–through Jesus Christ our Lord! So then, with the mind I

WORD STUDY
WILL

Will—*wishing, desiring, or choosing especially in reference to the will of God.* In the Gospels, primarily in John, Jesus is said to be acting not according to His own will, but according to the will of the heavenly Father (John 5:30; 6:38). Indeed, doing the will of the Father is Jesus' nourishment (John 4:34), and Jesus does nothing apart from the Father's will (John 5:19). Luke confirms this when he quotes Jesus' statement in the Garden of Gethsemane: "Father, if it is Your will, remove this cup from Me; nevertheless not My will, but Yours, be done" (Luke 22:42).[36]

myself serve the law of God, but with the flesh the law of sin. (7:24, 25)

Law-oriented living brings forth death. It can do nothing else. This is not an indictment against the holy law of God; it is only an admission that sin's power is greater than the law's power to free anyone from sin's grasp. No wonder Paul feels his wretchedness. To him, his existence is a body of death. Only in the actions of God Himself can he find hope.

This verse finds a parallel with the plight of humanity in Romans 3:20. In terms of judgment based on the law, there is no hope for humanity apart from Jesus Christ. Thus, the righteous actions of Christ and His atoning death free the sinner from condemnation.

Also, the actions of God are required to bring practical holiness into everyday life. No amount of will power will bring forth holiness. Rule-keeping and law orientation brings frustration and wretchedness. Only through the resurrected Christ is freedom from sin found in daily living.

By the end of chapter 7 we are left with a dilemma. The person who focuses on the law will be convinced of God's perfect plan for holiness, but that same person is powerless to live out this holiness due to the law of sin that operates through the flesh. The mind and the law are simply not powerful enough to win the battle with the flesh. The ultimate answer is found in chapter 8.

---

[36] Ronald F. Youngblood, general editor; F. F. Bruce and R. K. Harrison, consulting editors, *Nelson's New Illustrated Bible Dictionary:* An authoritative one-volume reference work on the Bible with full color illustrations [computer file], electronic edition of the revised edition of *Nelson's Illustrated Bible Dictionary*, Logos Library System, (Nashville: Thomas Nelson) 1997, © 1995.

QUESTIONS FOR PERSONAL REFLECTION AND GROUP DISCUSSION

Read Romans 7:1–25 and answer the following questions.

1. While Romans 7:1–3 does speak about marriage, its primary purpose is to teach about law. What do we learn about the law from these verses?

2. What is our relationship to the law according to Romans 7:4–6?

3. Is there any good purpose for the law (Rom. 7:7–12)?

4. What kind of a struggle does Paul go through in Romans 7:21–25?

5. How can it be said that the law is a good thing yet it has such a negative effect on us?

6. In what way can we learn from Paul's descriptions of his experience under the law?

7. Why would Paul say that he was a wretched man?

The New Way of Life by God's Spirit

Romans 8:1–39

This chapter is among the most powerful in the entire Bible. This is our declaration of freedom from sin. The victory over sin and death that Jesus accomplished in His death and Resurrection is now made real in the everyday world of believers. Here we find a discussion of the life fixed on the Holy Spirit versus the life fixed on the flesh, a declaration of our connection to the Father, a frank discussion of the present limitations of this world, and finally the total victory of God in every sense. So, Romans 8 ends with one of the Bible's greatest doxologies.

There is therefore now no condemnation to those who are in Christ Jesus, who do not walk according to the flesh, but according to the Spirit. (8:1)

What a great assertion this is! Those who are in Christ Jesus by faith need not worry about the condemnation that comes to those under law. The testimony of chapter 7 is that the law is powerless to liberate people from sin and death. But God liberates sinners through the righteous work of Christ. This fulfills all the demands of the law on our behalf. As a result, no condemnation proceeds to the believer because he or she has the righteousness of Christ. With such righteousness comes exoneration, not condemnation. Believers walk according to the Holy Spirit and not according to the flesh. Their minds are not fixed on the law but on the Spirit that liberates from sin.

For the law of the Spirit of life in Christ Jesus has made me free from the law of sin and death. (8:2)

A new law enters into the picture. The law of the Holy Spirit bursts on the scene with Christ's victory over sin and Satan and obliterates the law of sin and death. The very powers that brought shame and frustration in chapter 7 are now destroyed through the working of the Holy Spirit in the believer's life.

This liberation is twofold: the freedom from condemnation and the freedom from the bondage to sin and its deadly consequences. The way of the Holy Spirit is the way of freedom and righteousness. Law orientation does not bring such righteousness.

For what the law could not do in that it was weak through the flesh, God did by sending His own Son in the likeness of sinful flesh, on account of sin: He condemned sin in the flesh, that the righteous requirement of the law might be fulfilled in us who do

not walk according to the flesh but according to the Spirit. (8:3, 4)

God acted when humanity was totally helpless. Even though the law gave testimony to what God expected, the presence of sin and the flesh so weakened the law that it was powerless to bring life. Of course, as we mentioned before, a perfect obedience to the law justly brought life. Jesus demonstrated this. But since humanity sinned, the law did not have power to cleanse or redeem. But God can cleanse. God can redeem. He does so through the work of Christ, only through the work of Christ.

Jesus turned the tables on sin and the flesh. Instead of sin and flesh bringing condemnation upon all humanity, Jesus brought condemnation to sin and the flesh. He banished both for the sake of the believers. Sin and the flesh have dominion no longer; they are no match for the Holy Spirit's power.

Additionally, practical holiness is a reality for those who live by the Holy Spirit. The righteous requirement of the law is fulfilled, not because people strive to follow God's law, but because they rely on the Holy Spirit. The way of the Spirit is always perfectly in concert with God's wishes. So, a life focused on the Holy Spirit will by nature fulfill God's desires. There is, therefore, no warring between mind and flesh, but a sure, dedicated, methodical movement toward practical holiness. This is the way of true life and is in contrast with the law-oriented way that issues in death. Yet, these two are not even in the same world. Life by the Spirit totally out-performs law orientation. God is at work in the former and a single human being works in the latter.

For those who live according to the flesh set their minds on the things of the flesh, but those who live according to the Spirit, the things of the Spirit. (8:5)

What a fascinating turn of thought we have here. It is in sharp contrast with chapter 7. There, Paul wrote about how he fixed his mind on the law of God. This brought him frustration. Here, Paul addresses the fundamental problem: The mind is not powerful enough in itself to have victory over sin.

One might expect Paul to say that people should "set their minds on the things of the Spirit." Instead, he states that people who *live* according to the Spirit have their minds fixed on what the Spirit desires. Those who live by the flesh fix their minds on the things of the flesh.

A life in the Spirit is pleasing to God and fixes one's mind on the things of the Spirit. This order cannot be reversed. So-called spiritual thoughts do not produce a life in the Spirit. However, a life in the Spirit fixes one's mind on the things of the Spirit.

CROSS REFERENCE
Galatians 5:16

"I say then: Walk in the Spirit, and you shall not fulfill the lust of the flesh." Christ has freed us from sin, so we are no longer in slavery to sin. Christ has freed us to live a life according to the Holy Spirit. When we walk in the Spirit, we are guaranteed holy living. We will not sin if we are walking in the Holy Spirit. This is a promise. God mediates Christ's resurrected power through the presence of the Spirit in our lives. This is why it is so important to commit to live by the Spirit.

The Greek word *peripateo* is here translated to *live*. The same Greek word is also translated as *walk*. A daily walk motivated by the Holy Spirit brings forth transformation.

For to be carnally minded is death, but to be spiritually minded is life and peace. (8:6)

The words *spiritually minded* may be considered an unfortunate translation here. A literal translation might be "the mind of the Spirit." Nevertheless, life and peace flow from a mind fixed on the things of the Holy Spirit. There is no power in the mind apart from the Holy Spirit. But the mind of the Spirit in the believer allows the fruit of righteousness to dwell in the mind allowing frustration and shame to be replaced with life and peace.

Because the carnal mind is enmity against God; for it is not subject to the law of God, nor indeed can be. So then, those who are in the flesh cannot please God. (8:7, 8)

The mind of fallen humanity apart from the renewing of the Holy Spirit is set resolutely against God. Those whose minds are set on the flesh absolutely refuse to subordinate themselves to the law of God. The depth of sin and its orientation toward evil provoke enmity toward God. So much so, that everything is tainted with its twisted viewpoint. Even when unregenerate people do good things there remains a selfish, egotistical element that stains the effort. This does not mean that such good things are insignificant for humanity. They may be very beneficial. But they do not measure up under God's holy spotlight.

In these verses, the Spirit of God dramatically explains the absolute bankruptcy of the mind set on the flesh. Such a mind is totally unable to

WORD STUDY
ENMITY

Enmity—*deep-seated animosity or hatred*. The apostle Paul declared that the human mind in its natural state is in "enmity against God" (Rom. 8:7). This enmity can be changed only through the redemptive power of Christ.[37]

submit to God and, as a result, absolutely cannot please God. To be willing to do good cannot bring about inward change before God.

But you are not in the flesh but in the Spirit, if indeed the Spirit of God dwells in you. Now if anyone does not have the Spirit of Christ, he is not His. (8:9)

God makes the change that He requires of humanity. There is only one way to shift from being in the flesh to being in the Spirit. God is the only one that can bring this to pass. It is a work of God and not an act of willpower. When a believer embraces the Savior by faith, God's renewing work begins. Redemption, reconciliation, and justification are instantaneous works of the Holy Spirit, just as the Spirit's entry into the person is immediate. So, upon conversion the transformation from being in the flesh to being in the

Spirit is accomplished. This is why it is absurd to try again to live in the flesh. It is a denial of the reality of the Holy Spirit's work in a person. When we belong to Christ, the Spirit resides within us. Of course, that does not always mean we walk by the Holy Spirit in everyday living. That is a transformation that still must take place.

And if Christ is in you, the body is dead because of sin, but the Spirit is life because of righteousness. But if the Spirit of Him who raised Jesus from the dead dwells in you, He who raised Christ from the dead will also give life to your mortal bodies through His Spirit who dwells in you. (8:10, 11)

These two verses explain why the body, though destined for death due to sin, can be renewed. As mortal human beings we will not be freed from our fallen bodies until the final

---

[37] Ronald F. Youngblood, general editor; F. F. Bruce and R. K. Harrison, consulting editors, *Nelson's New Illustrated Bible Dictionary: An authoritative one-volume reference work on the Bible with full color illustrations* [computer file], electronic edition of the revised edition of *Nelson's Illustrated Bible Dictionary*, Logos Library System, (Nashville: Thomas Nelson) 1997, © 1995.

resurrection. Death still must occur. But there is still hope for righteousness within our mortal bodies. The indwelling Spirit is life. We have life in our mortal bodies because of the presence of the Holy Spirit. Certainly we are well aware of the deadness that resides in our bodies. But God intends to give life to the body through the Holy Spirit because of righteousness. And so, the expectation for holy living presented in Romans 6 finds fulfillment through the Holy Spirit's work. Indeed, there is no other way of bringing forth life in our mortal bodies. The same power that gave life to the dead body of Jesus is now resident in believers. Thus, the resurrected life of Christ is our assurance of a life that is pleasing to God. Only by the Spirit is this possible. Human will is destitute in this regard.

Therefore, brethren, we are debtors—not to the flesh, to live according to the flesh. (8:12)

Here Paul gives us the negative before the positive. We are truly debtors, but not to the old way of the flesh. We are debtors, he implies, to the Spirit of God. If we find we are living "according to the flesh" (Greek, *kata sarka*), it is evidence that we have submitted ourselves to the old manner where the flesh rules. But as followers of Christ, as brethren, we are to live by the Holy Spirit. The obligation to the flesh was terminated with our conversion.

For if you live according to the flesh you will die; but if by the Spirit you put to death the deeds of the body, you will live. (8:13)

True life is found through the life-giving Holy Spirit but the way of the flesh ends in death. Those who are without the renewing work of the Holy Spirit die without joy, peace, and eternal life. Their only expectation is wrath, distress, and condemnation. Yet, the deeds of the body which are akin to the works of the flesh are terminated through the Spirit who gives life. For we have been translated from the era of law and death to the era of the Spirit who brings life eternal.

For as many as are led by the Spirit of God, these are sons of God. (8:14)

Those who have the Spirit of God are sons of God. While Paul uses the term *children of God* to describe believers in v. 16, the use of the word *sons* here goes further to indicate the privileged standing of a son as the heir of a father. Thus, to be sons of God explains our relationship to the Father. As sons we fully receive of the blessings of heirs with full legal status to act on behalf of the Father. Believers, both men and women, possess such status.

WORD STUDY
ADOPTION

ADOPTION—*the act of taking voluntarily a child of other parents as one's own child; in a theological sense, the act of God's grace by which sinful people are brought into His redeemed family.*

In the New Testament, the Greek word translated adoption literally means, "placing as a son." It is a legal term that expresses the process by which a man brings another person into his family, endowing him with the status and privileges of a biological son or daughter.

In the Old Testament, adoption was never common among the Israelites. In the Old Testament, adoption was done by foreigners or by Jews influenced by foreign customs. Pharaoh's daughter adopted Moses (Ex. 2:10) and another pharaoh adopted Genubath (1 Kin. 11:20). Furthermore, there is no Hebrew word to describe the process of adoption. When the Pharaoh's daughter adopted Moses, the text says, "And he became her son" (Ex. 2:10).

By New Testament times, Roman customs exercised a great deal of influence on Jewish family life. One custom is particularly significant in relation to adoption. Roman law required that the adopter be a male and childless; the one to be adopted had to be an independent adult, able to agree to be adopted. In the eyes of the law, the adopted one became a new creature; he was regarded as being born again into the new family—an illustration of what happens to the believer at conversion.

The apostle Paul used this legal concept of adoption as an analogy to show the believer's relationship to God. Although similar ideas are found throughout the New Testament, the word "adoption," used in a theological sense, is found only in the writings of Paul (Rom. 8:15, 23; 9:4).[38]

For you did not receive the spirit of bondage again to fear, but you received the Spirit of adoption by whom we cry out, "Abba, Father." (8:15)

Paul borrows the concept of slavery here and dramatically contrasts it with adoption into a family. A slave in the first century had no assurance upon purchase that he might live beyond that day. The least

---

[38] Ronald F. Youngblood, general editor; F.F. Bruce and R.K. Harrison, consulting editors, *Nelson's New Illustrated Bible Dictionary*: An authoritative one-volume reference work on the Bible with full color illustrations [computer file], electronic edition of the revised edition of *Nelson's Illustrated Bible Dictionary*, Logos Library System (Nashville: Thomas Nelson) 1997, ©1995.

WORD STUDY
ABBA

ABBA [AB ah] (*father*)—*an Aramaic word that corresponds to our "daddy"* or "papa."
It is found three times in the New Testament: in the Garden of Gethsemane, Jesus prayed, "Abba, Father" (Mark 14:36); the apostle Paul linked the Christian's cry of "Abba, Father" with the "Spirit of adoption" (Rom. 8:15); and, again, Paul writes, "Because you are sons, God has sent forth the Spirit of His son into your hearts, crying out, 'Abba, Father!' " (Gal. 4:6). What a blessed privilege it is to be given the right to call the great Creator, daddy![39]

displeasure could bring the wrath of the slave-owner even to the point of death. The owner had complete authority over the slave and could for any reason, or even for no reason, kill the slave. But God's act of redemption does not bring such fearful slavery. The believer is brought into the family of God and God grants the presence of the Holy Spirit as proof of a new relationship.

Through that same Spirit we cry out, "Abba, Father." This crying out is reminiscent of the Psalms where crying out to God is part and parcel of a close relationship with God. The word "cry out" (Greek, *krazein*) is used at least forty times in the Greek version of the Old Testament. This urgent cry to the Father is sure to be heard. The warmth of the tender term *Abba* dramatically opposes the fear of the slave. Young children to address a loving father would have used this term. Our own access to God through Christ brings the closest of affectionate relationship. The Holy Spirit enables these relationships to not only begin, but to flourish.

The Spirit Himself bears witness with our spirit that we are children of God, and if children, then heirs—heirs of God and joint heirs with Christ, if indeed we suffer with Him, that we may also be glorified together.
(8:16, 17)

---

[39] Ronald F. Youngblood, general editor; F.F. Bruce and R.K. Harrison, consulting editors, *Nelson's New Illustrated Bible Dictionary: An authoritative one-volume reference work on the Bible with full color illustrations* [computer file], electronic edition of the revised edition of *Nelson's Illustrated Bible Dictionary*, Logos Library System (Nashville: Thomas Nelson) 1997, ©1995.

WORD STUDY
SUFFERING

Suffering—*agony, affliction, or distress; intense pain or sorrow.* Suffering has been part of the human experience since man's fall into sin (Genesis 3). The Psalms, one-third of which are laments, include graphic descriptions of suffering, including Psalm 22, a prophecy of Christ's suffering.

The Bible makes it clear that some suffering is the result of the evil impact of sin in the world, resultant from the Fall of man (Gen. 3:16-19). Some suffering is related to persecution and hardship, and a right response can shape and refine the character of the believer (1 Pet. 1:6–7; 5:10). The Book of Hebrews declares that Jesus learned obedience by the things which He suffered (Heb. 5:8) and that His suffering was key to perfecting His full provision for our need (Heb. 2:10).

The experience of suffering can lead to a fresh demonstration of God's power and grace in our lives (2 Cor. 12:7). Those who suffer learn a sensitivity and ability to comfort others who are suffering (2 Cor. 1:3-6).

Suffering often occurs through persecution and tortures people suffer for the sake of Christ and His kingdom (1 Pet. 2:18–22; Phil. 1:29; 2 Thess. 1:5; 2 Tim. 3:12). To do so is to suffer *with* Christ, and to enter into the "fellowship of His sufferings" (Phil. 3:10).

Christ's suffering, endured for the sake of those He redeems, is a promise of available release *from* suffering, with grace and power to go *through* suffering unto deliverance, since "By His stripes we are healed" (see Isaiah's portrayal of the Suffering Servant as both our sin-bearer and sufferer in our place, Is. 53:5).

The believer is not promised exemption from suffering, but we do have God's promise of triumph through trial (Rom. 8:28–37), healing when sick (1 Pet. 2:24; James 5:13–16) and deliverance from evil (2 Pet. 2:9; Matt. 6:13). This confidence is bequeathed to us as a redemptive resource through Christ: "Christ also suffered once for sins, the just for the unjust, that He might bring us to God" (1 Pet. 3:18). He not only has redeemed us from sin, but His redemption affords a resource of victory over or through suffering.[40]

---

[40] Jack W. Hayford, *Hayford's Bible Handbook* [computer file], electronic ed., Logos Library System, (Nashville: Thomas Nelson) 1997, © 1995.

The inner work of the Spirit of God testifies in our own spirits that we belong to God. This is the inner confirmation of the renewing work of God. The various manifestations of the Spirit are further evidence of our sonship. Of course, the children of the Father become His heirs as well. But not just any heirs; rather they are joint heirs with Christ. In this privileged position, what rightfully belongs to Jesus flows to us. This is extraordinary.

In the early part of the letter to the Romans, people are described as enemies of God, expecting wrath and destruction. Our transformation from wrathful enemies to fellow heirs with Christ is miraculous. This comes about purely by the love and grace of God applied by the Holy Spirit.

Being linked with Christ cuts two ways, however. We are certainly heirs, and will receive the glorification that Christ received through the resurrection from death. But we also are to share in His sufferings. One does not occur without the other. As His heirs, we equally receive glorification and suffering.

For I consider that the sufferings of this present time are not worthy to be compared with the glory which shall be revealed in us. (8:18)

We receive both suffering and glorification as Christ's heirs. However, these two are not at all equal in impact or character. The weakness and suffering are not worthy to be compared with the glory. True, we have to live through such sufferings and God meets us in such travail. But the future glorification is so great in scope and quality that comparison of the two is close to ridiculous. The revelation of glory in believers far outweighs any difficulties in this present age.

For the earnest expectation of the creation eagerly waits for the revealing of the sons of God. (8:19)

The created world itself, spoken of by Paul in almost personal terms, awaits the believer's future glorification because creation currently suffers along with the believers. The cosmos has been profoundly affected by sin's entry and rule. But the redemption of creation shall coincide with the final redemption of the believers.

For the creation was subjected to futility, not willingly, but because of Him who subjected it in hope; because the creation itself also will be delivered from the bondage of corruption into the glorious liberty of the children of God. (8:20, 21)

The emptiness and futility that now mark the created order due to sin will, in the future, be removed. This coincides with the release of the children of God from all the effects of sin. For, just as believers struggle with their current suffering, so also does creation suffer. Likewise, believers will find freedom from all of sin's tentacles and creation will also find such freedom.

Paul says the reason for this struggle is "because of Him who subjected it in hope." In other words, creation's suffering, like ours, is a hopeful action. God does not waste suffering. With it, He gives hope and provides grace by the Holy Spirit. But the future holds a sure and certain freedom from decay and the bondage to sin. The creation will share in this.

For we know that the whole creation groans and labors with birth pangs together until now. (8:22)

The created realm is in the midst of deep agony awaiting the dawn of the age to come. So the creation groans. From this Paul moves to our own experience in the midst of suffering.

Not only that, but we also who have the firstfruits of the Spirit, even we ourselves groan within ourselves, eagerly waiting for the adoption, the redemption of our body. (8:23)

Believers share the experience of creation as a whole. We groan within, because the agony of the fallen world touches us. We experience relational, emotional, as well as physical brokenness. And so, we groan, awaiting the end of decay. Even though we have the firstfruits of the Spirit as our guarantee of a blessed future, we still groan in concert with the world as a whole. The adoption spoken about here is the final restoration of the created realm, which includes a resurrected body that will not undergo decay. We embrace this resurrected body when we gain full adoption in the age to come. Today, the firstfruits of the Spirit are our guarantee of future perfection, even that of our bodies.

For we were saved in this hope, but hope that is seen is not hope; for why does one still hope for what he sees? But if we hope for what we do not see, we eagerly wait for it with perseverance. (8:24, 25)

A lie is perpetuated among Christians that causes us to think that if we suffer, the displeasure of God rests upon us. Paul, however, rejects this notion. He says that a believer suffers in hope. And we do not hope in something that may not happen. No, we hope in something sure. The redemption of our body will occur even though we do not yet see its fulfillment. So, we look for its fulfillment with dogged perseverance. Hope is not truly hope if we already have what we hope for.

Likewise the Spirit also helps in our weaknesses. For we do not know what we should pray for as we ought, but the Spirit Himself makes intercession for us with groanings which cannot be uttered. (8:26)

WORD STUDY
PREDESTINATION

Predestination—the biblical teaching that declares the sovereignty of God over all things in such a way that the freedom of the human will is also preserved.

Two views of predestination are prominent among church groups today. One view, known as Calvinism, holds that God offers irresistible grace to those whom He elects to save. The other view, known as Arminianism, insists that God's grace is the source of redemption but that man through his free choice can resist it. In Calvinism, God chooses the believer; in Arminianism, the believer chooses God.

Although the term predestination is not used in the Bible, the apostle Paul alludes to it in Ephesians 1:11: "We have obtained an inheritance, being predestined according to the purpose of Him who works all things according to the counsel of His will."

All Christians agree that creation is moving within the purpose of God. This purpose is to bring the world into complete conformity to His will (Rom. 8:28). From the very beginning of time, God predestined to save humankind by sending His Son to accomplish salvation. Thus, God "desires all men to be saved and to come to the knowledge of the truth" (1 Tim. 2:4).

The doctrine of predestination does not mean that God is unjust, deciding that some people will be saved and that others will be lost. Mankind, because of Adam's Fall in the Garden of Eden, sinned by free choice. Thus, no person deserves salvation. But God's grace is universal. His salvation is for "everyone who believes" (Rom. 1:16).

Paul also declared that he was a debtor under obligation to take the message of the gospel to other people (Rom. 1:14) so they might hear and obey.

Predestination is a profound and mysterious biblical teaching. It focuses our thinking on man's freedom and responsibility as well as God's sovereignty.[41]

---

[41] Jack W. Hayford, *Hayford's Bible Handbook* [computer file], electronic ed., Logos Library System (Nashville: Thomas Nelson) 1997, ©1995.

WORD STUDY
FOREKNOWLEDGE

Foreknowledge—*a fact of God's omniscience, which enables Him to know all events including the free acts of man before they happen.*
In Romans 8:29 and 11:2, the apostle Paul's use of the word foreknew means "to choose" or "to set special affection on," but is clearly shown not as a preemptive knowledge which judges in advance against some and for others. His predestination and salvation is pursuant upon His foresight of human action—not the cause but the effect of His electing love in Christ (Rom. 8:29–33). This same idea is used to express the nation of Israel's special relationship to God (Acts 2:23; Rom. 11:2; 1 Pet. 1:2, 20).[42]

Difficulties can cloud the mind. In deep travail it is difficult even to pray. In such extreme circumstances, the Holy Spirit, who is given as our guarantee of future glory, undertakes to pray for us. What a gift to know that God the Holy Spirit prays when we are too weak to do so. It is possible that the groaning of the Spirit becomes audible through speaking in tongues, although one cannot be sure about this point. The encouragement is not that we speak in tongues, but that God's own intercession is made for believers. Thus, the groaning prayers of the Spirit on our behalf join the groaning of creation and believers.

_____

Now He who searches the hearts knows what the mind of the Spirit is, because He makes intercession for the saints according to the will of God. (8:27)

God searches hearts. Through the Holy Spirit, God ministers to believers through perfectly focused intercession. The interceding work of the Holy Spirit is always in line with God's will. Even in our weakness (perhaps especially in weakness), God performs the work that is most needed by the believer. Since God always knows what we need, His intercession will effectively give us what we need. What assurance this is for us in our weakness.

_____

And we know that all things work together for good to those who love God, to those who are the called according to His purpose. (8:28)

[42] Jack W. Hayford, *Hayford's Bible Handbook* [computer file], electronic ed., Logos Library System (Nashville: Thomas Nelson) 1997, ©1995.

This verse has been an anchor for many people. It has also been seriously misunderstood throughout history. This is not a blatant announcement that everything that happens is God's desire. Evil still happens. But for those who have been reconciled to God, who love Him, true good will result from suffering. God is interceding by the Holy Spirit for those in weakness. No extreme experience is without consequent blessing from God because He brings gold out of the furnace of difficulty.

These sufferings work together for good. Isolated events may seem to be counterproductive to godly living; even contrary to God's ultimate plan. But put together by the loving hand of God, events work for God's design to bring blessings to believers. We may not know what is going on in our lives. But through this verse, God has given us His assurance that His ultimate plan for our lives will be worked out. Nothing escapes the eyes of God because His Spirit is within us. Therefore, He knows us intimately and knows what we need in the long run.

> For whom He foreknew, He also predestined to be conformed to the image of His Son, that He might be the firstborn among many brethren. Moreover whom He predestined, these He also called; whom He called, these He also justified; and whom He justified, these He also glorified. (8:29, 30)

These two verses provide the rationale for believing that God indeed works all things for the good of those who love Him. This is first seen in the verb tenses. Every verb is in the past tense. In other words, all these actions have already been accomplished: God foreknew us, predestined us to be like Jesus, called us to Himself, justified us, and glorified us. Note that glorification has been completed for the believer. This indicates that since all the other actions are past events, our glorification is certain. God's love is seen clearly through His wonderful action on behalf of the sinner who now is a follower of Christ. When God promises, He will bring it about. So, our glorification is sure and certain even though we see suffering, weakness, and difficulties.

> What then shall we say to these things? If God is for us, who can be against us? (8:31)

God's gracious work on behalf of believers totally overwhelms even the most extreme difficulties. God's love for humanity seen in the atoning, justifying work of Christ and indwelling presence and enabling of the Holy Spirit is proof that God's favor rests upon us. His certain and sure plan for the future allows peace to flow for us who look to His appearing and our full redemption and adoption.

The Ministry of the Holy Spirit in Life in Romans 8

Our triumph is gained and sustained:

1. By having the curse of condemnation broken from the soul, once and for all. Romans 8:1 asserts that there is a law of life in Christ Jesus. So, there is no longer in God's presence a record assigning sin to those who have received Him as Savior (3:24–26). Therefore, peace of heart and mind may be constantly experienced (5:1–11).

2. By allowing the Holy Spirit to fill, lead, and lift us above the desire of our flesh to master our body and soul and sustain patterns of sin in our lives (8:5–17). Walking in the fullness of the Spirit releases the power of Jesus' Resurrection life in us—power that will break the death-dealing force of sin and unworthy habits (8:11; 6:1–14).

3. By remembering that God has never promised trouble-free living, yet that He has guaranteed the certainty of our triumph through and beyond every trial (8:18–22). Remember to confront every stressful circumstance with Holy Spirit-begotten hope (8:23–25), and to enter into Holy Spirit-assisted intercession (8:26, 27). Do this in the confidence that these means will secure God's purpose for your life (8:28).

4. By rejoicing in the absolute commitment God has made to us to ensure our victory with Him through grace (8:29–32), and by answering any circumstance or lie of our Adversary (8:33, 34) with this grand, biblical hymn about certainty of conquering: Romans 8:35–39![43]

He who did not spare His own Son, but delivered Him up for us all, how shall He not with Him also freely give us all things? (8:32)

God did the hard work by sending His own Son. It is perfectly logical that we will receive all other things that are to our benefit; these all pale in comparison to the glorious gift of the Son of God. When Paul here says "all things" he is referring to those things which only enhance our lives, whether for now or for eternity.

Who shall bring a charge against God's elect? It is God who justifies.

[43] Jack W. Hayford, *Hayford's Bible Handbook* [computer file], electronic ed., Logos Library System (Nashville: Thomas Nelson) 1997, ©1995.

Who is he who condemns? It is Christ who died, and furthermore is also risen, who is even at the right hand of God, who also makes intercession for us. (8:33, 34)

The questions continue, but not in combative form, as they were earlier in the letter. These indicate praise for God's indescribable goodness toward humanity. So, the charge comes which seeks to condemn the believers in Christ, the elect of God, and no foundation is found that upholds the argument. For God Himself justifies the ungodly. Any charge regarding sin has already been punished at the Cross. The One who is the just One and the Justifier of the ungodly now sits at the right hand of God the Father. He has been given His rightful place as the Judge who can pronounce condemnation. But He acts with intercession for His elect, not in condemnation. So, God has already judged sin and brought

condemnation at the Cross. No foundation for any charges will be entertained against those who have the righteousness of Christ.

Who shall separate us from the love of Christ? Shall tribulation, or distress, or persecution, or famine, or nakedness, or peril, or sword? As it is written:

"For Your sake we are killed all day long; We are accounted as sheep for the slaughter." (8:35, 36)

Since we have already received blessing from God in the most extraordinary way, through the death and Resurrection of His Son, we are assured that His love shall continue no matter what. God adopted us, therefore, we need not fear anything. Tribulation and distress are not evidence of God's abandonment. No, in fact we should expect these things as part of the future of the people

ACCENT ON APPLICATION
The Defense of the Believer

Satan and the world of darkness accuse believers of not belonging to Christ through planting thoughts within their minds. People then doubt whether they have truly been redeemed. Satan loves to convince guilty sinners of their innocence and he loves to convince justified sinners of their guilt. People often wonder why they have the thought that they are far from God, even though they have believed in the Lord. This is nothing less than an assault upon the child of God by the realm of darkness. When such evil accusations are brought against a believer, he or she must banish them. They do not have a right to be raised.

of God on this earth. As Jesus Himself said, "In the world you will have tribulation; but be of good cheer, I have overcome the world" (John 16:33).

Yet in all these things we are more than conquerors through Him who loved us. (8:37)

Such conquering depends not on the circumstances we find on earth, but upon the love of God. When His love is poured into our lives, the victorious life results. Life, even in extreme difficulty, cannot limit the conquering love of God, which is in Christ Jesus.

For I am persuaded that neither death nor life, nor angels nor principalities nor powers, nor things present nor things to come, nor height nor depth, nor any other created thing, shall be able to separate us from the love of God which is in Christ Jesus our Lord. (8:38, 39)

What can you say about this? Everything is covered. The only thing left to do is to worship the great Redeemer and King!

With these verses Paul has provided a fitting climax to the first part of his letter to the Romans. We have moved from being justly condemned as sinners to being adopted into God's family. All the benefits of sin are replaced with the benefits of being joint-heirs with Christ. But there still are issues to address.

God has provided a way for sinners, but this may be misunderstood in regards to the privileged position of Israel. So, Paul must explain how God deals with Israel in order to uphold the absolute justice of God.

QUESTIONS FOR PERSONAL REFLECTION AND GROUP DISCUSSION

Read Romans 8:1–39 and answer the following questions.

1. Why is there no condemnation for those who are in Christ Jesus, according to Romans 8:1, 2?

2. In Romans 8:5–8, Paul characterizes the differences between a life according to the flesh and a life according to the Spirit. What are the characteristics of each?

3. What is the inward hope of the believer and what role does the Holy Spirit have in that hope (Rom. 8:23, 25)? What other responsibilities does the Holy Spirit have? (See Rom. 8:26, 27.)

4. What is the believer's assurance according to Romans 8:28? How should this affect our lives?

5. How should we respond to these truths in relation to God and to the outside world (Rom. 8:31–35)?

6. How does this section complement the teaching of Romans 7?

7. The importance of remaining in a life led by the Holy Spirit is echoed in Jesus' teaching found in John 15. Review John 15:1–8 and list the benefits of abiding in Christ.

8. How is it possible for the believer to persevere during his or her times of groaning to travail as verse 23 indicates? How does a future hope help us?

9. Some people have the attitude that all things will work out for the best. Is this true? Explain.

10. Paul describes some of his life's experiences in 2 Corinthians 11:24–28. What were some of these experiences and how did Paul view them? How was it possible for Paul to maintain a proper attitude within these trials?

Chapter 5

Romans 9—11

GOD IS RIGHTEOUS IN DEALING
WITH ISRAEL

*God's Justice and Mercy Are Seen in
God's Election*

Romans 9:1–33

Paul's concern for his own people and his desire to uphold the justice of God come together in chapters 9 through 11. In these chapters, Paul exhibits deep emotion and makes a focused argument about God's continuing righteousness and faithfulness regarding Israel. God has in no way failed Israel, but His great work in providing for sinners, Gentile and Jewish, has sidestepped the nation of Israel.

Some commentators regard this section as a parenthesis, not knowing how it fits the overall scheme of the letter. But this section is the crowning glory of the apostle's argument. In it, God shows His great handiwork in the midst of what appears to be utter failure. Nothing, not even the willful sinfulness and rebellion of the nation of Israel, will stop God from being merciful according to His own gracious promise. This brings Paul to a finale of unrestrained joyful exuberance.

As we have seen, each of Paul's arguments is part of a whole. Each step leads somewhere. In these chapters, Paul highlights the justice and mercy of the Almighty. This silences any charge of injustice in dealing with Israel and preserves the beauty of the provision of grace toward the Gentiles.

I tell the truth in Christ, I am not lying, my conscience also bearing me witness in the Holy Spirit, that I have great sorrow and continual grief in my heart. For I could wish that I myself were accursed from Christ for my brethren, my countrymen according to the flesh, who are Israelites, to whom pertain the adoption, the glory, the covenants, the giving of the law, the service of God, and the promises; of whom are the fathers and from whom, according to the flesh, Christ came, who is over all, the eternally blessed God. Amen. (9:1–5)

There is no question about Paul's concern for his brethren, the Jews. If it were up to him, he would sacrifice himself for their sake. Yet, we may ask why he would even say such a thing at this point. To answer this, let us gather the facts of the preceding eight chapters.

Paul has established that the Gentiles have not only abandoned God through their rejection of the knowledge of God, but they live in such a way that they should be condemned eternally (1:18–32). As the epistle progresses, we see that the Jews have not shown any less guilt. Both Jew and Gentile have shown outright disregard for what they know to be true about God. Both have exercised behavior that brings the condemnation of God. There is no difference here. Each deserves nothing less than wrath, condemnation, and death.

But if the Jews will not be justified by the possession of the law or the covenant, then certainly no one can be justified in God's eyes! Of course, this is true. Human effort or religiosity cannot claim justification before God. So, God justifies the wicked in a way entirely unexpected by the religious person. This is done in a way that is predicted by the Scriptures. The focus of justification is twofold: the faithfulness of God through the work of His Son, Jesus Christ, and upon the faith of the person who believes the gospel. This revolutionary thinking may imply that God's promised faithfulness to Israel has been set aside. But God does not forget His promises.

Paul had seen many Gentiles respond to this extraordinary and glorious message. Yet, the Jews did not embrace the gospel's message with the same joy. In fact, they largely rejected the message. Though the picture seems bleak, Paul sets the record straight about God's plans for Israel.

I tell the truth in Christ, I am not lying, my conscience also bearing me witness in the Holy Spirit, that I have great sorrow and continual grief in my heart. (9:1, 2)

Paul does not give in to wishful thinking when considering his countrymen. Most of them have rejected his message. Emotional appeals or positive thinking cannot change this. The truth in Christ and the inner testimony of his conscience bring anguish to his heart. He cannot deny the truth. Guilt, whether Gentile or Jewish, is still guilt. Nothing can change this. So, the Jews sit in the status of the guilty. They are not innocent and they are not redeemed, since they have not yielded to Christ by faith. This stirs the apostle's soul to deep concern. Even though he is the apostle to the Gentiles, Paul is Jewish and cares deeply for those among his people who have not responded to the message of justification through Christ.

For I could wish that I myself were accursed from Christ for my

brethren, my countrymen according to the flesh, (9:3)

Paul wishes that he were accursed. The Greek word that is translated *wish* is usually used in Paul's epistles for the word *pray*. Paul may be saying that he has prayed that he could exchange places with his brethren. This is like Moses' prayer on behalf of Israel in Exodus 32:31. There he asks God to destroy him rather than inflict wrath upon the Israelites. The story in Exodus is parallel to Paul's story of the Jew's rejection of the grace of God in Christ.

In Exodus, God brought Israel out of bondage in Egypt. Then, when Moses went up the mountain to receive the tablets of the law, the people rebelled and worshiped a golden calf. Such idolatry in the wake of grace kindled the wrath of God. Although God heard the prayer of Moses, He did not bring a curse on him instead of judging Israel. Thereafter, God continued

WORD STUDY
ACCURSED

Accursed (Gk., *anathema*)—*an animal to be slain as a sacrifice, devoted to destruction.* Because of its association with sin, the word had an evil connotation and was synonymous with a curse. In the sacrificial scheme, *anathema* meant alienated from God without hope of being redeemed.[44] Thus, in Romans 9:3 Paul presents the extent to which he would go to help out his countrymen.

---

[44] Jack W. Hayford, *Hayford's Bible Handbook* [computer file], electronic ed., Logos Library System, (Nashville: Thomas Nelson) 1997, © 1995.

JESUS CHRIST AS GOD

Jesus is called God in the New Testament. Thomas, convinced that the risen Christ stood before him, abandoned his doubts with the confession, "My Lord and my God!" (John 20:28).

But the classic text is John 1:1. John declared that the Word existed not only "in the beginning," where He was "with God," but also actually "was God." This is the Word that became incarnate as real man in Jesus Christ, without ceasing to be what He had been from eternity.

The Bible thus presents Christ as altogether God and altogether man—the perfect mediator between God and mankind because He partakes fully of the nature of both.[45]

to extend abundant grace toward Israel despite their abandonment of Him. Like Moses, Paul wishes to sacrifice himself for the people of Israel. But God has grander plans for them.

The apostle calls the Israelites his countrymen according to the flesh. This does not mean they are fleshly in a sinful sense. He is only indicating his link with them in his humanity. Both Paul and his brethren come from the Jewish heritage. He knows and understands their place, their heritage, their history, and their culture.

***

who are Israelites, to whom pertain the adoption, the glory, the covenants, the giving of the law, the service of God, and the

promises; of whom are the fathers and from whom, according to the flesh, Christ came, who is over all, the eternally blessed God. Amen. (9:4, 5)

Look at all that Paul has in common with the great nation of Israel: The adoption—God had chosen them to be His adopted children. The glory—God walked before the people of Israel in a pillar of fire by night and a great cloud by day. The covenants—To whom else did God give His great covenants? After Genesis 12, the covenants came for the Jews!

It is through the Jewish nation that such communication of the gracious hand of God comes to the world. The covenants refer to the covenants to

***

[45] Jack W. Hayford, *Hayford's Bible Handbook* [computer file], electronic ed., Logos Library System, (Nashville: Thomas Nelson) 1997, © 1995.

Abraham, Isaac, Jacob, and David. New Covenant is first mentioned in Jeremiah 31. It is through the nation of Israel that these came to the world. In the Old Testament, one would need to come under the blessing of the Jewish nation through the Covenant God Yahweh. Only through Him is there relief for sin. Only through the benefits of knowing this great God is there found hope.

The Jews also had the law—the people of God received the law of God, which gave explicit instructions to the people on how to live their lives in such a way that was pleasing to Him. The law gave a new knowledge of God that did not exist prior to that in any specific way. This caused great pride in Israel as we have seen in Romans 2 and 3.

They also had the service of God— this is a reference to the true worship of God. Paul refers to the daily ritual of the sacrificial system in the temple and tabernacle. The correct way of approaching the most holy God is proscribed. What a joy it is to know how to come near to God to have your sins forgiven. And this service of worship (which Paul picks up in Rom. 12:1, 2) is to be given great prominence.

The promises were given to Israel—God gave promises to Israel that could be relied upon. Paul certainly may have had in mind the promises given to Abraham in Genesis 12, 13, 17, and 22. But God's promises to Israel extend way beyond even these, though

these are great promises. There are promises of God's continual presence and blessing, promises of redemption, promises regarding the Messiah. These belong to Israel. No pagan nation can claim these.

Theirs is the fathers—even the patriarchs are of Israel. It is no wonder that Paul has such high regard for his own heritage and the history of his people. God's choice of Israel is not diminished in the least with the message of the gospel of Christ. Indeed, we are left with the final item on the list!

Christ—it is through Israel herself that the Messiah, the promised King, is given. According to the flesh, that is, in His humanity, Jesus the King is Jewish! That is no small claim. Paul knows full well that his own Lord and Savior is out of Israel. So, to have his own brethren reject the Lord of heaven and earth, who is of their own human stock, yields great sorrow in Paul's heart. Israel should have received the Savior. Instead they rejected Him.

———————

Christ came, who is over all, the eternally blessed God. Amen.

Here are two aspects of the person of Christ. First, He is over all. This is usually a designation of God. Second, He is the eternally blessed God.

Paul commonly expresses praise for God's wonderful works and pure character. These expressions are called doxologies. But this one is special among the doxologies because its focus is on Jesus, not the Father. One cannot have Christ as Savior and Lord without accepting Him as God. This one verse puts to rest any speculation that Jesus is anything less than God Himself.

Controversy attends the following verses. In them, one must discern whether God is referring to individual election and salvation or to nations through whom God works. We believe that Paul is addressing the nation of Israel and expressing his regret that the nation has rejected the Messiah. One cannot underestimate the ramifications of this understanding. If Paul is addressing individuals, then all references to election, predestination, and salvation must be applied to individuals. However, if Paul is writing about God's outworking of His redemptive plan through a specific nation, which He elects and predestinates, then an individual's choices are made in the context of God's redemptive work among the nations. God's choice of a redemptive nation does not nullify an individual's freedom to respond to grace.

It is not our intention here to undergo a thorough study of the subject of the election of the individual vs. the election of a nation. However, we must understand what the text is saying regarding these issues.

But it is not that the word of God has

ACCENT ON APPLICATION

Paul presents a wonderful example of the difference between trying to achieve the work of God by human effort over against the working of God Himself in the person of Abraham. Abraham had a son through human effort through Hagar. Even though God had promised offspring through Sarah, Abraham thought he must act on God's behalf since it seemed Sarah was too old to become pregnant and fathered a son through the maid Hagar (Genesis 16—17). But God was clear that the promise was to come through another son who will be born through miraculous working. So Isaac is born and the promised son will inherit the blessings given to Abraham and through whom the covenant will extend. The nation begins through this promised child. The working of God through His leading and promises surpasses the effects of any purely human effort. This, of course, requires the leading of the Holy Spirit to discern what actions are to be taken and when. But God has promised to lead and guide and we have the presence of the Holy Spirit in us if we believe in Jesus.

taken no effect. For they are not all Israel who are of Israel, nor are they all children because they are the seed of Abraham; but, "In Isaac your seed shall be called." That is, those who are the children of the flesh, these are not the children of God; but the children of the promise are counted as the seed. For this is the word of promise: "At this time I will come and Sarah shall have a son." And not only this, but when Rebecca also had conceived by one man, even by our father Isaac (for the children not yet being born, nor having done any good or evil, that the purpose of God according to election might stand, not of works but of Him who calls), it was said to her, "The older shall serve the younger." As it is written, "Jacob I have loved, but Esau I have hated." (9:6–13)

When God speaks, the world responds. Genesis chapters 1 and 2 provide abundant evidence of this. The Word of God, in Jesus, is further evidence, for nature itself is at the bidding of Christ who is called the Creator in John 1:1–3. Jesus proved His supremacy over nature in stilling the storm, multiplying the loaves, and healing the sick. These were accomplished by His Word. So, to imply that God's Word has no impact is ludicrous.

It appears on the surface that the failure of the Israelites to embrace Jesus as the Messiah is God's failure. But Paul provides evidence of the efficacy of God's Word through the channel of redemption. In Paul's day, only small numbers of Jews embraced the King of kings. Is this God's failure? Absolutely not! Here Paul traces the movement of God's redemptive work, which shows the fulfillment, not the failure, of God's working in the world. God has selected a line of redemption based on individuals and their faith, not always along the lines of nations.

---

nor are they all children because they are the seed of Abraham; but, "In Isaac your seed shall be called." (9:6b, 7)

Paul describes people who, though descendants of Israel, are not among the people who embrace the promise of God. So, while some within national Israel have rejected Messiah, others embrace Him. This should not be surprising; Israel's history has worked like this all along: Ishmael did not produce the nation of promise (the seed). The promised people of God have come through Isaac, not Ishmael.

That is, those who are the children of the flesh, these are not the children of God; but the children of the promise are counted as the seed. For this is the word of promise: "At this time I will come and Sarah shall have a son." (9:8, 9)

WORD STUDY
ELECTION

The word translated "election" in Romans 9:11 delineates God's powerful and gracious act of selecting a people through whom He will work out His redemptive purposes in the world. It is very important to understand that God is calling out a *people* for Himself here and that this is not referring to God calling individuals into a relationship with Himself. Much misunderstanding has been brought into the Christian church without such an understanding. God does not refer here to choosing individuals for salvation and leaving others to damnation. He does not wish that "any should perish but that all should come to repentance" (2 Pet. 3:9). He has provided the way through Christ and through a people given the joy and responsibility of reaching the world for God. Jacob represents the nation through whom God will work in the Old Covenant. His people today are the church, encompassing both believing Jews and believing Gentiles.

The key word in these two verses is *promise*. God's promise, His Word, will be fulfilled to the benefit of all humanity. Fleshly descent does not determine the path of blessing from God. Those who embrace God's promises by faith establish the place of God's work in the world. So, the children of promise take prominence in God's economy.

When God promised a son through Sarah, it was accomplished! Abraham believed God for this promise and was considered righteous as a result. God's promises make the difference in this world. Fleshly descent or religious tradition are irrelevant in terms of God's plan of salvation for humanity. Belief in the promised Messiah is paramount.

And not only this, but when Rebecca also had conceived by one man, even by our father Isaac (for the children not yet being born, nor having done any good or evil, that the purpose of God according to election might stand, not of works but of Him who calls), it was said to her, "The older shall serve the younger." As it is written, "Jacob I have loved, but Esau I have hated." (9:10–13)

One may conclude from the story of Abraham's experience and dealings with Isaac and Ishmael that God's choice was made according to human factors. That is, something in Ishmael was rejected. Therefore, an alternate path had to be found. But Paul subdues such speculation with another story of God's election.

The story of Rebecca in Genesis 25:21-24 shows that no human element could possibly influence God's choice of a path of redemption. For, contrary to custom, God chose the younger of Rebecca's twins over the older. God showed Rebecca that two nations were in her womb. In other words, the biblical text in Romans and in Genesis carefully highlights that individual election is not the issue. The choice of nations is clearly delineated by the Old Testament text; national election is at stake. If an individual in any nation will be saved from wrath is determined by that person's embrace or rejection of God's merciful and just plan of salvation.

God's call and His promises are preeminent. It is not whether one works but whether one responds to the call of God (9:11). Personal embrace of the Savior depends upon God's plan of election of a people through whom the message of mercy comes. At the time of Paul's writing, this channel of salvation was the Gentiles—a scandalous choice. But the choice of the younger brother Jacob was also scandalous as was the choice of Isaac over Ishmael who was the firstborn son of Abraham. It was scandalous but not unjust. God calling takes precedence over human convention and culture.

Some may object to the apparent harshness of God's decree regarding Esau. God hated Esau and loved Jacob in the context of His divine rejection and selection. His preference was made in order to gain an elect people through whom He could work. The rejection of Esau is related to the divine choice of a nation through whom the blessings of God could flow. However, the individual's choice to follow God remains.

Remember, at the time of the writing of Romans much of national Israel had rejected Christ and so was not among the people of promise. In other words, they were in the same place as the descendants of Esau! This idea would be tough for any Jew to accept. But the evidence of Jewish unbelief can lead to no other conclusion.

What shall we say then? Is there unrighteousness with God? Certainly not! For He says to Moses, "I will have mercy on whomever I will have mercy, and I will have compassion on whomever I will have compassion." So then it is not of him who wills, nor of him who runs, but of God who shows mercy. For the Scripture says to Pharaoh, "For this very purpose I have raised you up, that I may show My power in you, and that My name may be declared in all the earth." Therefore He has mercy on whom He wills, and whom He wills He hardens. (9:14–18)

Here we are introduced to the theme of God's mercy. This is the connecting theme for these three chapters (Rom. 9—11). Though many see God's harsh choice, Paul is presenting God's gracious mercy extended through an elect people to bring forth His presence on earth. So, far from pointing to a capricious choice of God, the Holy Spirit intends that we see God's grace.

What shall we say then? Is there unrighteousness with God? Certainly not! For He says to Moses, "I will have mercy on whomever I will have mercy, and I will have compassion on whomever I will have compassion." (9:14, 15)

As we have noted before, Paul's argument revolves around certain questions. In this case, the question is, "Is God unjust?" Paul vigorously denies such a proposition. God's election was made to provide us with mercy, not mete out justice. If justice were the

WORD STUDY
MERCY

Mercy—the aspect of God's love that causes Him to help the miserable, just as grace is the aspect of His love that moves Him to forgive the guilty. Those who are miserable may be so either because of breaking God's law or because of circumstances beyond their control.

God shows compassion toward those who have broken His law (Dan. 9:9; 1 Tim. 1:13, 16), although such mercy is selective, demonstrating that it is not deserved (Rom. 9:14–18). God's mercy on the miserable extends beyond punishment that is withheld (Eph. 2:4–6). Withheld punishment keeps us from hell, but it does not get us into heaven. God's mercy is greater than this.

God also shows mercy by actively helping those who are miserable due to circumstances beyond their control. We see this aspect of mercy especially in the life of our Lord Jesus. He healed blind men (Matt. 9:27–31; 20:29–34) and lepers (Luke 17:11–19). These acts of healing grew out of his attitude of compassion and mercy.

Finally, because God is merciful, He expects His children to be merciful (Matt. 5:7; James 1:27).[46]

---

[46] Ronald F. Youngblood, general editor; F. F. Bruce and R. K. Harrison, consulting editors, *Nelson's New Illustrated Bible Dictionary: An authoritative one-volume reference work on the Bible with full color illustrations* [computer file], electronic edition of the revised edition of *Nelson's Illustrated Bible Dictionary*, Logos Library System, (Nashville: Thomas Nelson) 1997, © 1995.

WORD STUDY
HARDEN

Harden—Many read this passage and see God's choice to harden Pharaoh so that he would be unable to respond to God's merciful call. The ultimate state of Pharaoh is not in view in these verses. Indeed, Pharaoh had a specific role to play in driving Israel out of Egypt and out of bondage. If it took the hardening of Pharaoh to work out a redemptive plan, so be it. The nation of Israel, and by extension, the world, received God's mercy because of the actions of Moses and Pharaoh.

motive, the letter to the Romans would have begun with nothing but bad news for all (1:18—3:20). If Paul were appealing for retributive justice from Almighty God, he would have been flirting with wrath, anger, judgment, and condemnation for the sinner. A demand for justice based on works leads only to hell! But God elected nations through whom He could provide mercy for the sinner.

It is the very nature of God to provide mercy (Ex. 33:19) according to Paul. The provision for salvation as established earlier in the Romans letter is totally dependent upon God and not upon us. We ought to be extremely grateful for this. Anything less than the work of God to provide salvation leaves humanity in a dismal state. Mercy, found in Christ and proclaimed among the Gentiles, is part of God's plan to bring salvation to the whole world.

So then it is not of him who wills,

nor of him who runs, but of God who shows mercy. (9:16)

Nothing people can do will merit the mercy of God. The word *mercy* implies as much. God is not coerced into being merciful. He doesn't have to be. It is His nature to be merciful. So, any charges of injustice on the part of God are ridiculous.

For the Scripture says to Pharaoh, "For this very purpose I have raised you up, that I may show My power in you, and that My name may be declared in all the earth." Therefore He has mercy on whom He wills, and whom He wills He hardens. (9:17, 18)

God's purpose for mercy is shown in the person of Pharaoh, who is often associated with the judgment of God. Instead of this, Paul associates Pharaoh with the provision of the mercy of God. He takes pains to show that the power exhibited by God through Pharaoh is for the salvation of captive Israel, not the destruction of Pharaoh. This quotation from Exodus 33:19 emphasizes the proclamation of the name of God through the showing of mercy. The power and mercy of God's name is seen in the miraculous deliverance of Israel and the destruction of those who threatened her existence as the people through whom God would work.

Romans 9:19–29 is a large section of Scripture, but its meaning must be taken as a whole. Paul is talking of those whom God calls, "My people." This is the nation set apart for His purposes. But the strange movement of history by God's merciful plan brings those who are not called God's people into the status of God's people. And those who God previously called, "My people," the people of Israel, lost this designation.

God's plan for mercy was not thwarted even by the sin of His people. Israel sinned against the Lord but God used their stubbornness to reach the Gentiles while preserving the remnant of those in Israel who had personal faith. Even though both Jews and Gentiles could be classified as sinful and vessels of God's wrath, He has been merciful. This displays the predominance of mercy as the crowning glory of God's actions.

———————

You will say to me then, "Why does

He still find fault? For who has resisted His will?" But indeed, O man, who are you to reply against God? Will the thing formed say to him who formed it, "Why have you made me like this?" (9:19, 20)

These are good questions that Paul refutes using a quotation from Isaiah 29:16. If God is all-powerful and has prepared a redemptive people through whom He can work, then why is one held accountable for sin? If God directed Pharaoh's steps, for instance, then why was Pharaoh accountable? But Pharaoh's personal sinfulness was established long before he arose to power. Romans 1:18–32 clearly shows this. His first sin was the refusal to acknowledge God as the revealed Creator. This is an internal understanding and is part of all Gentiles' experience. Pharaoh could not ask God, "Why did You make me this way?" But God, because of His mercy, used Pharaoh's power and stubbornness to bring Israel out of bondage. God uses even those who are sinful to work out His plan of salvation. In other words, God is free to use any means to show mercy to humanity. This illustrates the extent to which God went to bring redemption to this world.

———————

Does not the potter have power over the clay, from the same lump to make one vessel for honor and another for dishonor? (9:21)

Paul's imagery here is familiar and draws from Jeremiah 18:1–12. There it is fascinating to note the clay's amazing attitude, raising a clenched fist at the potter. It is absurd that such an attitude should be found in the clay. Yet, that is exactly the attitude of all humanity toward their Creator. Paul provides abundant evidence of this. The very ones who should be awestruck in worship scorn Him. Nevertheless, God has used nations to do His will. And we should not expect anything less from an all-powerful God. God's power is used to the benefit of those in desperate need of mercy, even those who shake a clenched fist toward Him.

What if God, wanting to show His wrath and to make His power known, endured with much longsuffering the vessels of wrath prepared for destruction, and that He might make known the riches of His glory on the vessels of mercy, which He had prepared beforehand for glory, even us whom He called, not of the Jews only, but also of the Gentiles? (9:22–24)

What is often missed in this exchange between Paul and his questioner is God's perspective on the vessels of humanity previously described as Jews and Gentiles. Both Jews and Gentiles are vessels of wrath prepared for destruction. It is not as though one group is any better than the other. Both groups are prepared for destruction due to disobedience. Yet God does not pour forth His wrath and power upon the vessels. He does not show judgmental power upon them. He endured them with much longsuffering. Yet both are prepared for the final judgment. In His patience, He provides an escape for those who find themselves prepared for destruction.

Such patience and longsuffering reveals God's ultimate plan: to bring mercy. As such, it is a glorious plan laid before the foundation of the world. What should be a world marked by judgment becomes a world with an ever increasing number of vessels of mercy. The targets of mercy are those who embrace the call to repentance and faith in Jesus Christ. These are both Jewish and Gentile vessels. God uses those who were previously disobedient to usher in the era of mercy. In other words, the sins of others do not restrict the working of God's mercy; rather God uses the sins of others to bring forth His mercy. Such is the glory of God.

As He says also in Hosea:
"I will call them My people, who
    were not My people,
And her beloved, who was not
    beloved."
"And it shall come to pass in the
    place where it was said to them,
'You are not My people,'

There they shall be called sons of the
living God."
Isaiah also cries out concerning
Israel:
"Though the number of the children
of Israel be as the sand of the sea,
The remnant will be saved.
For He will finish the work and cut it
short in righteousness,
Because the LORD will make a short
work upon the earth."
And as Isaiah said before:
"Unless the LORD of Sabaoth had left
us a seed,
We would have become like Sodom,
And we would have been made like
Gomorrah." (9:25–29)

Paul, by the Holy Spirit, proves
God's ultimate mercy using carefully
selected Old Testament texts. He
quotes from Hosea 1:10, Isaiah 1:9
and Isaiah 10:22, 23. The context of
the Hosea passage shows God addressing the northern kingdom of Israel. They are the rejected ten tribes of
Israel who are exiled among the
Gentiles, outside the realm of God's
special care for the kingdom of Judah.
Thus, the prophecy applies to those in
darkness. Yet the promise is for the
mercy of God to be extended to those
who live in such darkness. Their future is bright because of God's mercy.
God extends this mercy even to the
point of Gentiles being called "sons of
the living God." This is a theme in
Romans: God has adopted people
who were far off, making them His

children. Such adoption is inconceiv-
able in light of the sin of the people.
But God is not hindered by sin!

Paul follows the Hosea text with
two from Isaiah. Each has the same
point: God didn't have to spare any
people in Israel, but out of His mercy,
He did so. God redeemed a remnant
among those who had abandoned
God. That remnant has embraced the
Savior from among the Jews.

In the final section of chapter 9 (vv.
30–33), Paul concludes the issues of
God's mercy extended toward both
Jew and Gentile. While none deserve
the merciful actions of God, they receive mercy. While neither Jew nor
Gentile can claim special merit based
on behavior, God has elected to show
mercy through a people chosen for
His glory. The glorious ministry of
God to all humanity causes mercy to
reign.

What shall we say then? That
Gentiles, who did not pursue righteousness, have attained to righteousness, even the righteousness of
faith; but Israel, pursuing the law of
righteousness, has not attained to
the law of righteousness. (9:30, 31)

Here we have the greatest reversal
in history. The Jews had the Mosaic
Law, which defined how to live righteously under God's commands.
Through keeping this law, one could
be declared righteous. But if the law is

transgressed, condemnation results. So, the law that was intended to bring life brought death. Thus, the Jews did not attain what they sought. The law only led them to disaster.

But Gentiles found righteousness by faith even though God's law did not come to them nor did they seek it. Such law orientation was not part of the Gentile perspective. Gentiles attain righteousness through trusting in Christ. Here is the irony: What Jews sought through law-keeping, they did not obtain. What Gentiles didn't seek, they obtained through faith.

Why? Because they did not seek it by faith, but as it were, by the works of the law. For they stumbled at that stumbling stone. As it is written:
"Behold, I lay in Zion a stumbling stone and rock of offense,
And whoever believes on Him will not be put to shame."
(9:32, 33)

Paul has already established the sinfulness of all humanity, even those who possess the law and circumcision. He has shown that conformity to law does not gain the sinner anything and that sinners only have one destiny: death. No matter how many laws a sinner keeps, judgment and condemnation is sure. The law is only meritorious if one completely conforms to every requirement of the law.

The Jews have stumbled, according to 9:32. The prophet foresaw this

THE FOLLY OF LAW-ORIENTED LIVING

Here in Romans 9 we have a reminder of the folly of law-oriented living. The Jews, through such a law-orientation did not find what they so doggedly pursued: righteousness before God. Even though they sought to obey the Mosaic Law and enjoyed the benefits of God's gracious hand extended toward the Jewish nation, they did not arrive at a place of practical righteousness. They certainly attained a nation of practices which in many ways reflected God's law, but they did not obtain the holiness to which the law pointed. Israel should have known, for the prophets declared what Abraham knew: righteousness is only on the basis of faith extended by God's mercy. Law-oriented living will not bring forth practical holiness. Only life lived in the fullness of the Holy Spirit through those who have tasted God's mercy in Christ will exhibit practical righteousness on earth. Law-based living God rejects; Spirit-led living God accepts.

WORD STUDY
SHAME

Shame—*a negative emotion caused by an awareness of wrongdoing, hurt ego, or guilt.* In the Bible, the feeling of shame is normally caused by public exposure of one's guilt (Gen. 2:25; 3:10). Shame may also be caused by a hurt reputation or embarrassment, whether or not this feeling is due to sin (Ps. 25:2–3; Prov. 19:26; Rom. 1:16).

Joseph, not wishing to shame Mary, desired to divorce her secretly (Matt. 1:19). Ultimately, God will expose the guilt of the ungodly, putting them to shame (Dan. 12:2). God also puts to shame the wise of the world by exposing their guilt before Him and by choosing to save the foolish of this world by a "foolish" message (1 Cor. 1:18–31).

Finally, our Lord Jesus suffered the shame of the Cross because He was put on public display as the recipient of God's wrath (2 Cor. 5:21; Heb. 12:2).[47]

and by the Holy Spirit proclaimed this message. While tragic in one sense, their stumbling is not outside of the mighty work of God. In fact, God will use this to His ends. The same is true with the Jews' rejection of Messiah. They stumbled at the stumbling stone says the apostle, quoting Isaiah 28:16.

Those who did not have regard for God, though they were indeed Jews, were ruling Jerusalem at the time of the writing of this epistle. Their actions were marked by lies, deception, and trust in their own devices despite the fact that God's absolute justice and righteousness was their measuring

line (Is. 28:17). While they should have been entrusting themselves to the chief cornerstone, Christ, they were more committed to their own schemes.

But those who trust in this cornerstone will "not be put to shame." This is testimony that God's measuring stick is absolute righteousness based on law and not the subjective viewpoint of sinners who usually regard themselves as being "not so bad." But those who have come to grips with their sin, and impending judgment, gladly entrust themselves to the chief cornerstone and gain righteousness through Him.

---

47 Ronald F. Youngblood, general editor; F. F. Bruce and R. K. Harrison, consulting editors, *Nelson's New Illustrated Bible Dictionary:* An authoritative one-volume reference work on the Bible with full color illustrations [computer file], electronic edition of the revised edition of *Nelson's Illustrated Bible Dictionary,* Logos Library System, (Nashville: Thomas Nelson) 1997, © 1995.

QUESTIONS FOR PERSONAL REFLECTION
AND GROUP DISCUSSION

Read Romans 9:1–33 and answer the following questions.

1. What is Paul's attitude toward the people of Israel and how does Paul display his feelings for his people according to Romans 9:1–3?

2. List the good things which the people of Israel can claim for themselves. What does this tell you about God's attitude toward Israel?

3. Paul wants to show that God's Word does not fail. How does he do this in Romans 9:6–13? How can you summarize this in your own words?

4. Paul answers the charge that God is unjust in Romans 9:14–18. We can see the nature of God by examining the words that are repeated in this section. What is His controlling attribute in the section?

5. Is it possible for people to claim they are pawns of God (Rom. 9:19–25)? Why or why not?

6. What was the problem with Israel's attempts at pursuing righteousness to Romans 9:30–33?

7. How does Paul's discussion in Romans 2:25–29 help us understand what Paul means when he says in Romans 9:6 that not all who are descended from Israel are Israel?

8. What is the point of Paul's quotations in each of the following verses? (Rom. 9:25, 26, 27)

God's Justice and Mercy in Dealing with Israel's Unbelief

Romans 10:1–21

In God's plan, all humanity plays on a level playing field. The Jews, who were chosen by God, rejected His gracious provisions for them, while the Gentiles, those who were excluded from the people of God, became the primary conduits of His merciful plan of redemption. Yet, mercy is available for all, not through law-keeping, but through trusting Christ, who is the stumbling stone. For both Jews and Gentiles, this is the only way to find the remedy of redemption. This level playing field is laid out according to God's righteous mercy.

Brethren, my heart's desire and prayer to God for Israel is that they may be saved. (10:1)

Paul's evangelistic, compassionate heart evidences itself here. It must have seemed a strange irony that he, a Jew, would be the apostle to the Gentiles, while his own countrymen rejected his message. Yet, even though his apostleship was to the Gentiles, Paul maintained a deep concern for his own people. He was deeply aware of the blindness that affected his soul before he came to the Lord. So, He longs for their salvation.

For I bear them witness that they have a zeal for God, but not according to knowledge. For they being ignorant of God's righteousness, and seeking to establish their own righteousness, have not submitted to the righteousness of God. (10:2, 3)

Zeal for God is certainly good, but ignorance of God is not. The combination of ignorance with zeal results in disaster. The Jews ignorantly assumed that they were right with God and zealously promoted this righteousness. This is a little different than the Gentiles' situation exposed in 1:18–32. They spurned the knowledge of God as seen in creation and in the testimony of the conscience and behaved in abhorrent ways that demanded the wrath of God be revealed against them. The rebellion of religious people is just as bad, if not worse. They proclaim their righteousness rather than a submitting to the message of God's Word.

Paul says the Jews were ignorant of God's righteousness. He is referring to the theme of the whole letter to the Romans: the absolute justice of God in both condemning sinners, whether Jews or Gentiles, and providing salvation through the faithfulness of Jesus to all who believe. Justice according to law is good news for the perfect person but not for the sinner. The just working of God that brings salvation through Christ's perfect work is the Good News of salvation by faith. The tragedy is that the Jews did not submit to this righteousness of God. True knowledge of God is found in the faith-based relationship with God through Jesus Christ, the righteous One.

For Christ is the end of the law for righteousness to everyone who believes. For Moses writes about the righteousness which is of the law, "The man who does those things shall live by them. (10:4, 5)

There is disagreement about the meaning of this verse. At issue is the word *end* (Greek, *telos*), which can imply the fulfillment, the termination, the goal of the law, or any combination of these. If we examine each one, we find that there are aspects of each that are important. Of course, Christ fulfills the law. Although He is under the law, He is the perfect Man who is not in any way tarnished by sin. In other words, He perfectly maintains the standard of the law. Second, Jesus Christ terminates the relationship of the believer with the law. This is seen in Romans 7:1–6. In addition, 6:14 declares that the believer is no longer under the law. This implies the termination of the relationship of the believer with the law. Finally, the goal of the law is the perfection that is found only in Jesus Christ. All that is contained in the

law is found in Jesus' life of obedience. To this end, then, the law finds its perfect goal in the declaration of Christ as the righteous One.

Anyone living under the law must live by the demands of the law. This is fine for the sinless, but disaster for the sinner. The sinner, as Paul has made abundantly clear, finds only bad news under the law. The only person for whom the law is truly good news is Jesus Christ who maintained the law with perfect obedience and received glory, honor, and immortality. There is no doubt about which one is superior, the way of grace or the way of the law. Yet some people still choose the way of religious demands rather than a Holy Spirit-empowered life which is always consistent with the obedience of Christ.

But the righteousness of faith speaks in this way, "Do not say in your heart, 'Who will ascend into heaven?' " (that is, to bring Christ down from above) or, " 'Who will descend into the abyss?' " (that is, to bring Christ up from the dead). But what does it say? "The word is near you, in your mouth and in your heart" (that is, the word of faith which we preach): that if you confess with your mouth the Lord Jesus and believe in your heart that God has raised Him from the dead, you will be saved. (10:6–9)

These verses have puzzled many commentators. Paul quotes from Deuteronomy 30:12–14. Yet, the paraphrasing of the Old Testament text, and the answers given to its questions, have caused some to question Paul's use of the Old Testament. The original context of the quotation from Deuteronomy shows that the commandment and the law are near to us. Yet, here in Romans, Christ is the answer to the questions; He is near to us. Christ is the perfection of the law. So, it is not necessary to strive to keep the law since fulfillment of the law is so close to you. So, the incarnate, resurrected Christ is the divine answer to the question of how to pursue God.

Striving with the law can cease; embrace Christ. This is enough.

Continuing with the reference to Deuteronomy 30, Paul connects the "word" of verse 14 with the "word of faith" that he proclaims. The word of the law with all its demands for obedience is no longer a factor; rather, the message of Christ's righteousness that is acquired by faith fulfills the seeking heart. It is no longer necessary to have the right word in one's mouth and heart. The Christian message is enough. The Lord Jesus came down from heaven so we need not strive to bring Him down. He was raised from the dead so we do not need to bring Him up

CROSS REFERENCE
Joel 2:32

Paul quotes from the prophet Joel to support his point in Romans 10:13: "whoever calls on the name of the LORD shall be saved ... among the remnant whom the LORD calls." We should note the two-fold calling signified in this text. First of all, people call upon the living God for salvation. But at the same time God is at work calling people to Himself. How this works is a divine mystery. God's call never overpowers the freedom of the individual to choose the Lord. Yet God's call provides the invitation and necessary movement for the individual to receive the Lord.

We should also note here that the name of the Lord in Joel 2:32 is the personal name of the covenant God Yahweh. In Romans 10:13 this text refers to Jesus. In other words, Jesus is called Yahweh and is the same as the covenant God of Israel. The deity of Christ is clearly seen here as it is in John 1:1; Colossians 2:19; Philippians 2:6-11; Hebrews 1:8 among other verses. While the term "trinity" is not used in the Bible, the truth of the concept of the triune God is evident in God's Word.

WORD STUDY
SALVATION

The salvation that comes through Christ may be described in three tenses: past, present, and future. When people believe in Christ, they are saved (Acts 16:31). But we are also in the process of being saved from the power of sin (Rom. 8:13; Phil. 2:12). Finally, we shall be saved from the very presence of sin (Rom. 13:11; Titus 2:12–13). God releases into our lives today the power of Christ's resurrection (Rom. 6:4) and allows us a foretaste of our future life as His children (2 Cor. 1:22; Eph. 1:14). Our experience of salvation will be complete when Christ returns (Heb. 9:28) and the kingdom of God is fully revealed (Matt. 13:41–43).[48]

out of the abyss. He fulfills every requirement of God.

The designation *Lord Jesus* refers to the deity of Christ because to the Jews, the Lord was Yahweh the God of Israel. Here again, Christ is shown to be God. The message here is that the incarnate God can fulfill the demands of the law-giving God. The confession of Jesus as Lord is the evidence that one has the perfect commandment (embodied by the incarnated Christ) in the mouth. Belief is the evidence that one has the perfect commandment (embodied by the resurrected Christ) in the heart. This meets God's demand to have the law in one's mouth and heart. Confession and belief are all that is needed to please God. The result is that you will be saved. This salvation depends on the perfection of Christ and in His fulfillment of the law.

For with the heart one believes unto righteousness, and with the mouth confession is made unto salvation. For the Scripture says, "Whoever believes on Him will not be put to shame." For there is no distinction between Jew and Greek, for the same Lord over all is rich to all who call upon Him. For "whoever calls on the name of the LORD shall be saved." (10:10–13)

Paul gives scriptural proof for his statement that "with the heart one believes unto righteousness, and

---

48 Ronald F. Youngblood, general editor; F. F. Bruce and R. K. Harrison, consulting editors, *Nelson's New Illustrated Bible Dictionary: An authoritative one-volume reference work on the Bible with full color illustrations* [computer file], electronic edition of the revised edition of *Nelson's Illustrated Bible Dictionary*, Logos Library System, (Nashville: Thomas Nelson) 1997, © 1995.

CROSS REFERENCE
Isaiah 52:13—53:12

"Behold, My Servant shall deal prudently; he shall be exalted and extolled and be very high. Just as many were astonished at you, so His visage was marred more than any man, and His form more than the sons of men; ... And He was numbered with the transgressors. And He bore the sin of many, and made intercession for the transgressors."

This well-known messianic prophecy reveals God's plan for humanity's redemption. This is sometimes called the Servant Song. It declares how the Messiah will be exalted, will provide a blood atonement bearing our sins and sorrows, yet be rejected. He will take our guilt as His own, die, and be buried to save those who believe. This makes clear that the message of the gospel was declared to Israel seven hundred years before Christ's death and Resurrection.

with the mouth confession is made unto salvation." In Paul's version of Isaiah 28:16, he equates "not be put to shame" with righteousness by faith. One believes with the heart, thus, righteousness ensues when the heart believes in Christ. The statement, "whoever calls on the name of the LORD shall be saved" is drawn from Joel 2:32. This shows that place of confession unto salvation is the mouth.

The apostle is not simply providing a salvation formula as if mouthing, "Jesus is Lord," will make everything fine. However, a person who is really seeking the justification of God can find it in confessing the Lord Jesus who is the fullest expression and complete fulfillment of the law. Complete righteousness is guaranteed by true belief and confession. This satisfies the righteous demands of God.

In 10:14–21, the apostle furthers his argument by establishing the justice of God toward Israel. He grounds his reasoning in the scriptural passages that posit that Israel already knew of the promise of the Lord through the prophets. While the clear Word of God was there, the embrace of that Word was lacking. Therefore, the rejection of the plan of God was not God's fault, for He clearly told of His strategy to save sinners by faith in Messiah. So, Paul places the blame squarely at the feet of Israel. God's plan was rejected outright by Israel even though they knew of it. In some ways, this is analogous to Romans 1:18–32 where the knowledge of God was made plain to the Gentiles but was rejected by them.

How then shall they call on Him in whom they have not believed? And how shall they believe in Him of whom they have not heard? And how shall they hear without a preacher? And how shall they preach unless they are sent? As it is written:

"How beautiful are the feet of those who preach the gospel of peace, Who bring glad tidings of good things!" (10:14, 15)

The objection given here is that Israel could not have called upon the Lord because they did not believe in Him. Also, Israel could not believe in someone about whom they had not heard. This was not possible because there was no proclamation of the gospel message. If none were sent to Israel, then how can Israel be held accountable for the rejection of the message? Paul's quotation from Isaiah 52:7 is a hint of what is to come. For Paul, the proclamation of the lordship of Christ and His sacrificial work is found in the prophets of Israel. Thus, the prophetic word which was truly good news of the coming Messiah, Jesus, gave adequate opportunity for Israel to call upon the Lord and to believe on Him. So, the word had already gone forth to Israel.

But they have not all obeyed the gospel. For Isaiah says, "LORD, who has believed our report?" So then faith comes by hearing, and hearing by the word of God. (10:16, 17)

Paul puts the issue squarely where it should be. The problem has not been the absence of a proclamation of the gospel. The problem has been the lack of obedience to the gospel. Indeed, Isaiah speaks of the disobedience to the message of the coming Messiah in Isaiah 53:1. Faith comes through hearing the word of God and acting upon it. And the word of God came to Israel in abundance through the prophets. Yet, as Paul by the Holy Spirit has said before, possession of the Word of God does not equal obedience to the Word of God. In this case, the word of faith was not embraced and obeyed, even though Israel possessed it.

But I say, have they not heard? Yes indeed:
    "Their sound has gone out to all the earth,
    And their words to the ends of the world." (10:18)

Paul provides further evidence for the fact that Israel has heard the message of the gospel by quoting Psalm 19:4 to indicate how far the message reached; that is, to the ends of the earth. Israel certainly would have been within hearing distance of the message. The ends of the earth have heard the message of the gospel. As proof of this, many Gentiles have responded to the Messiah. Yet, Israel remains in disbelief and disobedience. The problem is not the lack of proclamation and, therefore, the opportunity to believe. It is the refusal of the Jews to embrace the message declared by the prophets, by Paul, and other Christian preachers.

> But I say, did Israel not know? First
>> Moses says:
> "I will provoke you to jealousy by
>> those who are not a nation,
> I will move you to anger by a foolish
>> nation."
> But Isaiah is very bold and says:
> "I was found by those who did not
>> seek Me;
> I was made manifest to those who
>> did not ask for Me."
> But to Israel he says:
> "All day long I have stretched out
>> My hands
> To a disobedient and contrary
>> people." (10:19–21)

Paul quotes three Old Testament texts to prove that the knowledge of the message was not an issue for Israel. He quotes Deuteronomy 32:21, Isaiah 65:1 and 65:2 to make his point. The first text shows that even a foolish nation can embrace this message. Israel claimed to be a guide to the blind and a corrector of the foolish (Rom. 2:19, 20). Yet as Paul and his readers knew full well, the Gentiles were embracing the message of the gospel. These supposedly foolish people embraced what the so-called wise from Israel had possessed since the prophets declared it. Israel's rejection of the message may have lead to anger and jealousy, but it did not allow a plea of ignorance.

Similarly, the prophetic words of Isaiah 65:1, 2 point out that the issue is not the knowledge of the gospel but the embrace of that knowledge. Those who did not seek God, found Him, and those who saw the revelation of God in the gospel didn't ask to see it. But it happened; the Gentiles did respond to the glory of the Living God. God's posture to Israel, however, has not changed. He continues to extend Himself to Israel; ready to receive them back when they embrace His message. The issue, as Isaiah 65:2 states clearly, is not ignorance, but the unbelief of a disobedient and obstinate people.

QUESTIONS FOR PERSONAL REFLECTION
AND GROUP DISCUSSION

Read Romans 10:1–21 and answer the following questions.

1. What is Paul's heart's desire for Israel in Romans 10:1?

2. What was the problem with Israel's approach to God? (Rom. 10:2–4)

3. What is involved in faith according to Romans 10:9, 10 and how does this affect our understanding of what it is to present the gospel?

4. What does Romans 10:14, 15 teach us about our responsibility in evangelism?

5. When did the Jews have the opportunity to hear the Good News of justification by faith according to Romans 10:16–18?

6. What was the response of the Jews and Gentiles to the message of the gospel and what was God's purpose in all of this according to Romans 10:19–21?

7. How does Acts 1:8 relate to this passage and what does it say about our responsibilities in evangelism?

God's Promise for the Future of Israel

Romans 11:1–32

In 11:1–10, the apostle answers this question: Has the disobedience of Israel so provoked God that Israel is now cast off as His people? The short answer is, No. Paul sees the hand of God in preserving those from among the people of Israel as those counted among the faithful. This is proof of God's ultimate working in Israel unto salvation.

I say then, has God cast away His people? Certainly not! For I also am an Israelite, of the seed of Abraham, of the tribe of Benjamin. (11:1)

Paul himself is the answer to this question. The apostle was called by the Lord on the road to Damascus and embraced not only the message of faith in the Messiah, but also the mantel of apostle to the Gentiles. His existence as an Israelite from the kingly tribe of Benjamin, the tribe from which Saul came, shows the certainty of God's embrace of His people, Israel.

God has not cast away His people whom He foreknew. Or do you not know what the Scripture says of

---

CROSS REFERENCE
Philippians 3:4–7

"Though I also might have confidence in the flesh. If anyone else thinks he may have confidence in the flesh, I more so: circumcised the eighth day, of the stock of Israel, of the tribe of Benjamin, a Hebrew of the Hebrews; concerning the law, a Pharisee; concerning zeal, persecuting the church; concerning the righteousness which is in the law, blameless. But what things were gain to me, these I have counted loss for Christ."

Paul here puts his Jewish heritage and privileged status as the Old Covenant people of God in perspective. Paul does not deny that he received blessings from such heritage but that he holds such privilege in contrast to all that he has receive in Christ. Thus, he considered such special status and training as "loss for Christ." His life was to receive a new focus, not on the issues in the Old Covenant, which led to death, but on the joy of the New Covenant through Christ which leads to life.[49]

---

[49] *The Holy Bible, New King James Version*, (Nashville, Tennessee: Thomas Nelson, Inc.) 1982.

Elijah, how he pleads with God against Israel, saying, "LORD, they have killed Your prophets and torn down Your altars, and I alone am left, and they seek my life"? But what does the divine response say to him? "I have reserved for Myself seven thousand men who have not bowed the knee to Baal." (11:2–4)

Paul likens his situation to that of Elijah in the days of the reign of King Ahab and his wife, Jezebel. Those were dark days for Israel. Elijah was convinced that he was the only one of God's prophets left. But God took pains to make sure that Elijah knew the truth of the situation. The reign of the disobedient does not at all negate God's work in the remnant of those who are pure before God. Any complaint by Elijah (and perhaps by Paul?) was met with the assurance of the divine protection of those who continue to be full of faith and obedience to God. Paul's own plea to give himself for the people of Israel is met with God's promise to preserve the remnant that continues to believe. This does not change throughout history.

Even so then, at this present time there is a remnant according to the election of grace. And if by grace, then it is no longer of works; otherwise grace is no longer grace. But if it is of works, it is no longer grace; otherwise work is no longer work. (11:5, 6)

In the age of grace, God has preserved a remnant of those from among Israel who have identified themselves with the Messiah. This group provides the seed of hope for the future of Israel as a nation. They are proof that God has not totally abandoned the people of Israel. It is true that mostly Gentiles have found a place in the election of grace, but Israel is not without its remnant there. Of course, as Paul established in chapter 9 regarding the election of nations, works have no part in preserving this remnant. These people are preserved by faith, not by their works. For only the election by grace will stand before God. Works demand justice; grace hopes in mercy by faith in Jesus. Faith and works are diametrically opposed to each other in election. The people through whom God works are selected based only upon God's free and unrestrained choice. It can be no other way.

What then? Israel has not obtained what it seeks; but the elect have obtained it, and the rest were blinded. (11:7)

The elect, both the remnant from among the Jews, and the many Gentiles, have obtained the righteousness that Israel sought. Israel sought such righteousness based upon the law, while the elect from Israel, and the Gentiles, sought it based on faith.

We must be careful here to place this verse in context. Israel in disobedience and unbelief rejected the message of the gospel from the beginning. Their

WORD STUDY
REMNANT

Remnant—*the part of a community or nation that remains after a dreadful judgment or devastating calamity, especially those who have escaped and remain to form the nucleus of a new community* (Is. 10:20–23). The survival of a righteous remnant rests solely on God's providential care for His chosen people and His faithfulness to keep His covenant promises.

The concept of the remnant has its roots in the Book of Deuteronomy (4:27–31; 28:62–68; 30:1–10), where Moses warned the people of Israel that they would be scattered among the nations. But God also promised that He would bring the people back from captivity and establish them again in the land of their fathers. This concept was picked up by the prophets, who spoke of the Assyrian and Babylonian captivities. The concept was extended to apply also to the gathering of a righteous remnant at the time when the Messiah came to establish His kingdom.

In Amos and Isaiah the remnant consisted of those chosen by God who were rescued from the impending doom of the nation (Is. 1:9; Amos 5:14–15). As such, they were labeled "the poor," those who suffer for God (Is. 29:19; 41:17). At the same time, they serve God and stand before the nation as witnesses, calling the people to repent of their rebellion.

In the New Testament the apostle Paul picked up the teaching of Isaiah and other prophets about the remnant and applied it to the church (Rom. 11:5). Paul showed that God's purpose is seen in the "remnant" out of Israel who have joined the Gentiles to form the church, the new people of God. Further, Jesus' choice of twelve apostles built upon remnant themes. Symbolizing the twelve tribes, the apostles became the remnant who erected a new structure, the church, upon the foundation of Israel. In the church, both Jews and Gentiles, circumcised and uncircumcised, find their true spiritual home when they believe in Christ.[50]

---

[50] Ronald F. Youngblood, general editor; F. F. Bruce and R. K. Harrison, consulting editors, *Nelson's New Illustrated Bible Dictionary:* An authoritative one-volume reference work on the Bible with full color illustrations [computer file], electronic edition of the revised edition of *Nelson's Illustrated Bible Dictionary,* Logos Library System, (Nashville: Thomas Nelson) 1997, © 1995.

rejection of God's plan caused God's blinding of them for a season. It is important to see the progression in this. The blindness came when the Jews rejected the knowledge of God. This pattern mirrors what the Gentiles did in Romans 1:18–32. First, the Gentiles rejected the knowledge of God. So, God gave them up to the consequences of their choice. Also, God gave Israel up because she rejected the knowledge of the gospel; this led to disastrous consequences. But the blindness wasn't capricious; it was a just payment for Israel's disobedience.

Just as it is written:

"God has given them a spirit of stupor,

Eyes that they should not see

And ears that they should not hear,

To this very day."

And David says:

"Let their table become a snare and a trap,

A stumbling block and a recompense to them.

Let their eyes be darkened, so that they do not see, and bow down their back always."

(11:8–10)

The apostle points out the sad consequences of disobedience and unbelief. He directs the readers to Isaiah 29:10 and Psalm 69:22, 23 for proof of the result of rejecting God's message; of not seeing as they ought and not hearing as they ought.

The first act was the Jew's rejection of the message of the gospel that came through the prophets and through apostolic preaching. This is similar to the Gentiles' rejection in Romans 1:18–32. As a result, blindness set in and the nation was set aside as the conduit of redemptive work. True, a remnant from Israel remained, but it was a small number compared to the number of Gentiles who embraced the gospel.

In Romans 11:11–18, Paul presents a warning to the Gentile believers who may be smug or haughty about their favored position as the new vessel for redemptive work. He carefully presents the case for humility among those who are not of Israel but are favored by grace. Israel still has a place in God's plan and the Gentile's place is tenuous if unbelief and disobedience set in among them. The position of the Gentile believers does not depend on them (for it is by grace). Thus, the focus is upon their gratitude toward God who extended Himself to them, though they did not deserve it. It was His purpose to work in this way for the ultimate benefit of all humanity, though some will choose not to believe.

I say then, have they stumbled that they should fall? Certainly not! But through their fall, to provoke them to jealousy, salvation has come to the Gentiles. (11:11)

Another accusation is made about the just working of God in this verse. The opponent charges that God desires the end that Israel now embraces: that they should fall. In other words, God's intentions are simply to have Israel in a fallen state outside of the grace of God. Of course, God by nature never enjoys the disobedience and the devastating consequences such disobedience brings. The state of being fallen is equally not desired. But that is the situation Israel chose. So, what does God do with Israel's choice? He redeems the choice for the sake of the Gentiles. This is to bring forth a jealousy among the Jews, which will finally lead them back to God. So, as God usually does in great grace, He brings good out of evil. This is God's specialty. He takes the scraps of disobedience and fashions a beautiful garment. The Gentiles, who wear this garment, will provoke Israel to return to God.

> Now if their fall is riches for the world, and their failure riches for the Gentiles, how much more their fullness! (11:12)

Here Paul uses a classic method of argument. While more extensive explanation of the text will wait until a discussion of 11:15, 16, the logic is simple. If God has so worked in wonderful fashion to bring Gentiles to Himself, how much more certain can we be that He will bring Israel back to Himself. So, since the fall of Israel brings riches for the world through grace and since the failure of Israel brings riches for the Gentiles, how much greater riches will come when the fullness of faith comes to Israel! In other words, you may think it is great how God is gracious to Gentiles through Israel's disobedience, just wait until you see the overabundant riches that will come when the Jews have the obedience of faith.

> For I speak to you Gentiles; inasmuch as I am an apostle to the Gentiles, I magnify my ministry, if by any means I may provoke to jealousy those who are my flesh and save some of them. (11:13, 14)

In speaking to his Gentile readers, Paul shows his heart for his countrymen. Sure, he is called to minister to the Gentiles and he obeys that call. But he also sees his ministry as a way of reaching some of his fellow Jews. For his successful ministry of grace will provoke some Jews to seek the grace of God that is found in Christ. It is as if Paul has a secondary ministry to Jews. Paul relishes this ministry, So, he magnifies his ministry. This is another reason why he is not ashamed of the gospel; it will bring some of his countrymen to faith in Christ, even by jealousy.

WORD STUDY
GRAFTING

Grafting—*in horticulture, the process of uniting a shoot or bud with a grow-ing plant so they grow as one.* The apostle Paul used this procedure to illustrate the relationship between Jews and Gentiles in God's plan. The natural branches of the good olive tree (Israel) were broken off (because of Israel's unbelief), and the alien branches of a wild olive tree (the Gentiles) were grafted onto the root of the good olive tree (because of the Gentiles' faith; Rom. 11:17–24).[51]

For if their being cast away is the reconciling of the world, what will their acceptance be but life from the dead? For if the firstfruit is holy, the lump is also holy; and if the root is holy, so are the branches. (11:15, 16)

Paul now proves the awesome power shown in the restoration of the Jews. Israel was cast away due to her disobedience to the Lord. But even this, which is surely tragic, brought something good in God's economy. Gentiles found a way of salvation through faith in Christ and are reconciled to God. But when Israel returns to God, it will be the nation's resurrection. New life, eternal life, will be brought to Israel when they embrace the gospel of the kingdom of God. Paul, and other Jewish believers in Christ form a firstfruit offering to God. Paul changes the metaphor from firstfruits to lump and then to root and branches to carry forward his argument. Since the partial lump is holy, the whole lump is holy; that is, set aside for God's work. So also if the root is set aside for God, so are the branches, even if some have not yet followed through in response to God.

And if some of the branches were broken off, and you, being a wild olive tree, were grafted in among them, and with them became a partaker of the root and fatness of the olive tree, do not boast against the branches. But if you do boast, remember that you do not support the root, but the root supports you. (11:17, 18)

Paul notes carefully "some of the branches were broken off" of the holy olive tree of God's redemptive plan. He

---

51 Ronald F. Youngblood, general editor; F. F. Bruce and R. K. Harrison, consulting editors, *Nelson's New Illustrated Bible Dictionary:* An authoritative one-volume reference work on the Bible with full color illustrations [computer file], electronic edition of the revised edition of *Nelson's Illustrated Bible Dictionary*, Logos Library System, (Nashville: Thomas Nelson) 1997, © 1995.

does not say that all were. For Paul and the remnant of Jewish disciples of Jesus remain as the first choice of God in being reconciled with God. Yet some who were disobedient were broken off. This has allowed room for Gentiles (a wild olive tree) to be grafted in. They not only become part of the tree, but partakers of the root and fatness of the olive tree. So the riches of grace from the root overflow even to those not originally connected to the tree.

No one would doubt that this is an overwhelmingly gracious act; but it is crucially important for the Gentile branches to keep a proper attitude. Arrogance at receiving grace finds no place in redemption. It is true that Gentile believers outnumber Jewish believers, but the fact that the tree originally had Jewish branches must not be forgotten. It is only by God's grace that Gentiles have a place on the tree. God was under no obligation to graft them in.

In Romans 11:13–27, the final resolution of the status of Israel is assured. Gentiles need to be aware of this fact. It may seem that Israel has become blind without any remedy. It may seem that Gentiles now occupy the prized position as primary vessels of the redemptive plan of God. But it shall not be the case forever. God's plan is to use Israel's disobedience and blindness to His own benefit for the sake of humanity. In such a way God will be able to be both just in His dealings with humanity, and gracious in

His redemptive work toward all people. Gentiles must understand that the current preference for Gentiles is only temporary in God's economy.

––––––––––

> You will say then, "Branches were broken off that I might be grafted in." Well said. Because of unbelief they were broken off, and you stand by faith. Do not be haughty, but fear. For if God did not spare the natural branches, He may not spare you either. (11:19–21)

One might point out that others were broken off that I might be grafted in. But this is not anything to boast about. In fact, in some ways it is quite sad for it was due to unbelief. The only reason Gentile believers have been grafted in is that they stand by faith. In other words, no merit brought about this change. Only the gracious hand of God caused Gentiles to have salvation. Thus, a posture of humility, not arrogance, must result. For when the Holy Spirit declares, "If God did not spare the natural branches, He may not spare you either," it is a warning to the Gentiles against taking for granted their standing. Natural branches have much more reason to stay on the tree. Grafted branches have no right to a natural standing. The grafted branch is only a guest and not entitled to the richness and fatness of the olive tree. Grace, only grace, brought about such grafting.

> Therefore consider the goodness and severity of God: on those who fell, severity; but toward you, goodness, if you continue in His goodness. Otherwise you also will be cut off. (11:22)

Paul points out basic facts about the character of God. Wrath is real and goodness is real. Wrath is part of the severity of God. Yet it is not capricious. Wrath comes justly upon those who are disobedient and who do not trust in the Lord. But goodness comes to those who have the faithfulness of Jesus Christ (Rom. 3:22) applied to their benefit through belief in Him. Such goodness is overwhelming but must not be taken for granted. Gentiles must remain in that goodness or suffer the consequences: being cut off.

> And they also, if they do not continue in unbelief, will be grafted in, for God is able to graft them in again. For if you were cut out of the olive tree which is wild by nature, and were grafted contrary to nature into a cultivated olive tree, how much more will these, who are natural branches, be grafted into their own olive tree? (11:23, 24)

We are now quite familiar with Paul's method of arguing. Paul points out that if there is the response of faith on the part of Israel, God will graft the Jews into the olive tree again. This should be no surprise. It is obviously easier to graft in the natural branch than to graft a wild olive branch into the tree. So, when Israel returns to her God by faith, such grafting will take place. Gentiles should not at all be surprised at the result. After all, it is their own [Israel's] olive tree.

> For I do not desire, brethren, that you should be ignorant of this mystery, lest you should be wise in your own opinion, that blindness in part has happened to Israel until the fullness of the Gentiles has come in. And so all Israel will be saved, as it is written:
> "The Deliverer will come out of Zion,
> And He will turn away ungodliness from Jacob;
> For this is My covenant with them, When I take away their sins."
> (11:25–27)

It should be no surprise that God has a plan. The mystery of God is to bring forth great things out of dust and ashes. The failure of the Jews to embrace the Lord has been used by God to bring many to salvation. This is the choice of the omnipotent God, not the choice of the Gentiles. So, it is absurd that anyone would be tempted to be wise in their own opinion. God's methods are way beyond the rationale of the Gentile believer (or Jew for that matter!).

The time when the fullness of the Gentiles has come in is a reference to the season set aside by God for Gentiles in great number to respond to the message of the gospel of grace. Yet that time does not extend forever. A time has been fixed to end that era. At that time, "the Deliverer will come out of Zion and He will turn away ungodliness from Jacob" (v. 26). A great movement of the Savior will occur which will be evident to Jews. In response to their faith, God will take away the sins of Israel. A great throng of Israel will believe in the Messiah, their King. The nation will again be brought to the prominent place of being the redemptive people of God. Such a day is sure.

Next, Romans 11:28–36 shows mercy ruling the day. God's desire is to show mercy rather than wrath, to Jews and Gentiles. We must remember that God is dealing with nations here, not individuals. And while nations are made up of individuals, nations provide the method of reaching people with the redemptive Word. So, here the amazing mystery is totally revealed. Mercy is to come upon Jew and Gentile alike. It is all by grace; nothing is merited. The beauty of God's mercy is evident to all; the wisdom of God's plan causes one to stand in awe.

Concerning the gospel they are enemies for your sake, but concerning the election they are beloved for the sake of the fathers. For the gifts and the calling of God are irrevocable. (11:28, 29)

What a view Paul gives of those Jews who oppose the gospel. These Jews are enemies for your sake. In other words, while you see them as enemies, the net effect of their rejection of the Messiah leads to your redemption. So, a compassionate view ought to be the result. While no one enjoys persecution, in the case of Jews objecting to the message of grace we must be ever mindful that their rejection brought faith to the Gentiles. But God's election still stands. God has deep love for His people Israel, even if disobedience and unbelief have taken them outside of His redemptive plan for the moment. But that shall not continue forever, because God's gifts and calling are irrevocable.

For as you were once disobedient to God, yet have now obtained mercy through their disobedience, even so these also have now been disobedient, that through the mercy shown you they also may obtain mercy. (11:30, 31)

Disobedience, whether on the part of Jew or Gentile, does not exclude a merciful and gracious work of God in the future. Gentiles were clearly shown to be disobedient in 1:18–32. Yet they found mercy. So will Jews find mercy, though they are currently disobedient to the message of grace. By the very mercy shown Gentiles, which will provoke jealousy, God will also bring mercy to the Jews. In other words, you can't hold back God's mercy. Mercy begets more mercy.

For God has committed them all to disobedience, that He might have mercy on all. (11:32)

All people, whether Jew or Gentile, are in disobedience. But this does not disqualify them from God's gracious work. In fact, God has used disobedience to bring both groups to Himself. Even rebellion against God does not restrict His gracious working.

Praise to God for His Wisdom and Judgment

Romans 11:33-36

Oh, the depth of the riches both of the wisdom and knowledge of God! How unsearchable are His judgments and His ways past finding out! (11:33)

"For who has known the mind of the LORD?
Or who has become His counselor?"
"Or who has first given to Him
And it shall be repaid to him?"
For of Him and through Him and to Him are all things, to whom be glory forever. Amen.
(11:33-36)

What a fitting ending to the story. God has even used sin to bring out more mercy. The complaint early on that God is unjust in dealing with His people is surely put to rest. For who can argue with a plan that takes the despicable deeds of people, freely chosen by them, and turns them around to bring redemption. No human plan could have brought forth such brilliance. Thus, Paul concludes with a doxology, a word of praise, which extols the greatness of God's mighty, redeeming work. It is all to God's glory.

Questions for Personal Reflection and Group Discussion

Read Romans 11:1–36 and answer the following questions.

1. Why would Paul cite himself as an answer to the question of Romans 11:1?

2. In what way is Elijah a further answer to the same question of Romans 11:1?

3. What has been the result of Israel's rejection of the gospel according to Romans 11:11, 12?

4. What is the proper response of the Gentile "branches" to Israel's actions? (Rom. 11:17–23) What kind of warning is given the Gentiles?

5. What will happen to Israel in the future according to Romans 11:25–32?

6. Romans 11:33–36 is called a doxology, which is a declaration of praise to God. What can we learn from this doxology about the nature of God?

7. What does the phrase *the fullness of the Gentiles* refer to in Romans 11:25?

8. The doxology of this section ends the first major division of the Epistle to the Romans. These first eleven chapters dealt with the doctrinal or theological foundation for understanding the gospel as it relates to the Jews and Gentiles. Summarize each of the following sections below to refresh your memory: Romans 1:16, 17; 1:18—3:20; 3:21—5:21; 6:1—8:39; 9:1—11:36.

Chapter 6

Romans 12—14

GOD'S JUSTICE AND MERCY
LEAD TO A LIFE IN THE SPIRIT

After arguing forcefully for God's complete justice and continuing grace toward Israel, Paul moves on to practical commands to help in the daily lives of believers. It is not a surprise to find Paul concluding the letter with specific commands for the church after a detailed theological explanation of the gospel. This is his pattern. Theological principles form the foundation for practical action. This is true in Romans, certainly, as well as in Ephesians and Colossians. It is also seen in the way Paul presents his thoughts on the issues raised by the Corinthians. He usually goes first to theological principles, which pertain to the practical issues at hand. Then he moves to application. So in Romans 12:1, when Paul says, "Therefore," he is basing the next section he says on all that went before.

The twelfth chapter brings a torrential flood of specific commands. Of course, Paul is not erecting a new law for the believer, for he knows quite well the impotence of law orientation. However, any command applied by the Holy Spirit carries power, not because of the command, but because of the Holy Spirit.

God's Mercy Leads to Transformation

Romans 12:1, 2

It is now time to address the Roman believers who have witnessed Paul erect a substantial and crucial treatise regarding the justice and mercy of God. These two verses serve as a foundation for all the directives that are to come forth from his pen. So, Paul urges the Christians in that great city to acknowledge not only the justice of God, but also to celebrate the mercy that emanates from the heart of the Almighty.

I beseech you therefore, brethren, by the mercies of God, that you present your bodies a living sacrifice, holy, acceptable to God, which is your reasonable service. (12:1)

He beseeches the Christians. The Greek word for beseech is *parakalo*. It bears the sense of a strong urging or pleading with the reader to act upon what has been said. Paul connects this exhortation with the word *therefore* as the key link to what goes before. All of 1:18—11:36 is in view here. For it is by the mercies of God that one is challenged to excel in living for Christ in daily life. In fact the whole letter tells of mercy coming after justice. Justice left humanity dead, condemned, and expecting wrath. But the just One, Jesus Christ, provides the way of being justified before God purely by grace through faith. His holy life is ours; His atoning, sacrificial death is ours; His resurrection life is ours. We have all we need to live for Christ in the present day.

Present your bodies a living sacrifice, holy, acceptable to God, which is your reasonable service.

The Greek word for *service* can also be translated *worship*. Worship is our most urgent service to God. The presentation of our bodies in worship is not simply a matter of showing up for church services. It is an active, conscious presentation of all of our being to God. David declared the power of our physical involvement in worship in this way: "The lifting up of my hands as the evening sacrifice" (Ps. 141:2). Only human pride and ignorance deny the forthright physical, biblical exercise of praise as the pattern of worship in the church today.[52]

Because of these things, we are to present our bodies as a living sacrifice.

---

52 Jack W. Hayford, *Hayford's Bible Handbook [computer file]*, electronic ed., Logos Library System, (Nashville: Thomas Nelson) 1997, ©1995.

Paul has already described the problem of the body. We are to present the members of our body as instruments of righteousness and not wickedness. For we now have the power over sin which we lacked before. Resurrection power, however, is good for dead bodies. So, first the believer must offer the body in sacrifice to the Lord. It is a living sacrifice. Literal death does not occur and yet the body is dead through the death of Christ. The individual must choose to bring this offering of the body. Indeed, this is called a holy and acceptable offering. God does not reject this humble, submissive act on the part of the disciple of Jesus.

This is also called reasonable service. In other words, it just makes sense to do this. What other path could be considered other than this? At this point Paul picks up a word he's used before. The word *reasonable* is translated from the Greek word *logiken*. We have seen words from this family many times before, as in

WORD STUDY
TRANSFORM

Transform—*to change radically in inner character, condition, or nature.* In Romans 12:2 the apostle Paul exhorted Christians, "Do not be conformed to this world, but be transformed by the renewing of your mind." Followers of Christ should not be conformed, either inwardly or in appearance, to the values, ideals, and behavior of a fallen world. Believers should continually renew their minds through prayer and the study of God's Word, by the power of the Holy Spirit, and so be transformed and made like Christ (2 Cor. 3:18). When He returns, Christ will "transform our lowly body that it may be conformed to His glorious body" (Phil. 3:21).

In 2 Corinthians 11:13–15 Paul warned his readers to beware of "false apostles, deceitful workers, transforming themselves into apostles of Christ" (v. 13). One should not be surprised, said Paul, at such false apostles—people who are counterfeit and phony but who wear masks to deceive others—for "Satan himself transforms himself into an angel of light" (v. 14). Satan's workers, in imitation of their ruler, also disguise themselves as agents of good.[53]

---

[53] Ronald F. Youngblood, general editor; F. F. Bruce and R. K. Harrison, consulting editors, *Nelson's New Illustrated Bible Dictionary:* An authoritative one-volume reference work on the Bible with full color illustrations [computer file], electronic edition of the revised edition of *Nelson's Illustrated Bible Dictionary*, Logos Library System, (Nashville: Thomas Nelson) 1997, © 1995.

WORD STUDY
CONFORMED

Conformed—(Rom. 12:2) *suschematizo*.
Compare "scheme" and "schematic." This refers to conforming oneself to the outer fashion or outward appearance, accommodating oneself to a model or pattern. *Suschematizo* occurs elsewhere in the New Testament only in 1 Peter 1:14, where it describes those conforming themselves to worldly lusts. Even apparent or superficial conformity to the present world system or any accommodation to its ways would be fatal to the Christian life.[54]

the phrase, "Abraham believed God, and it was *accounted* to him for righteousness" (Rom. 4:3). This word indicates that the transaction is complete, logical, reasonable. So, our offering of the body is a reasonable, logical action in response to mercy.

And do not be conformed to this world, but be transformed by the renewing of your mind, that you may prove what is that good and acceptable and perfect will of God. (12:2)

Believers can take two directions: One, we can allow the world to press us into its mold. This is too common a sight. There are powerful forces in this world. Paul has in mind all of the evil elements of this present age. Paul does not decry the physical world; he points out the disastrous effects of "this age" with all of its

darkness and demonic activity and human beings sold into slavery in sin. Such forces are powerful. But they are to be rejected as the primary influencers of the soul.

Two, believers are to be transformed (Greek, *metamorphousthe*) bringing a radical change in the fundamental nature of their beings. This occurs by the renewing of your mind. The mind is not renewed by self-will. No, only the Spirit of God can do such renewing. Only the Holy Spirit has the power to bring forth the metamorphosis from slave to sin to joyful servant of righteousness.

In being transformed, we prove (or demonstrate) what it is to be perfectly conformed to God's will. External laws are powerless to bring this about. But God, by His Holy Spirit, does it. When people see this demonstration, the verdict on a person's attitudes and behaviors is that they are good and

---

[54] Jack W. Hayford, *Hayford's Bible Handbook* [computer file], electronic ed., Logos Library System (Nashville: Thomas Nelson) 1997, ©1995.

acceptable and perfect. God's will is seen in the behavior of those whose minds are fixed on the Spirit.

God's Mercy Leads to New Life Principles

Romans 12:3–21

As the apostle describes the practical expressions of what it means to be transformed by the renewing of your mind, he focuses on the body of believers within the local church. There are fundamental principles that must be in operation for the fullness of Christ to be revealed among these disciples of Jesus. In this short section the main emphasis is on how Christ has graced the believers with gifts. Such gifts have a dramatic impact on transformation of the body of Christ.

For I say, through the grace given to me, to everyone who is among you, not to think of himself more highly than he ought to think, but to think soberly, as God has dealt to each one a measure of faith. (12:3)

As usual, any commands Paul gives are based in grace and not on law. Here he admonishes the Romans "through the grace given me." He has the right as an apostle to exhort purely based on his standing as an apostle. But he does not do this here. Rather, he bases his authority on the grace of Christ given to him. This includes the grace of the empowerment as an apostle to the Gentiles. The Roman church was made up of mostly Gentiles.

The apostle pleads for the believers to consider each one as equal under the grace of Christ. He appeals to them to think soberly. Fundamental to sober thinking is equality within the ranks of the church. Such careful thinking will lead to right understanding for a mind that is set on the Spirit and yield the revelation that God has dealt each believer with a measure of faith. Paul is not talking about a quantity of faith here. He is speaking how each has the same measure of faith. When we see that each brother and sister in Christ is given the same measure of faith, there is no room for arrogance or haughtiness. The field is level. Neither Jew nor Greek has any credit before God before coming to Christ, so there is no superiority after coming to Christ. An equal measure is given to all. Therefore, sober judgment leads to equal consideration for all the brothers and sisters in Christ.

For as we have many members in one body, but all the members do not have the same function, so we, being many, are one body in Christ, and individually members of one another. (12:4, 5)

Equality in the church does not mean uniformity in the church. The

CROSS REFERENCE
1 Corinthians 12:4-6

"There are diversities of gifts, but the same Spirit. There are differences of ministries, but the same Lord. And there are diversities of activities, but it is the same God who works all in all ..."

Let us clarify the distinct role each member of the Godhead plays in giving gifts to mankind. God the Father gave us our existence (Gen. 2:7; Heb. 12:9). He also gave His only begotten Son as the Redeemer for mankind (John 3:16). God the Son gave us eternal life (John 5:38-40; 10:27, 28) and gave His life to give us redemption (John 10:17, 18; Eph. 5:25-27). The Father and Son jointly sent the Holy Spirit (Acts 2:17, 33) to advance the work of redemption through the church's ministry of worship, growth, and evangelism.

There are three categories of gifts: the Father's (Rom. 12:6-8), the Son's (Eph. 4:11) and the Holy Spirit's (1 Cor. 12:8-10). These gifts provide for our unique purpose and fulfillment. Each category illustrates the unique work of each member of the Trinity.

Romans 12:3-8 sequentially describes the gifts given by God as Father. They characterize the inherent tendencies that characterize each person through the Creator's unique workmanship. While only seven categories of gifts are listed, few people are fully described by only one. A mix of gifts is commonly found. While different traits of each gift are present to some degree, usually one is a person's dominant trait. It is a mistake to suppose that when an individual responds to a specific gift, this fulfills the Bible's call to "earnestly desire the best gifts" (1 Cor. 12:31). These gifts show us our place in God's created order. They are foundational.

The nine gifts of the Holy Spirit are listed in 1 Corinthians 12:7-11. Their purpose is to profit the body of Christ. These nine gifts are available to each believer as the Holy Spirit distributes them (1 Cor. 12:11). They are not to be acknowledged in a passive way, but rather to be actively expected and welcomed (1 Cor. 13:1; 14:1).

The Son of God's gifts apply the first two categories of gifts to the body of Christ. Ephesians 4:11 lists the offices that Christ has given as gifts to the church: apostles, prophets, evangelists, pastors, and teachers. The ministry of these offices equips the saints to know their place in the body and to know God's creative workmanship in them. Then the saints can know the possibilities that are open to them. These four offices enable the believers to receive the power of the Holy Spirit and respond to His gifts, which are given to expand each believer's capabilities beyond the created order. They give each saint a way to serve in the redemptive dimension of ministry for edifying the church and evangelizing the world.[55]

commonality of being in one body is similar to having the same measure of faith. The differentiation is seen in the various roles and functions of believers. These different functions are crucial to the effective operation of the fellowship of believers. But these various functions do not negate the basic premise: we are individually members of one another. Nothing can negate this bedrock truth. The power comes not from people's individual gifts, but from the unity of faith by the power of the Holy Spirit. This connection between believers is a vital aspect of the Christian life.

Having then gifts differing according to the grace that is given to us, let us use them: if prophecy, let us prophesy in proportion to our faith; or ministry, let us use it in our ministering; he who teaches, in teaching; he who exhorts, in exhortation; he who gives, with liberality; he who leads, with diligence; he who shows mercy, with cheerfulness. (12:6–8)

The unity of the body is nurtured by the different gifts (Greek, *charismata*). Yet, even these gifts depend upon the grace (Greek, *charis*) that God has given. Gifted individuals come from God who has given grace in Christ. The gifts differ but the primary grace that brought about one body of Christ creates the unity of Christ's body even if there are differences in gifts. The believers' soberness of mind relates to the unity in the body that comes from the same measure of faith given to all in the midst of the diversity of gifts.

Paul continues to describe some of these gifts. He does not give an exhaustive list. These are representative of many gifts that God has given to the body. A particular gift is always given and exercised in a manner consistent with our common gift of grace. So, if the gift is prophecy, it is used according to the basic issues of faith. The prophet is not to deviate from what is the essence of faith that we hold in common. For those

---

55 Jack W. Hayford, general editor; consulting editors, Sam Middlebrook...[et.al.], *Spirit-Filled Life Study Bible* [computer file], electronic ed., Logos Library System (Nashville: Thomas Nelson) 1997, ©1991.

who serve, that is, minister, they are to do so with the common serving attitude that we all have. Those who teach must stay within the teaching of faith we hold in common. Those who have a ministry of comfort or exhortation must remain within the ministry of the divine Comforter. There is a consistency to exhortation when it is Spirit-led.

While there are various gifts, the unity of these gifts is the common standard of the faith. This highlights unity in the midst of diversity. So, the gifts of giving, leading, or showing mercy are to be exercised with the common measure of liberality, diligence, and cheerfulness that we all have by faith. In this way, the focus is not on the particular gift, but on the common element of the faith that we all share.

Romans chapter 12 continues with a flood of exhortations for the Roman believers. It is as if Paul was just waiting for the foundational work of Romans to be

WORD STUDY
GIFTS

The Greek word for the word "gift" is *charisma* from which we have the plural *charismata*, "gifts." The word "charismatic" in English often signifies a person of significant influence who has an ability to persuade through personal power or oratory. We sometimes hear of the "charismatic" gifts, often referring to the so-called "sign" gifts of tongues, prophecy, healing, etc. People even, at times, evaluate themselves to find out what gifts they have. But we should understand the word *charisma* before we try to bring application of certain "gift" texts to our lives. The word *charisma* is constructed from the root *charis*, which means "grace," and the particle, or suffix, *ma*. This suffix brings a sense of movement to the noun that it is attached to. Thus, it would be appropriate to understand the word "gift" as a "movement of grace." Think about how this would revolutionize our understanding of the "spiritual gifts" if we would think of these as "movements of God's grace" in our lives. No longer would we think in terms of what "gifts" we have. We would be moved to consider being open to any movement of the grace of God in ways that build up the body of Christ. The debates of what "gifts" are "best" (which the Corinthians were concerned about in 1 Corinthians 12—14) fade into the background as we are available in any way for God's gracious actions taking place in us for the benefit of others. Rather than possessors of certain gifts, we become channels of the grace of God.

THE GIFTS OF GOD IN ROMANS 12:6–8

1. PROPHECY

a. To speak with forthrightness and insight, especially when enabled by the Spirit of God (Joel 2:28).

b. To demonstrate moral boldness and uncompromising commitment to worthy values.

c. To influence others in one's arena of influence with a positive spirit of social or spiritual righteousness.

2. MINISTRY

a. To minister and render loving, general service to meet the needs of others.

b. Illustrated in the work and office of the deacon (Matt. 20:26).

3. TEACHING

a. The supernatural ability to explain and apply the truths received from God for the church.

b. Presupposes study and the Spirit's illumination providing the ability to make divine truth clear to the people of God.

c. Considered distinct from the work of the prophet who speaks as the direct mouthpiece of God.

4. EXHORTATION

a. Literally means to call aside for the purpose of making an appeal.

b. In a broader sense it means to entreat, comfort, or instruct (Acts 4:36; Heb. 10:25).

5. GIVING

a. The essential meaning is to give out of a spirit of generosity.

b. In a more technical sense it refers to those with resources aiding those without such resources (2 Cor. 8:2; 9:11–13).

c. This gift is to be exercised without outward show or pride and with liberality (2 Cor. 1:12; 8:2; 9:11–13).

6. LEADERSHIP

a. Refers to the one "standing in front."

b. Involves the exercise of the Holy Spirit in modeling, superintending, and developing the body of Christ.

c. Leadership is to be exercised with diligence.

7. MERCY

a. To feel sympathy with the misery of another.

b. To relate to others in empathy, respect, and honesty.

c. To be effective, this gift is to be exercised with kindness and cheerfulness—not as a matter of duty.[56]

taken care of so he could tell of the practicality of the Christian life. These practical commands cover quite a lot of ground. They are meant to be part of the common experience of the people of God living in the Holy Spirit.

Let love be without hypocrisy. Abhor what is evil. Cling to what is good.
(12:9)

It is not surprising that love is the first command. "Love one another" is the key ethical command of God, just as to love God with our whole mind and strength and will is the key command in regard to our relationship with God.

Love here must be without hypocrisy. In the Greek text, the literal rendering of this is "the sincere love." While it is certainly reasonable to consider this a command, it is also possible to regard this whole section as a description of true love. True love, which is without hypocrisy, is summarized in two things: abhorrence of what is evil and clinging to what is good. These describe the essence of what it means to have pure love both of God and of others. The rest of the commands are descriptions of how this works out for the believer.

Be kindly affectionate to one another with brotherly love, in honor giving preference to one another; not lagging in diligence, fervent in

---

[56] Jack W. Hayford, *Hayford's Bible Handbook* [computer file], electronic ed., Logos Library System, (Nashville: Thomas Nelson) 1997, © 1995.

LOVE AND THE COMMANDS

In Romans 12:9 the word "love" leads the list of commands. Love (Gk., *agape*) designates God's kind of love which is self-giving, concerned for the needs of the other person primarily. The concept of "love" binds the whole section from 12:1—15:13. Love, true, God-like love, behaves a certain way. In fact, 12:9 probably ought to be translated, "God's kind of love is without hypocrisy." Technically, this is not a command but a description of how the church of Jesus Christ is to behave in the midst of a world that works against such love. That is why Paul says in Rom. 13:9–10 that all the commandments of God are "summed up in this saying, 'You shall love your neighbor as yourself.' Love does no harm to a neighbor; therefore love is the fulfillment of the law." All that follows about how a believer behaves within the church and in society stems from the first concept: God's kind of love is to be shown for we have received such love and mercy (as Romans 10:18—11:36 clearly demonstrates).

---

spirit, serving the Lord; rejoicing in hope, patient in tribulation, continuing steadfastly in prayer; distributing to the needs of the saints, given to hospitality. (12:10–13)

These three verses may better understood if we examine the word order of the Greek text. Paul begins the sentence with what is most important. It may be better to read the sentence as follows:

In the brotherly love for one another, you are to be affectionate.
In the honor for one another, you are to be giving preference to each other.

In diligence, you are to not be lagging.
In the Spirit, you are to be fervent.
In the Lord, you are to be serving.
In the hope, you are to be rejoicing.
In the trials, you are to be patient.
In the prayer, you are to be steadfastly continuing.
In the needs of the saints, you are to be sharing in.
In the hospitality, you are to be pursuing.

Certain qualifiers and characteristics need to be examined further in Romans 12:10-13 to gain a more complete picture of what true love among the brethren ought to be. Brotherly love (Gk., *philadelphia*), for instance, is used to designate:

the love of brothers (or sisters) for each other; the love of fellow Christians for one another, all being children of the same Father in a special sense. Occasionally the New Testament uses the word "brother" to refer simply to another human being, whether a Christian or not (Matt. 25:40), or to one's fellow countryman (Rom. 9:3). Usually, however, it is used of a fellow believer in Christ. This is true of all places where the concept of brotherly love, or brotherly kindness, appears.

In the Old Testament, Israelites were taught not to hate their brothers: "You shall not hate your brother in your heart … but you shall love your neighbor as yourself" (Lev. 19:17–18). This emphasis is continued and is made even more positive in the New Testament. Believers are exhorted to "be kindly affectionate to one another with brotherly love" (Rom. 12:10), to "let brotherly love continue" (Heb. 13:1), to "love the brotherhood" (1 Pet. 2:17), and to "love as brothers" (1 Pet. 3:8).

Brotherly love is to be the badge, or hallmark, of a Christian (John 13:35).[57]

As people of the Spirit of God we are to be "fervent." This word highlights the place of intense emotion with reference to life in the Holy Spirit. We are not to be Stoic in demeanor as followers of Jesus. We are to have the burning zeal of the moving of the Spirit of God in our midst.

Tribulations and afflictions will come into the Christian's life. How the believer handles them will show to what extent there is trust in the omnipotent God to do what is right. The response to tribulations is to be "patient." The Greek word for patience here is *hypomone*. It generally expresses patience with regard to things. It may be described as the quality that enables a person to be "patient in tribulation" (Rom. 12:12). The Christian has for his example the patience of Jesus, who "endured the cross" (Heb. 12:2). Christians are challenged to run with endurance the race that is set before them (Heb. 12:1)."[58] Thus, we are to have a long-term view of situations that tend to be very trying upon us, perhaps even quite distasteful.

In prayer (literally, "in the prayer") believers are to continue steadfastly. This word is used in the Book of Acts to refer to the disciples who continued in prayer steadfastly after the ascension of Christ (Acts 1:14). It is also the same word used in Acts 2:42 and Acts

57 Ronald F. Youngblood, general editor; F.F. Bruce and R.K. Harrison, consulting editors, *Nelson's New Illustrated Bible Dictionary: An authoritative one-volume reference work on the Bible with full color illustrations* [computer file], electronic edition of the revised edition of *Nelson's Illustrated Bible Dictionary*, Logos Library System, (Nashville: Thomas Nelson) 1997, © 1995.

58 Ronald F. Youngblood, general editor; F.F. Bruce and R.K. Harrison, consulting editors, *Nelson's New Illustrated Bible Dictionary: An authoritative one-volume reference work on the Bible with full color illustrations* [computer file], electronic edition of the revised edition of *Nelson's Illustrated Bible Dictionary*, Logos Library System, (Nashville: Thomas Nelson) 1997, © 1995.

2:46 to indicate the continual attention to the apostles' teaching, the fellowship of believers, and the breaking of bread, as well as in prayers.

In the ministry of hospitality the believers are to show their love and concern through relentless pursuit of what is helpful to people.

All of these are pictures of what true, un-hypocritical love looks like.

Bless those who persecute you; bless and do not curse. (12:14)

Paul further defines what active, self-giving love is all about. In this case, he refers to those who are outside the community of faith, admonishing the reader to speak well of (bless) those who bring persecution. Paul knows about persecution since he was a persecutor of Christ and Christians before becoming a pursuer of Christ and servant of Christians. It is interesting that he says the word *bless* twice. The opposite command, "do not curse," is a negative injunction. Notice the similarity of this with v. 9:

Let love be without hypocrisy. Abhor what is evil. Cling to what is good. (v. 9).
Bless those who persecute you; bless and do not curse (v. 14).

Rejoice with those who rejoice, and weep with those who weep. Be of the same mind toward one another. Do not set your mind on high things, but associate with the humble. Do not be wise in your own opinion. Repay no one evil for evil. Have regard for good things in the sight of all men. If it is possible, as much as depends on you, live peaceably with all men. (12:15–18)

Again, it may be easier to see this section if we examine the word order of the Greek text in view of the method and manner of living out the commands of verses 15–18:

Rejoicing with those who rejoice.
Weeping with those who weep.
Being of the same mind toward one another.
Not being proud in your own mind.
Being associated with the humble.
Not being wise in your own mind.
Repaying no one evil for evil.
Having a regard of what is good before all people.
Striving for peace as much as possible.

The key to the structure above is one's blessing and not cursing others. While it is easy to see these as commands, they are really descriptions of a manner of life that is full of blessing. This life carries power in the eyes of the outsider. It also brings life and health to the fellowship of believers.

Beloved, do not avenge yourselves, but rather give place to wrath; for it is written, "Vengeance is Mine, I will repay," says the Lord. (12:19)

The next admonition in the sequence is a continuation of the above description of a Christian manner of life. The structure of the sentence is literally, "not avenging yourselves, beloved, but ..." So, the manner of life is one of continued blessing even though one might desire vengeance. Paul counts on the justice of God. It is essential to be reminded that God is still the Judge of all humanity. Sinners will be judged and condemned. So, the believer gives place to God's wrath.

Scripture itself supports this proposition. God promises to repay people for wrongs done in this life. And that is an unsettling proposition, because God is not ignorant to injustices and wrongs which are done to us by others. His eyes see both the wrong and the future punishment for that wrong. But this is not a reason for smugness. The next verse shows the manner in which we should behave towards those who harm us.

Therefore

"If your enemy is hungry, feed him;
If he is thirsty, give him a drink;
For in so doing you will heap coals of fire on his head."
(12:20)

We disciples should inflict good upon those who do us harm. This is a redemptive action because our hope is in the God of peace and justice. We needn't seek revenge; God will repay.

WORD STUDY
VENGEANCE

Vengeance—*punishment in retaliation for an injury or offense; repayment for a wrong suffered.* The Levitical law prescribed, "You shall not take vengeance" (Lev. 19:18). Only God was qualified to take vengeance, because His acts were based on His holiness, righteousness, and justice, which punishes sin and vindicates the oppressed and the poor in spirit (Deut. 32:35; Rom. 12:19).[59]

---

[59] Ronald F. Youngblood, general editor; F.F. Bruce and R.K. Harrison, consulting editors, *Nelson's New Illustrated Bible Dictionary*: An authoritative one-volume reference work on the Bible with full color illustrations [computer file], electronic edition of the revised edition of *Nelson's Illustrated Bible Dictionary*, Logos Library System, (Nashville: Thomas Nelson) 1997, © 1995.

We seek goodness towards those who do not treat us well.

The coals of fire in this verse are a reference to the shame that is brought upon the one who is unjustly bringing forth evil upon the believer. This shame is the response to love and peace. While this shame does not guarantee repentance, it may be a key toward submission to God.

Do not be overcome by evil, but overcome evil with good. (12:21)

The final verse in the chapter is a fitting summary to what has been said about our attitude toward the enemy of faith. It also rightly sums up the way of love, which embraces love and shuns all forms of evil.

QUESTIONS FOR PERSONAL REFLECTION
AND GROUP DISCUSSION

Read Romans 12:1–21 and answer the following questions.

1. In Romans 12:1, Paul states, "In view of God's mercy." Of what mercy is he speaking? What does Paul want us to do in view of this mercy according to verses 1, 2?

2. Paul wants believers to not think of themselves more highly than they ought to think. What is a good attitude to have according to Romans 12:4, 5?

3. As we think about the gifts God gives us, it would be a temptation to think that some gifts are more important than others. How does 1 Corinthians 12:4–7 help us counter such thinking?

4. In Romans 12:9, Paul declares, "love must be without hypocrisy." What are the characteristics of this kind of love?

5. How can we show our devotion to one another in a practical way according to Romans 12:10, 13?

6. How are we supposed to act in the midst of affliction according to Romans 12:12? What makes this difficult to do?

7. How should we act when people oppose us even though we are acting rightly according to Romans 12:17–21?

8. How are we to understand the command given in Romans 12:17, "Have regard for good things in the sight of all men"?

9. Notice the important qualifying phrase, "as much as depends on you," in Romans 12:18. Why is this important?

God's Mercy Leads to Submission to Authorities and to the Law of Love

Romans 13:1–14

In this chapter, Paul addresses the importance of living rightly in the world because of God's mercy. In light of what God has done, and due to the fact that we are part of His glorious plan, God's people are to live in a radical way. This life is a dramatic departure from the norm of society. The way we live under the constraints of government also speaks volumes to the world.

Let every soul be subject to the governing authorities. For there is no authority except from God, and the authorities that exist are appointed by God. (13:1)

First, we must remember what the governing authorities were like during Paul's day. While it is true that the individual cultures within the Roman Empire were left largely unchanged, Roman rule dominated the spheres of law, taxation, etc. In many places, religious orientations were left unchanged as long as proper taxes were paid and order was kept.

Paul appeals to the believers in Rome to subject themselves to the civil authorities. The Greek language allows us to get the nuance of this command. It literally says, submit yourselves to the authorities. This is a voluntary choice. Believers who acknowledge a new King

WORD STUDY
AUTHORITY

Authority—*the power or right to do something, particularly to give orders and see that they are followed.* The word "authority" as used in the Bible usually means a person's right to do certain things because of the position or office held by that person. This word emphasizes the legality and right, more than the physical strength, needed to do something.

The two basic forms of authority are intrinsic authority (belonging to one's essential nature) and derived authority (given to one from another source). Since "there is no authority except from God" (Rom. 13:1), every kind of authority other than that of God Himself is derived and therefore secondary to God's power (John 19:11).[60]

---

[60] Ronald F. Youngblood, general editor; F.F. Bruce and R.K. Harrison, consulting editors, *Nelson's New Illustrated Bible Dictionary: An authoritative one-volume reference work on the Bible with full color illustrations* [computer file], electronic edition of the revised edition of *Nelson's Illustrated Bible Dictionary*, Logos Library System, (Nashville: Thomas Nelson) 1997, © 1995.

in Jesus could be tempted to rebel against the earthly authorities.

Believers are dual citizens: citizens in heaven and on earth. So, men and women must have a proper regard for these civil authorities. Paul elevates his command by asserting that the authorities are appointed by God. So, to rebel against them would be a rebellion against God.

Therefore whoever resists the authority resists the ordinance of God, and those who resist will bring judgment on themselves. (13:2)

No one wishes to resist God. Therefore, one must be very careful about going against the governing authorities. Paul is not saying that we should submit to every sort of action of a governing authority. Indeed, Peter rebelled against the governing authorities by refusing to heed their demand in Acts 5:27–29. But Paul describes certain activities that must be respected and obeyed.

For rulers are not a terror to good works, but to evil. Do you want to be unafraid of the authority? Do what is good, and you will have praise from the same. For he is God's minister to you for good. But if you do evil, be afraid; for he does not bear the sword in vain; for he is God's minister, an avenger to execute wrath on him who practices evil. (13:3, 4)

CROSS REFERENCE
Ephesians 5:21

"Submitting to one another out of reverence to Christ."

Paul uses the same Greek word in Ephesians 5:21 as he does in Romans 13:1. We should note that the apostle does not use the word "obey" in either of these two passages, though he had access to words that would clearly mean "obey" rather than "submit." The focus of the word "submit" is the voluntary choice to be subject to the person or authority. It is not the demand of the other that brings the submission but the desire within the person that produces the submissive posture. So, therefore, this is not a weak response to power but a powerful gesture of love. This posture of loving submission, even to the authorities of the government, is not without limits. The believer still makes choices of what are appropriate areas for submission. The believer is not to break God's moral requirements for the sake of secular authorities or for the sake of a husband.

The issue of civil and criminal justice is in view in these two verses. If evil is done, then it ought to be punished. This is an appropriate view of the role of the civil authorities. In this case, they truly are in the place of a minister of God to the believers. The word "minister" (Greek, *diakonos*) is the same word we use for deacon. Thus, there is a sense in which God is ministering through these authorities on behalf of righteousness. We are very aware of the concern for righteous justice in the Epistle to the Romans. When God's justice is meted out through human justice, we ought to rejoice.

For those who do evil we ought to be afraid, for the authority does not bear the sword in vain. So, when the righteous act righteously and are either rewarded or ignored by the civil authorities, they rejoice. When the righteous people see injustice and evil punished by civil authorities, they also rejoice. The authorities are ministering for God.

Therefore you must be subject, not only because of wrath but also for conscience' sake. (13:5)

The first part of this verse is quite simple to understand. Because of the presence of wrath in the world, civil authorities are necessary and one must be subject to them. But what does Paul mean when he says, "but also for conscience' sake"? He is referring to the higher motivation of the believer who may simply fear the authority's wrath if they do wrong. But the believer has a higher view of the governing authorities, for they are God's ministers. So the believer submits to them, not in fear, but out of reverence to God. In some ways, acknowledging God and His rule when acknowledging civil rule is an act of worship.

For because of this you also pay taxes, for they are God's ministers attending continually to this very thing. Render therefore to all their due: taxes to whom taxes are due, customs to whom customs, fear to whom fear, honor to whom honor. (13:6, 7)

God's ministers must be supported. Thus, taxes are important. No one prefers to pay taxes, but they are due the authorities. Paul insists we recognize this. He moves from taxes to customs to fear to honor. The taxes and customs are due all of Rome's authorities. Such is a given. Fear is due for those who do evil, for they expect to receive wrath. Paul may also be recognizing that in the civil arena, not all are due honor. Yet some are due such respect because of their upright actions. Believers should not dismiss the authorities, especially the upright, benevolent ones. Rather, they are due honor.

> Owe no one anything except to love one another, for he who loves another has fulfilled the law. (13:8)

While Paul is advocating a life without personal debt, the focus here is upon the positive debt of love for one another. While Paul usually is referring to believers when he uses the phrase *one another*, here he is thinking beyond the believing community. He is thinking about the neighbor he mentions in verse 9. In following this command about love, the law is fulfilled. This higher law goes beyond civil law and keeps one from the wrath of the civil authorities. This law is far more important and weighty than giving taxes, customs, fear, or honor to the authorities.

We must not divorce this verse from what has come before. Paul moves the reader beyond civil authority to neighborly issues. One may be able to avoid civil trouble but the interaction with one's neighbor is constantly an issue.

> For the commandments, "You shall not commit adultery," "You shall not murder," "You shall not steal," "You shall not bear false witness," "You shall not covet," and if there is any other commandment, are all summed up in this saying, namely, "You shall love your neighbor as yourself." Love does no harm to a neighbor; therefore love is the fulfillment of the law. (13:9, 10)

This collection of commands resonates in the Christian and Jewish mind because they are among the Ten Commandments. Leviticus 19:18 and its re-statement by Jesus in Luke 10:25–37 show their importance. Commands dealing with the worship of God are absent because the focus here is on the horizontal relationships between human beings. Such loving actions on the part of believers fulfill God's commands concerning behavior. Of course, no harm ought to be done. But it won't be done if love rules the ethical life of the follower of Christ.

> And do this, knowing the time, that now it is high time to awake out of sleep; for now our salvation is nearer than when we first believed. (13:11)

The believer is to give attention to this primary principle of ethical behavior, not out of fear of judgment, but because of the nearness of Christ's return. If one has Christ's return in view, then the commands are pertinent and compelling. Slumber must wait; we must awaken and be about the task of living in a way that is fitting for the recipients of mercy. The reason for this is that "our salvation is nearer than when

WORD STUDY
PUT ON THE LORD

We are reminded of the armor of God of Ephesians 6:11, 13, which was "an expression that symbolizes the combat equipment of a Christian soldier who fights against spiritual wickedness; the full resources of God that are available to all who take up the cross and follow Christ. Because our spiritual enemy is stronger than we are, we must 'put on the whole armor of God' (Eph. 6:11, 13)."[61] Here in Romans 13:4 the embrace of the Lord Jesus Himself is the answer to the fiery darts of the evil one. But there is certainly practical overlap in these two concepts. The elements contained in Ephesians 6:10-18, such as truth, righteousness, faith, and prayer, all are means by which we put on the Lord Jesus Christ.

we first believed." Paul here does not mean that the Romans are not already saved. There is a present aspect of salvation that they already possess because they have been made right with God. Yet there is a future aspect of salvation that they will soon enjoy; they will see Christ face to face and have a redeemed body (Rom. 8:23). The nearness of this aspect of salvation is important to grasp. It is a motivating force for action.

The night is far spent, the day is at hand. Therefore let us cast off the works of darkness, and let us put on the armor of light. (13:12)

Paul gives some final commands for those wishing to live well in society. He motivates them with two reminders: One, the day is at hand. Two, the light of Christ has come to the world so it is important to live as people of the light. Thus, one is to cast off the works of darkness. People of the light reject deeds of darkness. They are new creatures in Christ and not among the old, unredeemed creatures. Their transformation by the renewing of their minds by the Holy Spirit leads them to new ways of living. This living is by nature and not by law. So they put on the armor of light. This armor includes instruments by which the believer defends oneself from evil and fights for what is good.

---

61 Ronald F. Youngblood, general editor; F.F. Bruce and R.K. Harrison, consulting editors, *Nelson's New Illustrated Bible Dictionary*: An authoritative one-volume reference work on the Bible with full color illustrations [computer file], electronic edition of the revised edition of *Nelson's Illustrated Bible Dictionary*, Logos Library System, (Nashville: Thomas Nelson) 1997, © 1995.

Let us walk properly, as in the day, not in revelry and drunkenness, not in lewdness and lust, not in strife and envy. But put on the Lord Jesus Christ, and make no provision for the flesh, to fulfill its lusts. (13:13, 14)

Paul presents a concluding, all-encompassing command. The followers of Jesus are to walk properly, as in the day. Such a living is either in the daylight, which does not have revelry and drunkenness, or in the coming day of the Lord when all such behavior is unknown, for we shall be like Christ. Indeed, the believer's behavior is to exhibit the new kingdom of God and not the old dominion of the Evil One. When such a kingdom life is present, these old behaviors will vanish.

Paul uses three pairs of nouns to describe a wide variety of evil behaviors. In this way, Paul summarizes three main areas of sin—the indulgence of the body in revelry and drunkenness, the involvement in the sexual sins typified by lewdness and lust, and the destruction of relational sins of strife and envy. It is certain that Paul is not trying to construct a complete list of vices; he does wish to show the dangerous deeds of darkness from which believers should flee.

The believer combats these urges by putting on the Lord Jesus Christ. Daily, vigorous embrace of Christ is the first step in living in the day and in putting on the armor of God. Consequently, one also rejects the deeds of the flesh. The way of the Spirit of Christ is to live by the Spirit and not by the lusts of the flesh. Such behavior is against the new nature of the follower of Christ.

QUESTIONS FOR PERSONAL REFLECTION
AND GROUP DISCUSSION

Read Romans 13:1–14 and answer the following questions.

1. Why, according to Romans 13:1, 2, should we submit to governing authorities? What is the purpose that God has established for the authorities (13: 3, 4)?

2. Why would a person fear the authorities (13:3, 4)?

3. What should our attitude be toward the paying of taxes as Romans 13:6, 7 indicates?

4. What kind of debt should we retain according to Romans 13:8?

5. What does Paul mean when he says, "the night is far spent" (13:12)? What should we do in light of this fact?

6. Remember that Paul not only saw the benefits of Roman rule, he also saw the drawbacks of living under the domination of the Roman Empire. He was at times protected by law and, in the end, was put to death by that same law. In light of this, how is Acts 4:18–20 an important qualification for what we read in Romans 13?

7. Are there times when we must intentionally disobey the governing authorities? When and why?

8. Read Luke 20:20–26. How does this passage help us understand more fully the Christian's attitude toward the authorities? Is this an important teaching for today? Why or why not?

9. How can we actively put on the Lord Jesus Christ? What does this mean in the context of 13:12–14?

God's Mercy Leads to the Acceptance of One Another

Romans 14:1–23

In 14:1—15:13, Paul addresses the conflict between the so-called weak believers and the strong believers in the church in Rome. While it is not certain how to characterize all of the facets of this disagreement, certain points are evident. First, there were deep issues of conscience. Second, Jewish lifestyles probably came into conflict with the Gentile surroundings of Rome. Third, the church was made up of both Jews and Gentiles so a certain regard for Jewish ceremonial law probably was present within the church. Fourth, these issues had created a separation between the believers. Paul found it necessary to bridge the gap between these two groups in an effort to further the unity of the Spirit in the bond of peace.

In 14:1–13, Paul presents a summary of the issues, first addressing the so-called strong element of the church. Here we are given a picture of what is at stake. Issues of eating or not eating certain foods are a part of the conflict as are the observation of special days. The important things were ignored by these arguing believers.

Receive one who is weak in the faith, but not to disputes over doubtful things. (14:1)

ACCENT ON APPLICATION

One should note the limits of the admonitions in this section. Many have used them to argue against any offense that is brought to light. In other words, if someone's feelings are hurt by another's free behavior, people cry foul. Yet that is not the issue. It is not that someone may have hurt feelings or disagree with another's freedom. The key is this: Is someone's faith jeopardized by another's freedom? The offended ones are often those who would never be tempted to do what the person of freedom is doing. In other words, the offense results from a deep disagreement over the extent of freedom one may exercise in these disputable matters. But those who are offended are not at all threatened in their faith. They are simply angry.

Another issue here is the church's responsibility to teach the freedom that is in Christ. Paul did not shy away from describing that all foods are clean. The issue of truth must dispel matters of dispute. The ones with responsibility for teaching ought to be sure that the weak do not remain in that state. Of course, the strong must be taught to abandon selfish behaviors as well.

The first part of this sentence is quite clear: the strong are to receive the weak in the faith. The second half says they are not to do this while judging the weak about unimportant things. In other words, the strong should not receive the weak with a haughty attitude. Such arrogance is not appropriate in the kingdom of God. Yet, it is a temptation for those who are supposedly strong in the faith.

Let not him who eats despise him who does not eat, and let not him who does not eat judge him who eats; for God has received him. Who are you to judge another's servant? To his own master he stands or falls. Indeed, he will be made to stand, for God is able to make him stand. (14:3, 4)

Paul states both sides of love in these verses. For the strong, it is vitally important not to develop a hardened attitude towards the weak believer who does not eat meat. But it is equally important that the weak not judge the ones who eat meat. The reason is compelling: God has received both the weak and the strong. This would certainly be a shock to both groups. Each is convinced of the rightness of his position. But God is the ultimate arbiter, not the believer.

The Holy Spirit issues a powerful statement through the apostle Paul. God receives both the strong and the weak. Then Paul asks a great question: "Who are you to judge another's servant?" God judges His own servants. Only God makes just discernment in such matters. Yet, in these matters, God will make the believer stand. Which one? Both stand righteously before God because the eating of meat is not a vital matter.

For one believes he may eat all things, but he who is weak eats only vegetables. (14:2)

Some believers thought it prudent to avoid eating meat and simply eat vegetables. In this case, some Jewish believers may have been considering the Mosaic Laws against improperly slaughtered animals. Some may also have rejected meat that was used in the context of idol worship (see 1 Cor. 8—10). In either case, there is sensitivity to the Mosaic Law. We should note here that the text does not specifically single out Jewish believers. Indeed, Gentile believers may have been particularly sensitive to the issue of meat sacrificed to idols if they had come out of such a practice. So, it is not possible to be certain of what is at stake here. But we can conclude that such an issue was deeply rooted in the conscience of some believers in Rome. These believers are here called weak.

One person esteems one day above another; another esteems every day alike. Let each be fully convinced in his own mind. He who observes the

---

CROSS REFERENCE
1 Corinthians 8:8, 9

"But food does not commend us to God; for neither if we eat are we the better, nor if we do not eat are we the worse. But beware lest somehow this liberty of yours become a stumbling block to those who are weak."

The issues found in 1 Corinthians 8—10 are remarkably similar to what we find in Romans 14. The Corinthians disputed over whether or not a person should eat food that had been offered in pagan sacrifice and then sold in the marketplace. Paul's response was clear: Eat it unless it provokes a brother or sister in Christ to slip back into idolatry. God wants us to use our freedom to partake of all good things unless it is a spiritual detriment to others. Food is not the issue. God desires a spiritual maturity that moderates our behavior to edify others. Paul's own life demonstrated this principle. Paul could have lived in a way quite different than he did (1 Cor. 9) but he adapted his life to bring the gospel to as many as possible.

---

day, observes it to the Lord; and he who does not observe the day, to the Lord he does not observe it. He who eats, eats to the Lord, for he gives God thanks; and he who does not eat, to the Lord he does not eat, and gives God thanks. (14:5, 6)

Here we have a further refinement of the positions of the weak and the strong. The weak regarded one day above another and the strong regarded every day alike. But Paul urges a deep belief in the Lord regardless of the believer's position. In fact, observations of a certain day or dietary regulations are acceptable to the Lord. Not observing these things is also acceptable to the Lord. For if a person has a good conscience about these things before the Lord, that person is accepted by the Lord.

Each gives thanks to God. This is the key. Both honor God, even if they disagree on these matters that are not primary faith issues.

For none of us lives to himself, and no one dies to himself. (14:7)

This is the main principle. We do not live in isolation. The believers must banish any hint of rugged individualism. It does not belong in the household of faith. We live before the Lord.

For if we live, we live to the Lord; and if we die, we die to the Lord. Therefore, whether we live or die, we are the Lord's. For to this end Christ died and rose and lived again, that

He might be Lord of both the dead and the living. (14:8, 9)

We live in full view of the Lord Jesus Christ. This is not affected by our position and practice of disputable issues. The word *Lord* is used four times in these two verses. It is obvious that Paul wishes the believers to grasp the essence of the Christian life. That is, we live before the resurrected Lord Jesus Christ. He is our King. Nothing and no one usurps that position. Therefore, no individual can take the Lord's role in these disputes. Whatever our state, alive or dead, Christ is Lord. This puts all disputable issues in perspective.

But why do you judge your brother? Or why do you show contempt for your brother? For we shall all stand before the judgment seat of Christ. For it is written:
"As I live, says the LORD,
Every knee shall bow to Me,
And every tongue shall confess to
    God." (14:10, 11)

Paul shows both sides of the offense here. Some had contempt toward those who were weak. Others judged those who were strong. In the minds of the weak, the strong were operating outside the will of God. In the minds of the strong, the weak were operating without appropriate knowledge and freedom in Christ. Yet, Paul insists that we let God be the believer's judge in such

matters. He reminds the Romans that they will all stand before the judgment seat of Christ. God is perfectly capable to judge such things. We do not have to do so. In support of this statement Paul quotes Isaiah 45:23, which shows the necessity for all to give account before the Lord Jesus Christ at Judgment Day.

So then each of us shall give account of himself to God. Therefore let us not judge one another anymore, but rather resolve this, not to put a stumbling block or a cause to fall in our brother's way. (14:12, 13)

Paul summarizes his position, pointing out the necessity of placing our focus on our life before the Lord, not before people. The Judgment is coming when God will evaluate our actions. This evaluation is not for merit to gain eternal life, but for reward. He then points out that we still have responsibility towards brothers and sisters in Christ in these matters and should avoid causing them to stumble.

In 14:14–23, the focus moves from the issues to the believers' responses to these issues. Paul insists on the primacy of love in their actions toward one another. It is not appropriate to act in selfish disregard for the brothers who may be compromised by heartless behavior. Nonetheless, one must insist upon the essence of what is true. What one eats is irrelevant in comparison to the main issues of the faith. Paul desires to provoke love and under-standing among the believers who are conflicted in these secondary issues.

I know and am convinced by the Lord Jesus that there is nothing un-clean of itself; but to him who con-siders anything to be unclean, to him it is unclean. (14:14)

Paul is not trying to introduce a relative morality here. The Lord Je-sus has convinced him that nothing in itself is unclean. This is a primary statement of truth. All that God has made is good. Genesis 1 and 2 prove this. Ritualistic observations that de-clare distinctions between good food and bad food do not hold theological water. However, Paul is concerned for the spiritual life of the weak be-liever. He does not wish to trample upon the conscience of the weak be-liever simply because he has a clearer understanding of the truth.

Yet if your brother is grieved be-cause of your food, you are no lon-ger walking in love. Do not destroy with your food the one for whom Christ died. (14:15)

Paul uses strong words to describe the effect the actions of the strong have upon the weak. A brother is grieved and might be destroyed due to the selfish be-havior of the strong believer. In other

words, the one who is weak in faith goes back into paganism or idolatry. The strong believer should not risk such a thing simply because he or she has the freedom to eat meat. One's behavior re-garding food must not be the cause of sending a fellow believer into doubt.

This is not an issue of simply hurting someone's feelings by one's freedom. The spiritual ruin of the weak is at stake here. We do not have a simple disagree-ment about practice but deeply held convictions that could send some people back into sin. Paul speaks of the conse-quence of jeopardizing a person's faith through selfishness. It is incomprehensi-ble to do this to a person for whom Christ died. In other words, if Christ went so far as to die for the sake of a weak believer, surely you can abstain from meat. The sacrifice you make is nothing compared to the Lord's sacrifice.

Therefore do not let your good be spoken of as evil; for the kingdom of God is not eating and drinking, but righteousness and peace and joy in the Holy Spirit. (14:16, 17)

In yielding to the needs of the weak is the greater good that must always be kept in view. Paul urges the strong to keep a proper perspective. Such issues pale in comparison to the kingdom of God. It does not consist of eating and drinking certain foods, but righteousness and peace and joy in the Holy Spirit. Freedom has its place, but it must not be at the cost of someone's faith. Yielding to others' needs is neither weakness nor evil. It is compassionate and fully in line with God's overflowing mercy.

> For he who serves Christ in these things is acceptable to God and approved by men. Therefore let us pursue the things which make for peace and the things by which one may edify another. (14:18, 19)

Such an attitude of service frees the strong to edify, that is, build up, the weak and pursue the things that make for peace. What a wonderful testimony before outsiders when such issues are not contentious or divisive in the Christian community. God is pleased when selfishness is in the background and mutual edification is in the foreground.

> Do not destroy the work of God for the sake of food. All things indeed are pure, but it is evil for the man who eats with offense. (14:20)

Paul again sets forth this truth: All things are pure. Yet, it is irresponsible to push this point if a believer is brought to spiritual ruin by the exercise of one's freedom. To deliberately eat meat knowing it will offend another is evil. In other words, to push one's selfish freedom because one knows the truth that all things are pure is a tragedy. It is evil when people are destroyed in their faith

as a result. Food and other secondary matters are not worth the destruction of someone's faith.

> It is good neither to eat meat nor drink wine nor do anything by which your brother stumbles or is offended or is made weak. (14:21)

Here is the overriding principle: Don't do anything that causes the spiritual ruin of a believer in Christ. While this seems obvious, when people push their freedom, such concern for the brethren can disappear. But Paul will not allow such blatant disregard for weaker believers. Their well-being is paramount.

> Do you have faith? Have it to yourself before God. Happy is he who does not condemn himself in what he approves. But he who doubts is condemned if he eats, because he does not eat from faith; for whatever is not from faith is sin. (14:22, 23)

This is a beautiful conclusion to this section. The strong are to fully act in accordance with freedom before God. Such actions, outside of view of the weak, are accepted and encouraged. But it is equally true that the weak should avoid violating their conscience. The sensitivity to the conscience is not to be abrogated. In faith the weak can abstain and be pleasing to the Lord Jesus Christ. Each find favor with God.

QUESTIONS FOR PERSONAL REFLECTION
AND GROUP DISCUSSION

Read Romans 14:1–23 and answer the following questions.

1. In Romans 14:1 what is the command concerning people who may have a different belief and practice concerning disputable matters?

2. What hindrances do we encounter when trying to accept people with minor differences?

3. What characterizes the weak person and the strong person according to Romans 14:1–3, 5–6?

4. Why should we not judge those who do differ from us in minor ways? (14:4)

5. How can you summarize the teaching of Paul contained in Romans 14:13–18 in your own words?

6. How can Romans 14:19, 22 be the controlling factors for dealing with minor differences?

7. Why do minor differences come between Christians? How can we avoid this trap?

8. In the midst of Paul's statement of being tolerant with others in the case of minor issues, he issues this command: "Let each be fully convinced in his own mind" (v. 5). How can we apply this and still be tolerant?

9. What are some nonessential issues among Christians and how can you demonstrate the reality of Christian tolerance in the midst of differing issues?

Chapter 7

Romans 15:1—16:27

PAUL'S CONVICTIONS
AND FINAL COMMENTS

Paul's Calling and the Roman Believers

Romans 15:1–33

The fitting conclusion to the issue of disputable matters comes in 15:1–13. Paul points out the necessity to edify all in the fellowship of believers because all are responding to the unmatched mercy of God. In light of such mercy, what is the importance of such disputable matters? The pure and beautiful worship of God among all believers should be celebrated.

We then who are strong ought to bear with the scruples of the weak, and not to please ourselves. Let each of us please his neighbor for his good, leading to edification. For even Christ did not please Himself; but as it is written, "The reproaches of those who reproached You fell on Me." (15:1–3)

Paul places himself among the strong in this section, for he has appropriate knowledge of the truth in these matters. But he does not push the issue. It is imperative that the strong bear with the scruples of the weak. It is impossible, at this stage, for the weak to find the freedom of the strong. They will simply be brought to ruin. The strong on the other hand are not in the least jeopardized by showing grace and patience to the weak.

Selfishness has no place in the kingdom of God; the strong do not act to please themselves. For mutual edification, acting for another's good is the goal. The actions of Christ control the methods and motives of the strong believer. Christ did not do what would be to His gain, but to our gain. He gladly took on the punishment that was due others for their sake. This self-sacrifice is in contrast with the selfishness of those who make a point of freedom and, in the process, bring to ruin someone's faith in Jesus.

> For whatever things were written before were written for our learning, that we through the patience and comfort of the Scriptures might have hope. (15:4)

Paul refers to the quotation in verse 3 from Psalm 69:9. He desires that believers become like Jesus in the way they respond to opportunities to do good and to deny selfishness with all its evil tentacles. The Scriptures admonish us to have patience and comfort in the midst of everyday life. In this case the strong believers exercise patience and comfort toward those who are weak. These actions edify the church.

> Now may the God of patience and comfort grant you to be like-minded toward one another, according to Christ Jesus, that you may with one mind and one mouth glorify the God and Father of our Lord Jesus Christ. (15:5, 6)

Like-mindedness comes from one's submission to the God of patience and comfort. If there is a concern for such patience and comfort, then mutual edification results. When mutual edification results, then the working of Jesus Christ among the believers through the Holy Spirit produces unity. Consequently, the world sees in the beautiful testimony of unified worship a disparate people who are one in Christ. Such worship is pleasing to the "God and Father of our Lord Jesus Christ." True worship results from the obedience of sacrifice not from the insistence of positions of freedom.

> Therefore receive one another, just as Christ also received us, to the glory of God. (15:7)

Thus, the essential principle remains: Receive one another. Whether strong or weak, we must embrace the oneness that believers have in Christ. Not a single disputable matter can be allowed to destroy this essential truth. The glory of God is at stake. Receiving one another is the mighty statement of the glorious work of God to the world.

Now I say that Jesus Christ has become a servant to the circumcision for the truth of God, to confirm the promises made to the fathers, and that the Gentiles might glorify God for His mercy, as it is written:
"For this reason I will confess to
    You among the Gentiles,
And sing to Your name." (15:8, 9)

Christ is a servant on behalf of both Jews and Gentiles. His work as a servant leads to the glorification of the Gentiles and the pure worship of God. At the same time Jesus Christ confirms the promises made to the fathers of Israel. In other words, the hope and fulfillment of the patriarchs is found in Christ. So, Jews who are prone to disputable matters of the law and Gentiles who are prone to freedom from the law worship as one people of God.

And again he says:
"Rejoice, O Gentiles, with His
    people!"
And again:
"Praise the LORD, all you Gentiles!
Laud Him, all you peoples!"
And again, Isaiah says:
"There shall be a root of Jesse;
And He who shall rise to reign over
    the Gentiles,

In Him the Gentiles shall hope."
    (15:10–12)

These Old Testament passages are a subtle reminder to the Gentiles. They have great freedom because God provided for their salvation. God was not bound by common opinions of what was acceptable, but brought the Gentiles to faith without undermining His work among the Jews.

Now may the God of hope fill you with all joy and peace in believing, that you may abound in hope by the power of the Holy Spirit.
    (15:13)

Paul concludes this section by focusing on the unity we have in Christ. Through believing both the weak and the strong have joy and peace. When people live by Holy Spirit disputable matters fade into the background. The work of God the Father, the faithfulness of Christ the Son, and ministry of the Holy Spirit are the most essential things in the Christian life.

Next, Paul moves from the specific issues between the weak and the strong to a more general response to the Roman believers. Paul had had no personal contact with them, but he had heard of their faith and obedience to the Lord Jesus Christ. So he expresses his broad concerns and specific plans he has regarding the believers in Rome.

Now I myself am confident concerning you, my brethren, that you also are full of goodness, filled with all knowledge, able also to admonish one another. Nevertheless, brethren, I have written more boldly to you on some points, as reminding you, because of the grace given to me by God, that I might be a minister of Jesus Christ to the Gentiles, ministering the gospel of God, that the offering of the Gentiles might be acceptable, sanctified by the Holy Spirit. (15:14–16)

Though Paul admonishes his fellow believers in Rome, he does not take the role of the only minister among them because they are full of goodness and all knowledge and so are able to admonish one another. He does not denigrate the ability and responsibility of the Romans to have mutual ministry. In other words, Paul is not coming to them as the single authority to whom alone they must listen. No, the whole church is involved in ministry to one another. Yet, Paul does write boldly because of the grace given to him by God. He takes his own apostolic ministry very seriously and does not shy away from doing what he ought to do before God. His Gentile ministry is to the Romans and the other parts of the world as well. He is ever mindful that his offering is to the Lord and his ministry is worship, which is sanctified by the Holy Spirit.

Therefore I have reason to glory in Christ Jesus in the things which pertain to God. For I will not dare to speak of any of those things which Christ has not accomplished through me, in word and deed, to make the Gentiles obedient—in mighty signs and wonders, by the power of the Spirit of God, so that from Jerusalem

CROSS REFERENCE
Acts 2:43

(See also Acts 4:30; 5:12; 6:8; 14:3; 15:12)—"Then fear came upon every soul, and many wonders and signs were done through the apostles."

God worked miracles at the hands of the apostles. These signs authenticated the apostles' ministry. God also, through the Holy Spirit, promised that gifts of the Holy Spirit would include miraculous workings and signs. Thus, we should expect that God would manifest Himself through power in the present age. There is no indication in Scripture that such signs and wonders would cease. In fact, church history proves their continuance.

and round about to Illyricum I have fully preached the gospel of Christ. (15:17–19)

Paul may seem to be boasting here, but he is simply establishing his apostolic authority in the presence of his Roman readers. He glories in the works of God; he is not acting in selfish freedom but is edifying others. Paul's actions are marked out in mighty signs and wonders because his is a ministry for God. This does not mean that people must be in awe of Paul. No, we must be in awe of God for Paul works by the power of the Spirit of God. Paul is the living example of self-sacrifice for the sake of those who were far off from God. Yet, he is simply obedient to the call of God and wishes that those in Rome to do the same thing.

And so I have made it my aim to preach the gospel, not where Christ was named, lest I should build on another man's foundation, but as it is written:
"To whom He was not announced, they shall see; And those who have not heard shall understand." (15:20, 21)

Paul's calling was to those among the non-Jewish nations, the Gentiles. He endeavors to live out that mandate. So, Paul defends his actions before the Roman believers by quoting Isaiah 52:15, which highlights the response of the Gentiles to the gospel. Because of the mandate that Paul minister to the Gentiles, Paul acts in ways that are beyond the judgment of others.

For this reason I also have been much hindered from coming to you. But now no longer having a place in these parts, and having a great desire these many years to come to you, whenever I journey to Spain, I shall come to you. For I hope to see you on my journey, and to be helped on my way there by you, if first I may enjoy your company for a while. (15:22–24)

Indeed, Paul's delay in visiting the Romans is linked to his apostolic mandate. His calling has kept him on a path that has not, to this point, brought him near Rome. But he has a great desire to visit them and minister to them (Rom. 1:11–13). He is hoping that his current plan will include them. If he does come, he expects to enjoy the company of the Romans and that they will aide his journey to Spain. Paul values the financial contributions and edification by these brothers and sisters in Christ.

But now I am going to Jerusalem to minister to the saints. For it pleased those from Macedonia and Achaia to make a certain contribution for the poor among the saints who are in

Jerusalem. It pleased them indeed, and they are their debtors. For if the Gentiles have been partakers of their spiritual things, their duty is also to minister to them in material things. (15:25–27)

Paul's first task is to take a contribution to the poor believers in Jerusalem. It is not at all improper for Gentile believers in one part of the world to have significant ministry among Jewish believers in Jerusalem. In fact, as we have seen in this epistle, through the work of God among the Jews that grace has overflowed to the Gentiles. God began with His people, the Jews. But due to their unbelief, he brought the Gentiles to faith in Jesus. Thus, since the Gentiles have taken spiritual things from the Jews, they should gladly participate in the ministry of material things to the Jews.

Therefore, when I have performed this and have sealed to them this fruit, I shall go by way of you to Spain. But I know that when I come to you, I shall come in the fullness of the blessing of the gospel of Christ. (15:28, 29)

Paul's intent is to visit Rome as he goes to Spain. He is confident that he will have the fullness of the blessing of the gospel of Christ when he comes there. In other words, there will be much ministry of mutual edification when he comes to them. They will not lack due to his apparent delays in visiting them because the fullness of grace will overflow to them also.

Now I beg you, brethren, through the Lord Jesus Christ, and through the love of the Spirit, that you strive together with me in prayers to God for me, that I may be delivered from those in Judea who do not believe, and that my service for Jerusalem may be acceptable to the saints, that I may come to you with joy by the will of God, and may be refreshed together with you. Now the God of peace be with you all. Amen. (15:30–33)

Paul concludes with three specific prayer requests. First, he asks that he be delivered from those in Judea who do not believe in Jesus Christ. Paul is well aware that those Judeans were his partners in the persecution of the saints. Paul knew many of them by name and they probably participated with him in imprisoning and perhaps murdering the saints. But Paul is convinced of the efficacy of prayer in this regard. So, he covets the Romans' prayers for this. Yet, he also wishes to be received well by his believing countrymen. He considers it a joy to risk his life in order to bring financial resources to those who have little. Finally, Paul also wants to make it to Rome to have his soul refreshed. He longs to be received by the believers to whom he now writes.

QUESTIONS FOR PERSONAL REFLECTION
AND GROUP DISCUSSION

Read Romans 15:1–33 and answer the following questions.

1. How should we act towards others according to Romans 15:2, 3?

2. What should our goal be in acting properly amongst each other (Rom. 15:5, 6)?

3. How should we respond to the fact that God has accepted us in Christ, according to Romans 15:7–13?

4. Notice that in the first section of this chapter the apostle Paul is speaking of the ministry of edification, which is the building up of one another. What are some practical ways that can be employed to edify others?

5. Paul gives us a look at what motivated him for serving Christ in Romans 15:14–22. What are these motivations?

6. What did Paul hope to gain by going to Jerusalem (Rom. 15:23–28)?

7. In what ways does Paul want the help of the Roman believers (15:30–32)?

Paul's Greetings and Encouragement

Romans 16:1–20

Now we are confronted with a barrage of the names of those who are dear to the apostle Paul. But most of the names are quite unknown to us. This is instructive because Paul labored with many people who are unknown in the subsequent centuries. Yet, they were crucial to the work of the ministry in Paul's day.

We today labor to have an impact in our present era for the age to come. History may record our names, but it probably will not. Though each worker has an impact, each must be content to be without much recognition, though God will say, "Well done," and those whom we serve may show gratitude. As we read the names in Romans 16 and the comments attached to them, we must be content to labor not for the attention of others, but purely for the pleasure of God.

I commend to you Phoebe our sister, who is a servant of the church in Cenchrea, that you may receive her in the Lord in a manner worthy of the saints, and assist her in whatever business she has need of you; for indeed she has been a helper of many and of myself also. (16:1, 2)

The first person to be mentioned is Phoebe, a woman who has been a servant of the church. What better commendation than to be a servant of Christ's church! The Greek word for "servant" is *diakonos*. Elsewhere Paul uses this term to indicate a person who holds the office of deacon (Phil. 1:1; 1 Tim. 3:8–13). Many have associated the events of Acts 6:1–6 with the formation of a group of people who were especially suited to serve the practical needs of the church. These were the deacons. Phoebe probably fulfilled the role of deacon elsewhere in the Christian community. She has now come to Rome where the church is asked to receive her as a fully recognized fellow-worker and to give her money and other practical support. Her past effectiveness and her future ministry to the saints require practical support.

The word "helper" (Greek, *prostatis*) indicates that Phoebe had a high social standing or a position of power within society. This Greek word is used in a different form in Romans 12:8, referring to one who governs or who is an administrator. Phoebe may be uniquely suited for effective service within the community since she has already gained social acceptance and is seen by the overall society as a woman of influence. Such well-placed people can help much by their steady, faithful service to the church.

Greet Priscilla and Aquila, my fellow workers in Christ Jesus, who risked their own necks for my life, to whom not only I give thanks, but also all the churches of the Gentiles. Likewise greet the church that is in their house. (16:3–5a)

Now Paul greets people in Rome itself. It is quite possible that Paul is recognizing people who have gatherings of the believers within their homes. Of course, church buildings did not exist, but that did not limit the expansion and ministry of the believers in Rome. Paul begins by greeting Priscilla and Aquila. We've met Priscilla and Aquila elsewhere in Scripture (Acts 18:2, 18, 26; 1 Cor. 16:19; 2 Tim. 4:19). They were influential in the teaching of Apollos in the way of the truth (Acts 18:26) and, as a result, Apollos' ministry was even more influential among the Jews (Acts 18:28). After being expelled from Rome (Acts 18:2, 3), Priscilla and Aquila hosted Paul in Corinth, ministered in Ephesus (Acts 18:18–26) and then found their way back to Rome. Priscilla is mentioned first, possibly she had the primary role of service to Paul with Aquila serving alongside her.

We know nothing of how Priscilla and Aquila risked their necks for Paul's life. The church obviously was aware of the risk taken on Paul's behalf. Thus they would have enjoyed great favor and blessing among the believers in Rome, and rightfully so. Their ministry continued in Rome, even amidst certain conflict with prevailing

negative disposition among the secular rulers.

Greet my beloved Epaenetus, who is the firstfruits of Achaia to Christ. (16:5b)

Paul wishes to note each person's contribution for his or her own edification. Epanaetus was one of the first to believe in Jesus in Achaia. Firstfruits have a special place in the sight of God for they are the guarantee of further reaping in an area. Epaenetus is special due to his status as a firstfruit offering to God.

Greet Mary, who labored much for us. Greet Andronicus and Junia, my countrymen and my fellow prisoners, who are of note among the apostles, who also were in Christ before me. (16:6, 7)

Mary is noted for her labor and Andronicus and Junia are noted for being fellow Jews and fellow prisoners with Paul. We don't know when Andronicus and Junia were imprisoned. We don't know if this was with Paul literally in the same prison or if they were also imprisoned for the sake of Christ and Paul was aware of their suffering and sacrifice as one who also had been imprisoned. They are both noted as being of note among the apostles. This man and woman were both considered apostles. This term referred to the original twelve apostles, but it also referred to a wider group of people who traveled as missionaries and planted churches. It was an office of importance and honor. Andronicus and Junia were both outstanding in their roles as apostles in the early church.

Greet Amplias, my beloved in the Lord. Greet Urbanus, our fellow worker in Christ, and Stachys, my beloved. Greet Apelles, approved in Christ. Greet those who are of the household of Aristobulus. (16:8–10)

Amplias was probably a slave. He, along with Urbanus and Stachys have names associated with slaves in the first century. Yet they are beloved and fellow-workers in the Lord. Paul says that Apelles is approved in Christ. He received honor for his actions as a follower of Jesus. Aristobulus may have been dead and those remaining were his heirs and relatives who belong to Christ. But Aristobulus may have been alive and not a believer though many in his household were. First-century society was focused on the identity of the husband and father of the household. Thus, the identity of the family was linked to him, even if he was dead.

Greet Herodion, my countryman. Greet those who are of the

household of Narcissus who are in the Lord. Greet Tryphena and Tryphosa, who have labored in the Lord. Greet the beloved Persis, who labored much in the Lord. Greet Rufus, chosen in the Lord, and his mother and mine. Greet Asyncritus, Phlegon, Hermas, Patrobas, Hermes, and the brethren who are with them. Greet Philologus and Julia, Nereus and his sister, and Olympas, and all the saints who are with them. (16:11–15)

The names continue to flow from Paul's pen. These people labor hard for Jesus, are beloved, in the Lord, chosen, etc. Rufus' mother even provided motherly kindness towards Paul! Paul wants each to know their special place in his heart. We are struck by the simplicity of the commendations. Few are noted for their outstanding leadership. Most are commended for their diligence and faithfulness. Some names are common, some are of those who are almost certainly citizens of Rome, some are slaves, but all have a place in the kingdom of God and in the functioning of the church of Jesus Christ generally and locally in Rome.

Greet one another with a holy kiss. The churches of Christ greet you. (16:16)

Paul has great concern for the peace of the assembly of believers. Thus, their greeting of one another and their reception of Paul's greetings further the peace of the church at large. Culturally, the kiss was a gracious way of bringing a heartfelt message of acceptance and welcome. When the church gathers in the local assembly around the Lord's Table, peace, acceptance, and welcome should be apparent. The work of Jesus Christ breaks down the worldly barriers between people that existed in the world. The local church should be the epitome of welcome and forgiveness.

Now I urge you, brethren, note those who cause divisions and offenses, contrary to the doctrine which you learned, and avoid them. For those who are such do not serve our Lord Jesus Christ, but their own belly, and by smooth words and flattering speech deceive the hearts of the simple. For your obedience has become known to all. Therefore I am glad on your behalf; but I want you to be wise in what is good, and simple concerning evil. And the God of peace will crush Satan under your feet shortly. The grace of our Lord Jesus Christ be with you. Amen. (16:17–20)

Paul now provides a cautionary note. Not all of those in Rome are looking out for the welfare of the church. Some are attempting to deceive the church. Paul's admonition guards the believers from those who wish to do evil

among them. Paul is sure of their obedience to the Lord and the Lord's ultimate victory over evil. Because of this, Paul is confident in their future.

Now I urge you, brethren, note those who cause divisions and offenses, contrary to the doctrine which you learned, and avoid them. For those who are such do not serve our Lord Jesus Christ, but their own belly, and by smooth words and flattering speech deceive the hearts of the simple. (16:17, 18)

Paul gives a very strong admonition here. Paul has used the words *I urge you* before in the epistle. It is a strong word (Greek, *parakalo*, "heed immediately." In Romans 12:1, Paul urged believers to present their bodies a living sacrifice, holy, acceptable to God. Paul here urges the believers to note those who cause division. We don't normally see that these are parallel. Paul has great concern for the integrity and health of the local church, yet there are those who only have a concern for themselves, wishing to obtain power and influence.

Paul urges the Roman believers to mark the divisive ones and to resist them. They cause division, propagate false teaching, and wish to sway the hearts of the simple. True leadership not only provides a call to follow, but also protects those in the flock of God. We don't know exactly what the focus of the false teaching was, but it is possible that the so-called strong believers mentioned in Romans 14, 15 were emphasizing their agenda, leaving behind the basic truths of the gospel of God. They were persuasive, to be sure, but by smooth words and flattering speech alone. These people were not true servants.

The essential nature of Christian truth, identity, and expansion of the kingdom were at stake in Rome. There was danger that secondary issues would become primary ones and derail the efforts of the church. A person's diet became a point of contention in the Roman church. But Paul rebukes the strong believers and lifts up the weak ones for the sake of the whole church. It is easy to become conceited and judgmental about issues that are not essential to the gospel. There may be a hint of holiness in the talk, but the end is divisiveness.

he urges wisdom in what is good and simplicity concerning evil. This recalls Matthew 10:16 where the disciples of Jesus are urged to be as wise as serpents and as innocent as doves. While Paul is not quoting the text from Matthew, the sentiment is the same. Wisdom in the protection of the church is crucial as is coldness toward evil desires. Believers ought to be blameless and shrewd. The world and its ways wish to deceive the church of God. But true leaders are not ignorant of the ways of the Evil One. Indeed, the God who brings peace will also bring peace when Satan is crushed. Such peace is the hope of every believer and of every local church. We can rest in the grace of our Lord Jesus Christ, which is present for every body of believers around the world.

Final Words

Romans 16:21–27

For your obedience has become known to all. Therefore I am glad on your behalf; but I want you to be wise in what is good, and simple concerning evil. And the God of peace will crush Satan under your feet shortly. The grace of our Lord Jesus Christ be with you. Amen. (16:19, 20)

Paul obviously has great confidence in the Roman believers in saying their obedience has become known to all. He is glad for this, but urges them to be diligent in their walk with God. Particularly

Next we are introduced to more people affiliated with Paul. It is now time to bring final greetings and a benediction to the believers in Rome. Paul has spent much time to this point bringing commendation to the Roman believers. Now he and those with him send their own personal words of blessing.

Timothy, my fellow worker, and Lucius, Jason, and Sosipater, my countrymen, greet you. (16:21)

Each of these people is dear to Paul and important to the work of the Lord. Timothy is one who truly was a fellow-worker for Paul. The epistles bearing Timothy's name indicate the level of trust put in him by the beloved apostle. The qualities of Timothy made him wonderfully suited for leadership in the church. But Lucius, Jason, and Sosipater are not so well-known. There is a Jason referred to in Acts 17:5–9. This Thessalonian brother in Christ welcomed Paul into his home for a short-lived stay in Thessalonica. Sosipater (Sopater) is found in Acts 20:4 along with Timothy and Paul. The picture given is one of a handful of faithfully devoted companions to Paul who are eager for the work of the gospel to continue.

_____

I, Tertius, who wrote this epistle, greet you in the Lord. Gaius, my host and the host of the whole church, greets you. Erastus, the treasurer of the city, greets you, and Quartus, a brother. The grace of our Lord Jesus Christ be with you all. Amen. (16:22–24)

Tertius is the one who wrote this epistle. He actually brought the ink to the paper but these are Paul's words. They are staying at the home of Gaius. This is not the same person as is in 3 John. It is more likely that this is the man found in 1 Corinthians 1:14. Paul was instrumental in Gaius' conversion

and baptism in the early days of the Corinthian ministry.

Erastus was an official of some standing in the city. He thus had influence and was a man of some means. Paul was equally at home with slaves and noblemen, poor and wealthy. Quartus is designated as a brother in Christ. This certainly was not minimizing Quartus' role; Paul simply wishes to bring greetings from his own coworkers. One would think that if Paul wished to explain all the benefits of each of the coworkers the epistle would be lengthier. The point of the letter as a whole was not to bring greetings but to bring instruction. But in all things the church is dependent upon the grace of our Lord Jesus Christ. Grace brings us to Christ and grace leads us in the work of the kingdom.

_____

Now to Him who is able to establish you according to my gospel and the preaching of Jesus Christ, according to the revelation of the mystery kept secret since the world began but now has been made manifest, and by the prophetic Scriptures has been made known to all nations, according to the commandment of the everlasting God, for obedience to the faith—to God, alone wise, be glory through Jesus Christ forever. Amen. (16:25–27)

Paul completes his epistle appropriately with a doxology, in essence saying, "Praise God from whom all blessings flow!" At the end of this magnificent letter Paul brings the focus back to the awesome God of the universe. It is God alone who is able to establish the believer.

While Paul's gospel and the preaching about Jesus are the means by which people know the mystery of God, it is God alone who makes people stand in right relationship before Him. It is through the gospel that the world has received the revelation of the mystery kept secret since the world began. Paul here gives the biblical definition of the word *mystery*. It is something that was secret but is now seen. In our contemporary understanding *mystery*, secrecy is emphasized. In the biblical understanding of *mystery* the manifestation of what used to be hidden is emphasized. It is now seen for all to see. In the preaching of the gospel of the kingdom of God this mystery presents itself to all. The secret is out. God is at work in Christ, reconciling the world to Himself. He is sending His Holy Spirit to enliven believers to make an alternate society where kingdom values and kingdom power are evident.

This is the same message that the prophetic Scriptures proclaimed. Thus, the message of Christ is not new at all. The saving work of the one true God is evident to all in a veiled way in the Old Testament. But Paul, through the proclamation of the gospel, opens up the mystery for all to see. All nations now are able to have peace with God through our Lord Jesus Christ.

Finally Paul returns to his opening idea that Gentiles (the nations) would come to the obedience of the faith. Belief begets obedience. The crowning glory of the omnipotent God is the work of salvation through Christ. God's wisdom, power, mercy, and grace are all seen in the dramatic act of bringing the reign of sin and death to an end. He is the victorious One. He is the Reconciler. He is the Propitiation. He is the Redeemer. All power, majesty, and glory rightfully come to Him. He reigns above and rightly receives the glory.

Thus ends this glorious epistle. Glory to God in the Highest. Amen.

QUESTIONS FOR PERSONAL REFLECTION
AND GROUP DISCUSSION

Read Romans 16:1–27 and answer the following questions.

1. How does Romans 16:1–16 demonstrate the care and encouragement Paul gave to those under his charge?

2. How does Paul describe Phoebe, Priscilla, and Aquila? What can we learn from these people's examples?

3. Notice that the church in Rome was not free from problems. What kinds of problems existed and how did Paul deal with them according to Romans 16:17–20? How does Paul demonstrate a triumphant attitude in the middle of difficulties?

4. Which of the people listed in Paul's final commendations most appeal to you as an example of steadfast discipleship?

5. How do we carry out the command to be wise in what is good, and simple concerning evil?

6. In what ways is Erastus a great example of Christian service and character?

7. Paul seemed to live a life full of doxology (words of praise). How can you incorporate a viewpoint similar to what Paul expresses in 16:25–27?

A Systematic Review of Themes
in Romans

The purpose of a commentary on a biblical book is primarily to understand what the inspired text is saying in its own context. Once this is embraced, the reader can, under the guidance of the Holy Spirit, move to the realization of what God would have people do with specific principles and applications of the text in the current era. This process of interpretation protects people from simply identifying and excising verses or phrases from the Bible and creating non-biblical ideas that were never intended. People often find "proof-texts" to support unusual ideas and these lead to all manner of errors.

It can be very instructive, however, to organize specific verses focusing on particular topics to see how God wishes us to embrace these truths from a thematic perspective. In this section we wish to examine some of these themes that are present in the epistle of Paul to the Romans in order to gain overall portraits that may not be seen from a simple reading of the text. In a sense, we systematize these truths for the benefit of celebrating and appropriating God's truth for us. We will look at what God is saying more broadly about Himself, about the person and work of Jesus Christ, the Holy Spirit, and about humanity. We will also look at the response of believers to God's truth in salvation and in living as His people as revealed in Romans. This is not a re-telling of the epistle but an organized examination of these truths along thematic lines.

God

The apostle Paul uses the word God (*theos*) in over 140 verses in Romans. For this reason many say that he is primarily "theocentric" in his presentation. God is at work. He is on the move bringing forth His will in the world through His Son, Jesus, who is the Christ, and in the present age by the Holy Spirit. While we would never diminish the work of Christ as portrayed in Romans, we must see the work of God the Father as well. Too often this is put in the background to some of the other themes that similarly are important. Romans presents a profoundly Trinitarian view of God. So we ought to start with God the Father.

Even at the very beginning of the epistle (1:1–3) Paul emphasizes that God is:

- Father of the Lord Jesus Christ
- The author of the gospel of the kingdom of God
- The One who reveals His plan to the prophets in the Scriptures.

The plan of salvation has its origin in God the Father Himself, who was at work from of old. Planning gives birth to action in Christ at the impetus of the Father. In this way the love of God is seen. He could easily have been the far-off God of Greek literature who had no contact or interest in the affairs of humanity.

But that is not our Father. The God who is the Father of the Lord Jesus Christ has infinite love towards humanity, even to the point of working out a plan of redemption. Indeed, Romans 9—11 is full of OT quotations that show the merciful plan of the Father. Such revelation through the prophets demonstrates God's attempt to make His people, the Jews, aware of salvation by grace through faith in the Christ.

God is seen not only as the revealer of His plans in the past, but also as the present revealer of His own nature. Creation and conscience join together as twin witnesses to the concerns of the Almighty God (1:18-20; 2:15). The created realm shouts out the very majesty of God, showing His infinite power. While humanity does not receive this well (to say the least), the message is available for all to see. Thus, revelation of the Father has occurred here apart from the Scriptures by His will. While it would be hard to imagine, God could have created a world that did not have any hint of revelation. But He willed the creation to have such a revelatory nature for our benefit.

So, too, conscience (2:15) is the blessed witness of the nature of God. This time, however, the message is not so much about the power of God and His majesty, but about His moral character and the nature of His justice and His hatred of evil. Thus, men and women have an inner testimony of

God showing them what is right and wrong. Through this conscience God gives testimony to people when they have done right according to their enlightened consciences. Of course, the conscience is not always correct, since in our fallen state we may become quite convinced of our own righteousness against the inner witness of God.

In either case, whether through creation or through conscience, God reveals to sinners that wrath is the consequence of wrong actions. And, as was stated above (see comments at 1:20–21), the primary wrong action is the rejection of the knowledge of God Himself. This leads to further behaviors that in themselves are part of the revelation of His wrath. Choosing the path of the rejection of the knowledge of God leads to consequences that show the sinner that the way of darkness ends dismally. Even this is a blessed revealing of God through judgment. While God has certainly revealed His will in the law, He also shows His nature in the fact that His justice is absolutely consistent with that law (2:17—3:20).

His justice is also revealed in the gracious way of salvation He provides through Christ (3:21–26). But even this revelation is consistent with the message of grace given to Abraham and David (4:1–25). So, the Father is continually revealing Himself to humanity, both in gracious wrath (since we are brought to our senses in seeing our demise), as well as in "wrathful" grace (since through the wrath of God that came on the Son of God we are brought to a place of peace with God [5:1–21]). All of this highlights the fact that God is the ultimate revealer. He is not silent in communicating either His nature or His will. He has provided testimony perfect for our own humanity.

Ultimately, however, we are shown the extent of the love of the Father. Humanity is lost in sin if not for God's redemptive, outrageous love. Love that leads to the death of the Son of God (5:8; 8:32) brings people back into a peaceful relationship with the Father (5:1). Believers then continue in an endless stream of the love of God that runs deep. Such love is so rich and deep that there can be no end to it, no matter what circumstances befall believers (8:28–39). This love also extends to the people of God's favor, the Jews, as Romans 9—11 show. God's mercy and love pour forth to bring people to Himself from both the Gentiles and the Jews. But His mercy does not end there, for He also brings forth gifts for believers to use to further the advance of the kingdom of God (12:6–8).

Jesus Christ

The person and work of Jesus Christ is very prominent in this epistle. But given the discussion above, we are able to see the partnership with the

Father in the plan of redemption. Of course, Romans does not stop with redemption that is found in Christ; indeed the whole of the Christian life depends upon the work of the resurrected Lord (6:1–6). Apart from His powerful work seen in the Resurrection (1:4), we would not have the evidence of His lordship over all creation. Even in the description of Jesus in 1:3 we find the riches of who He is:

- *His* Son, that is, God's Son invested with all the authority of the son of a regent
- *Son* of God, not a servant of God or even a prophet (as the Book of Hebrews brings out in full contrast)
- *Jesus*, or "God who saves"
- *Christ*, the promised One from of old who is more than a mysterious future conqueror, but a King in His own right.

It is a given that all we have as believers we have "in Christ." But Romans brings this before us in dramatic splendor. Before the grand entrance of Christ at 3:22 into the body of the letter, the name of Christ only appears once (2:16). Once He makes His entrance into the scene, He takes center stage as the obedient One (3:22), the One in whom we believe for salvation (3:22), the One who provides redemption (3:24) and propitiation (3:25) through the His shed blood.

It is only through Christ that we have peace with God (5:1), and only through Him are we even granted access to God the Father (5:2). Reconciliation to the Father (for we who have been enemies of God) comes through Christ alone (5:8–11). We become identified with Christ in His death (6:5) as well as with Christ's resurrection (6:5–6). He lives the life we should have lived in order that we might be freed from the dominion of the law and the chains of the flesh. We are granted freedom through His gracious work. Thus, there is "no condemnation to those who are in Christ Jesus" (8:1). Christ is the fulfillment and the fulfiller of the law (10:5), so that we who believe may be counted as innocent before God the Father. In response, the believer is to "put on the Lord Jesus Christ" (13:14) and, in so doing, abandon the life that is oriented toward sinful desire. It is no wonder that Paul breaks out into spontaneous praise at the work of God the Father as seen in Christ at the end of chapters 8 and 11. Doxology is the only proper response to such resplendent work.

The Holy Spirit

It should be obvious to any reader of Romans that the Holy Spirit is a key figure in the epistle. But that does not begin to touch the importance of the Spirit of God for the believer. We begin with the profound thought that

Jesus, also, was obedient to the Holy Spirit while He was found to be "according to the flesh," that is, while He lived on earth as a human being (1:3-4). If living through the empowering of the Holy Spirit was important to Jesus Christ, then it is vital for believers. Let us first consider some aspects of the Holy Spirit as presented in this epistle. The Holy Spirit is:

- The "Spirit of holiness" of Jesus (1:4).
- Given to the believer and enables us to sense God's love (5:5).
- The One who breaks the bond of believers serving "in the oldness of the letter" of the law (7:6).
- The "Spirit of life" (8:2).
- The One through whom we "put to death the deeds of the body" (8:13).
- The "Spirit of adoption" that brings a sense of being a child of God, and, therefore, "heirs of God and joint heirs with Christ" (8:15–17).
- Interceding for the believers who are caught in the bondage of decay along with all of creation (8:26–27).

The key to living a life pleasing to God is to live it according to the Holy Spirit. While much more could be said here (and is said in the appropriate places of this commentary), suffice it to point out that a life lived by the Holy Spirit will be a Christ-like life. Of course, no one lives perfectly that way, but the Spirit of Christ, the Holy Spirit, is the same Holy Spirit that indwells believers. This "Spirit-life" brings freedom from the old way of living by the written code, the law.

The Spirit not only breaks our bondage to the written law, He also brings an intimacy with God that could not be gained through obedience to the law. Intimacy implies relationship. Relationship is gained through the Spirit of the living God Himself. Our spirits are joined with His Spirit to bring a sense of peace and reconciliation that allows us to address God as Father in the dearest terms: "Abba" (8:15). The Spirit is the divine help during times of weakness in this era of having tastes of kingdom living but not the fullness of the kingdom of God. He is our intercessor and our strength (8:26–27).

The Human Condition and the Believer's Response

Humanity is in trouble. That sums up the first major block in the body of the Epistle to the Romans. From 1:18 to 3:20 we are greeted with a host of bad news. Paul sums up the general human response of those called "the Gentiles" in 1:18–32. He concludes that:

- People reject the knowledge of God revealed by Him (1:18–21).

- They "exchange the truth of God for the lie" (1:25).
- They also commit shameful acts in defiance of God (1:26–27).
- Human beings engage in all manner of sinful activity (1:28–32).
- They are aware, at least to some extent, of their guilt (1:32).

Self-righteous, religious people, however, are not exempt from God's judgment. Such people, typified in the confident, religious Jews, embrace certain characteristics. These people:

- Are confident (ignorantly) that God will overlook sin because of their special status (2:3–4)
- Believe that only real "sinners" should receive God's punishment (2:1–2)
- Think that God favors them because of their tradition and race (2:17–29)
- Don't realize that true favor comes from repentance and a recognition that apart from God's grace there is no hope (3:9–20).

Believers in Christ, whether Jew or Gentile, have a new outlook because they have been given a new Spirit (5:1–5). Believers recognize that it is only by grace and through faith that they have the right to become children of God (3:21–26). As such they are freed from sin, from the bondage to the law, and are given the Holy Spirit to live as people for God. Chapters 6, 7, and 8 of Romans read like a declaration of independence from sin and a marriage covenant to God. God has stepped in through the work of Christ to bring forth a new status and a new way of life for believers. Those who embrace Christ by faith live in the full reality of being God's children. They may occasionally be tempted to live underneath the old burden of law orientation, as chapter 7 indicates, but the Spirit of God wants to free us from that dismal existence. And He shall.

Believers are also given a glimpse in the final four chapters of the epistle of how kingdom living is supposed to look. Our basic outlook is changed (12:1–2). We serve in the newness of the Spirit that has changed our relationship with God and with others. The many commands of chapter 12 show that life in Christ looks different from when we are conforming to the world's ways. We live with new obedience to the principles of God's holiness as revealed to us by the Holy Spirit. Believers are empowered to be the gifts of the Father in this present age (12:3–8). We view the governing officials differently (13:1–7) and interact with the world at large with the love of Jesus Christ and full of the goodness of God (13:8–14). We no longer act with self-interest, but with the interest of building others up (14:1—15:13). In short, all things have changed because of our relationship with Christ and living under the power of the Holy Spirit.

NOTES

NOTES

NOTES

NOTES

NOTES